RE-VIEWING RECEPTION

Re-viewing Reception: Television, Gender, and Postmodern Culture
is volume 18 in the series

Theories of Contemporary Culture

Center for Twentieth Century Studies
University of Wisconsin–Milwaukee

General Editor, Kathleen Woodward

RE-VIEWING RECEPTION

TELEVISION, GENDER, AND POSTMODERN CULTURE

LYNNE JOYRICH

INDIANA UNIVERSITY PRESS
Bloomington and Indianapolis

The paper used in this publication meets the minimum requirements
of American National Standard for Information Sciences—Permanence
of Paper for Printed Library Materials, ANSI Z39.48–1984.

MANUFACTURED IN THE UNITED STATES OF AMERICA

Library of Congress Cataloging–in–Publication Data

Joyrich, Lynne, date

Re-viewing reception : television, gender, and postmodern culture
/ Lynne Joyrich.

p. cm. — (Theories of contemporary culture : v. 18)

Includes bibliographical references and index.

ISBN 0–253–33076–9 (alk. paper). — ISBN 0–253–21078–X (pbk. :
alk. paper)

1. Television and women—United States. 2. Television viewers—
United States. 3. Television criticism—United States.
4. Feminist criticism—United States. I. Title. II. Series.

HQ1233.J75   1996

306.4'85'082—dc20   96–6931

1   2   3   4   5   01   00   99   98   97   96

For Esther Zyskind (1904–1995)

CONTENTS

ACKNOWLEDGMENTS

For a "paused" look at a number of fleeting texts, this book was long in the making, and many people contributed to its production. I would like to thank my family—Myron, Ida, Richard, Wendy, and Naiomi Joyrich—all of whom offered support and encouragement, some of whom offered particular suggestions, comments, and TV trivia. My affiliation as a graduate student with the Pembroke Center for Teaching and Research on Women at Brown University allowed me first to formulate my thoughts about television and gender, and my continued affiliation with the Center for Twentieth Century Studies at the University of Wisconsin–Milwaukee has helped bring these ideas into fruition; in particular, I am deeply grateful to Kathleen Woodward for her unwavering support, and to all of the others at the Center for Twentieth Century Studies who have made this book possible. I am also grateful for the encouragement I've received from other colleagues at the University of Wisconsin–Milwaukee, especially from my friend Jane Gallop; from my time as a visiting professor at Brown University; and from the many students at both institutions who have not only lent me their enthusiasm, but have contributed important insights about television, gender, and postmodern culture.

A number of people have provided me with incisive comments and thoughtful suggestions, and I owe many thanks to the readers I have had over the years. Robert Bechtel, William Boddy, Mari-Jo Buhle, Paul Buhle, Jamie Daniel, Mary Ann Doane, Sandy Flitterman-Lewis, Amelie Hastie, Denise Mann, Gloria Jean Masciarotte, Patricia Mellencamp, James Naremore, Thomas Piontek, Lynn Spigel, Jeffrey Walker, Angela Wall, Kari Weil, Mimi White, and two anonymous reviewers have all offered useful advice about particular chapters and/or the book as a whole. In addition to a few of those already acknowledged, David Crane offered help with illustrations; excellent technical support for capturing the images was provided by John Grozik and especially Bob Schmidt. In all of these things, my research assistant, James Castonguay, amazed me with his tireless efforts and startling perceptions; without his assistance and good humor, completing this book would have been a much more arduous task. And Nicole Cunningham not only read every chapter in the manuscript several times over, providing a needed sounding board, insightful comments, stylistic suggestions, and editorial aid, but she also maintained a steadfast support for this project through both good and bad times.

Earlier versions of chapters 3, 4, and 5 appeared in *Camera Obscura* and the anthologies *Logics of Television* (Mellencamp) and *Modernity and Mass Culture* (Naremore and Brantlinger), respectively. Some material from chapter 1 appeared in *Cinema Journal,* and some material from chapter 7 appeared in *Discourse.*

RE-VIEWING RECEPTION

(Im)mediate reception: Deanna Troi in *Star Trek: The Next Generation*.

A mediated universe: *Max Headroom*'s futuristic TV landscape.

I

UNIVERSAL RECEPTION

Television and the Occupation of Femininity

In the 1987–1988 academic year, the Center for Twentieth Century Studies devoted a year of research to television and television studies that culminated in a conference entitled "Television: Representation/Audience/Industry." Presenting a paper which interrogated these terms of analysis, Stephen Heath explored the ways in which the U.S. broadcast television industry has shifted the very meaning of representation from a political and/or textual concept to what is now, in effect, a purely market index, thereby transforming the audience to whom TV's representations are addressed.[1] According to Heath, television constructs viewers not as stable, individualized subject-citizens, but as parts of a consumer network defined only by their pure "receptive capacity" (277):

> [W]e need . . . to understand the institution [of television] in respect of its fundamental universalizing function, universalizing not in the sense of the creation of some one coherent subject, some representative reason for its orders, but in that, more basically, of the universalization of the function of reception. Television exists first and foremost as availability, as saying everything to everyone, all of us receivers. (270)

Both confirming and negating this promise of free availability (since, though we all pay for TV in the elevated prices of goods advertised on television, there is no direct charge for broadcast reception), television enmeshes its viewers in an endless cycle of consumption and commodification, implicating us further and further in the logic of late capitalism. Given television's crucial social and economic role, is it not surprising then, asks Heath (in a line borrowed from Jean-Luc Godard), that viewers are not paid for watching TV, for engaging in this "productive" service (278)? For according to Heath, television is indeed "an occupation, in both senses: it takes up our time, employs us, and it holds the ground, defines the terrain" (297).

Television, of course, does not lack for its own images of what it might mean to "hold the ground," "define the terrain," and even extend its frontiers. In fact, just a few months prior to the aforementioned conference, a much awaited television event presented viewers with a literalized embodiment of Heath's universal receiver, one who was even paid for this effort. In the fall of 1987, *Star Trek: The Next Generation* (*ST-TNG*) debuted, populating a revamped starship *Enterprise* with a new crew eager "to explore strange new worlds . . . [and] boldly go where no one has gone before." *Star Trek* has always had a large and active female fan community, and as the change in the opening voice-over—from the original series' "no *man*" to the more egalitarian "no *one*"—indicates, ST-TNG seemed particularly concerned about its appeal to and representation of women.[2] The inclusion of crew member Deanna Troi (played by Marina Sirtis) was thus of great interest to female viewers, myself included.[3] A natural "empath," Troi functions as the starship's psychological counselor: half human and half Betazoid, a telepathic species, Troi can sense the emotions of the living beings around her, making her both an ideal confidante for the *Enterprise* crew and a running (if sometimes unnecessary) interpreter for the show's viewers. She therefore stands as a prime example of the interpenetration of therapy and television discussed, for instance, so insightfully by Mimi White (see *Tele-Advising*).

But perhaps even more noteworthy than Counselor Troi's official function as analyst/advisor is her gender role; indeed, the former seems to emerge from the latter. For in addition to being an empath, Deanna Troi is also the most conventionally "feminine" of all of Starfleet's female officers, noticeable for her extravagant hairstyles and her singular neglect of regulation uniform in favor of low-cut costumes that emphasize her body. In fact, the evolution of Troi's hairdo and wardrobe provides enough material for an essay in itself:[4] every season brings another cut and shape to her hair, neckline, hemline, color and fabric to her clothes—a remarkable contrast to the occasional change in collar for the rest of the crew. In this way, ST-TNG's presentation of Troi's outfits mimics the women's fashion industry in terms of the promotion of seasonal change.[5] What seems to me to be most intriguing about this character then is not simply the way in which, as "the ultimate helping professional," she illustrates television's deployment of therapeutic discourse, but even more fascinating, the way in which she personifies the professionalization of femininity itself.[6] In other words, Troi is valued more for her ability simply to sense feelings and incite them in others than for anything she might do in an actual office; employed for her pure emotive capabilities, she embodies rather than performs work per se.[7] Here femininity, defined precisely as a "receptive capacity," is thus (to reiterate Heath's words) both literally "universalized"—operative throughout distant galaxies—and "occupationalized"—constructed as a respected career.

Perhaps it is not so surprising that this image of professionalized feminine receptivity would appear in the late 1980s, near the end of a decade marked by heightened ambivalence about women's sexual and socio-economic status, their personal and professional locations. The original *Star Trek* had always had a penchant for engaging with current social issues by projecting them onto alien cultures and the future, and *Star Trek: The Next Generation* (under the executive production of *Star Trek*'s own creator, Gene Roddenberry) seemed to continue this same strategy. Furthermore, the intervening years between the two series (from classic *Star Trek*'s 1966–1969 run until ST-TNG's 1987 debut) saw an enormous change in the political, socio-economic, and cultural position of women: from the rise of the contemporary women's movement in the late 1960s to its besiegement in the 1980s by the forces of the new right galvanized under the Reagan/Bush regimes, its depreciation within the conservative retreat that has been labelled "postfeminism," and its erosion under the weight of its own contradictions and exclusions.[8] By incorporating a character whose professional role is defined by her ability to exemplify those traits considered most inherently "feminine" (empathy, nurturance, emotionality, intuition), *ST-TNG* could construct a "progressive" image of a twenty-fourth-century career woman while still alleviating twentieth-century anxieties about working girls.

Yet *ST-TNG*'s representation of Counselor Troi may be read not only in light of the 1980s ambivalence around women, work and home, feminism and postfeminism, but also in terms of the intersecting contradictions plaguing television's own relationship to femininity. In other words, not only might she equip *ST-TNG* with a way to manage recent discourses of gender, she also enables it to come to terms with the framing discourse of TV itself. Indeed, as indicated by Heath's definition of television viewing as "pure receptivity," the same properties that *ST-TNG* marks as essentially feminine have been aligned with TV itself: the almost uncanny correspondence between his description of the quintessential TV viewer (receptive, consuming, already bearing the marks of feminization), and *ST-TNG*'s figuration of its universal receiver (highlighted explicitly as gendered) reveals the way in which notions of the medium may themselves be implicated within television's own portrayals.[9]

What I am suggesting here is not that Heath's theory of television, however provocative, can serve to "explain" *ST-TNG* (or other 1980s TV programs) nor that 1980s television can somehow "explain" Heath. Rather, I am attempting to read the logics of criticism (the representations deployed in interpretation) and the "logics of television" (TV's own representations) against one another to see what they reveal about the epistemological and discursive order of postmodern American culture—specifically, what they reveal about the places and uses of sexual difference(s) within that order.[10] For disputes over the gendered subject—*women*'s place in the public and private spheres—have been complemented by similar disputes over the subject of reception—*woman*'s place within the discourses of and about television. Just as the figure of Deanna Troi, the professional empath, both strengthens and defamiliarizes the "natural" connection between "female subjects" and "feminine sensitivity" (calling attention to stereotypical traits that usually go unremarked), she also both underscores and unsettles the alignment between television and femininity as she embodies the receptivity posed as crucial to survival in a fully mediated environment (that of the *Enterprise* itself, with its complex array of screens, remotes, communication networks, and simulation apparatuses).[11]

Indeed, even though female characters are still limited in their roles on the new *Enterprise*, this very receptacle is permeated by a maternal presence (perhaps at times yielding the defensive "masquerade" of an excessive narrative concern with trajectories of fatherhood).[12] I'm referring here to the place on *ST-TNG* of Majel Barrett, the actress slated by *Star Trek* creator Gene Roddenberry to play the role of the powerful "second-in-command" officer, "Number One," in the first series, as she did in the pilot, before she was demoted to head nurse on NBC's orders (thus falling victim to what Tony Bennett and Janet Woollacott provocatively term the industry's own "occupational ideologies").[13] Barrett later married Roddenberry, and she fills a number of roles on *ST-TNG*. The extratextual "symbolic mother" of the series, Barrett is also an intratextual parent, playing mother both to Counselor Troi and, as the voice of the *Enterprise* computer, to the starship itself (suggesting a kind of supermom image since the computer always knows the exact location and activity of everyone on board). She might thus be seen as maintaining a maternal sway not only over the figure of feminine receptivity, but over the entire mediated environment *on*, as well as the whole fictional universe *of*, the program.[14]

Furthermore, *ST-TNG*'s pretension to universal representation (literally so, as it focuses on interplanetary affairs) implies that the relationship between television and femininity thus established through these alignments of women and receptivity, maternity and mediation, is operative across all cultural divides (be these the exotic distinctions between alien life forms or the more "mundane" differences of Earthly culture, class, and race). In 1988, *ST-TNG* introduced the semi-regular character Guinan (played by Whoopi Goldberg), another remarkably intuitive and receptive woman, here identified by dramatic costumes that resonate with mythologized images of "wisewoman" and "African matriarch" and a name pronounced like a derivative of the root *gyn*, the Greek stem for *woman*. Together with gendered intuition, something almost insinuated as "racial instinct" is therefore also occupationalized (if not, indeed, colonized, to invoke another sense of the word "occupation"), albeit through more modest means of employment. Assuming an all too familiar service position, Guinan works as the starship's bartender but seems to fulfill the same listening and advising functions of Deanna Troi.[15] In addition to racial and sexual stereotypes, she thus authorizes another media cliché as well, here about therapy in "low culture" (the bartender as the poor man's shrink). In other words, whether personified as a professional psychologist or an amateur counselor, tied to upscale privilege or downscale "aptitude," figured as a respected career or a barroom pastime, feminine receptivity in *ST-TNG* is vocationalized, universalized, and affirmed as an intrinsic aspect of a networked, technologized, and mediated world.

As represented by *ST-TNG*, this world is fully encompassing and wholly providing as all people are plugged into a great network of reception. But while there seemed to be little doubt in the 1980s popular imagination about the universal presence of television (and other electronic telecommunications devices), there was much less certainty about the place of women (their material presence within domestic space). As mentioned above, with the shift from "pre-feminism" to (second wave) feminism to postfeminism, from the old traditionalism to the new, women's position in the home was becoming less and less assured exactly as television's domestic location, now embellished by a full range of technological possibilities (satellite, cable and subscription services, VCRs, camcorders, and video games), was strengthened. The association between television and femininity, the latest variation on the long-standing association between women and mass culture, has therefore offered a phantasmatic way to think through historical concerns (be they sexual or technological, post-feminist or postmodernist).[16] As I plan to demonstrate in this book, such projections and displacements were operative in both the popular and critical discourses of the period which contributed to the conceptual matrix whereby TV representation and reception were figured as some-how feminine. Within its own discourses, television also played out the connections and disjunctions, associations and contradictions, between itself and its gendered receivers; less a "self-reflexivity" (television's awareness of its imagery) than a "self-receptivity" (television's awareness of the imagery of viewers), television has managed conceptions of its audiences within its very texts.[17]

As I have indicated, *Star Trek: The Next Generation* provides a particularly interesting example of this in its characterizations, even if not directly in its plots. Set in the twenty-fourth century, the *Enterprise* is not actually furnished with television as we know it, and thus, for all of its focus on the values of reception, there are no representations of TV per se.[18] The *Enterprise* does, however, have something even better—an entertainment apparatus which promises to fulfill all of our technological dreams of TV's interactive potential. I'm referring, of course, to the "holodeck," where characters from *ST-TNG* can interact with holographic beings of their own (and the computer's) creation, often, like TV, nostalgically recreating and recycling mass cultural products (hardboiled film noirs, Sherlock Holmes mysteries, Western shoot-outs, Robin Hood adventures, romance à la *Casablanca*, et cetera). More than just providing viewers with a vision of futuristic diversion, the holodeck then reiterates the logic of television (and the *Next Generation*) itself, providing the *Enterprise* crew with the ability to engage actively with illusionary characters much as *Star Trek* fans themselves are accused of doing.[19] In other words, crew members bring fictional characters into their lives just as we viewers bring these series regulars into our own. But while "official" discourses of both psychology and cultural taste might denigrate "Trekkies" for their over-involvement with the text, typically portraying them as either emasculated men or over-sexed women (and I purposely use here the pejorative term *Trekkies*, rather than the fans' preferred *Trekkers*, to suggest the way in which these fans are infantilized, belittled, and indeed feminized in most stereotyped characterizations), *ST-TNG* itself provides a more generous reading (Jenkins 10, 15). In fact, Starfleet's psychological expert, Counselor Troi herself, is generally quite approving of the recreational and therapeutic rewards to be gained by immersing oneself in a fictional world.

However, in one episode, "Hollow Pursuits," the specific contradictions that techno-fictional texts (holographic or televisual) may pose for women are suggested, making this a particularly instructive show for considering the relationship between television and femininity.[20] The episode (titled by a phrase that many would claim describes the empty lure of TV, the promised "tube of plenty" itself [Barnouw]) doesn't actually revolve around a female character (or even a ST-TNG regular); rather, it explores the fears and fantasies of an engineering officer, Reginald Barclay (disparagingly called Broccoli) who suffers from what crew members refer to as "holodiction" (the apparent cause of the media-induced "vegetative" state designated by the epithet).[21] In a plot twist that demonstrates the way in which the holodeck may function as a self-reflexive commentary on the series itself, rather than using the computer's simulation capabilities to invoke explicitly fictional beings, Barclay recreates fabricated versions of the "real" Enterprise crew, allowing him to interact with the ST-TNG team in ways that he finds more satisfying than the options available to him in his human encounters. He is thus represented, as Rhonda Wilcox has written, as exactly "the misfit dreamer that many Trekkies are accused of being," engaging, like the ST-TNG viewers themselves, in "a synthetic relationship" with the characters of the show (60).[22]

Concerned about the situation, the ship's chief engineer Geordi LaForge (Barclay's immediate supervisor) consults Counselor Troi about his behavior. In typical therapeutic fashion, she assures him that there is nothing necessarily wrong with submerging oneself in such simulations, that engaging with mediatized illusions might even help people resolve the issues that disturb them in their "real" relations. A similar defense is offered by Guinan who (here as usually) stands up for the rights of misunderstood misfits. Yet Troi's opinion changes when she enters the holodeck and sees how she has been represented in his media creation: as an alluring fantasy figure swathed in silky Greek robes, proclaiming herself as "the Goddess of Empathy" as she urges Barclay to "cast off [his] inhibitions and embrace love" (which he interprets as a clear sexual invitation).

Reduced from a qualified professional into merely a muse of sexual healing (an even more exaggerated feminine stereotype than that of empath), Deanna Troi is portrayed in this diegetic fantasy as a mythical but nonetheless reassuring erotic object—precisely the kind of comforting, emotional/sexual image that she may be for many of ST-TNG's own viewers. She might mediate the conflicts between feminism and post-feminism as she manages the psychological stress plaguing the Enterprise crew (and the viewers themselves), but her ability to assure women's (and television's) place in both the public and private spheres is dependent upon her own self-effacement. She must be willing to "receive" impressions that define her as simply a receptacle for others' fantasies (sexually objectifying and/or narcissistically consumerist). In other words, underpinning the seemingly "positive image" that Troi provides is a discursive and representational system that functions in quite ambivalent ways. Thus revealing the conflicts and contradictions in simply aligning televi-

Deanna Troi as the Goddess of Empathy in "Hollow Pursuits."

sion with women (let alone with anything that might be labelled "women's interests"), this episode indicates the ways in which, even as media receptivity is figured as feminine and/or feminizing, television's own figurations are more apt to operate at women's own expense. Deanna Troi might get reimbursed for her services for Starfleet, but here on Earth, women are perhaps the ones most likely to pay for the television industry's "universal occupation."

Industry/Viewers/Texts

Star Trek: The Next Generation demonstrates exceptionally well the tensions and contradictions that define the relationship between women and television, the continuities and gaps in the alignment of femininity and reception. Reception may be figured as feminine "occupation"—in the sense of a career on *ST-TNG*, but in more typical (and typically misogynist) popular images of television viewing, as an emasculating (woman's) pastime and a feminizing territorialization—yet, as the episode discussed above suggests, this female occupation is nonetheless colonized by and for men. Such a figuration thus illuminates U.S. television's shifting, indeed embattled, status in the 1980s, a period marked both by changes in women's position in the public and private spheres and by permutations in television's own cultural, domestic, and technological position.

Just as 1980s television then maneuvers between the discourses of feminism and postfeminism, alignments with women and government by men, it also mediates notions of the modern and postmodern, the past and the future. Although this book primarily focuses on major network television (my introduction by way of the syndicated-only *ST-TNG* notwithstanding), it was during the 1980s that the capabilities of the entire apparatus of television reached far beyond broadcast network reception and almost exploded into warp drive: the Reagan-era push for deregulation inaugurated a period of intense competition among new and improved technologies (cable systems, satellite linkages, interactive CD and video game equipment, camcorder and VCR innovations, et cetera), leading to a vastly different television landscape.[23] On the institutional front, massive mergers paved the way for the hegemony of a handful of multimedia and multinational conglomerates; but in regard to TV's output, the multiplicity of channels, offerings, and technological options (from the more striking subscription services and specialty stations, rented or self-produced videos, pay-per-view movies, and home shopping clubs to simply "channel surfing," time-shifting, and zapping out commercials) appeared to promise a bounty of choices. In other words, the unification at the economic level seemed to be matched by an equally marked diversification at the level of viewing: no longer claiming to consolidate the audience through broadcasting, the industry (with demographics as its key phrase) now raved about its ability to "narrowcast."

Involving a varied array of modes of production, distribution, presentation, and address, and thus promoting a wide range of styles of "watching TV" (some of which may not include looking at the screen at all, while others involve a more absorbed attention), television has been linked to the dispersed, decentered, consuming—indeed, "pre-occupied"—subjectivity associated not only with figurations of femininity, but also with postmodern pastiche.[24] In discussing a number of texts and genres that have been linked to the postmodern, I explore this relationship in more detail in the chapters to follow. But this is not simply to analyze television's own representations; I am also concerned with analyzing how television has been represented in mass cultural as well as scholarly debates, and therefore, attention to the way in which television has been taken up as a symbol of "our culture" and "our times" is crucial. Specifically, I am interested in what investments such a figuration of television allows—that is, in how this representation of television encourages viewers and critics to "read" TV according to sexual as well as other cultural differences that have been used both to symbolize and to manage historical change. For I argue that gender affects the reception, not simply of particular programs, but of TV as a whole, defining not only viewer positioning but television's own cultural location (its popular and critical reception).

To explore these dynamics, I investigate the inscription of gender in a number of discourses surrounding recent television, considering popular and critical discourses about TV in order to trace the ways in which television has been figured as feminine in representations of the medium (chap. 2); I then turn to the discourses within television texts themselves in order to examine how television's own strategies of representation work (or fail) to manage the contradictions of gender and spectatorship that arise as a result of TV's cultural position. With this in mind, I analyze a number of television's genres and representational forms: melodramas which have historically been associated with female viewers (chap. 3); action and crime dramas that attempt to deny television's "feminine" connotations in order to construct a masculine spectator and achieve the status of "quality" television (chap. 4); programs that maintain television's traditional emphasis on the familial even as they redefine the family in order to contain those disruptions of race, class, and gender that threaten TV's dominance (chap. 5); and finally, texts which self-consciously announce television's "difference" through the use of postmodern and reflexive strategies which call attention to the specificity of the medium and/or broadcast institutions (chap. 6). Though I do not extend it in the chapters to come, my previous example of *Star Trek: The Next Generation* might serve further to illustrate my project and clarify my interest in such texts: while other scholars have researched the ways in which women viewers interpret and appropriate shows like *Star Trek* and *ST-TNG*, I am intrigued by the way in which these texts themselves re-interpret women's viewing, in how (as I elaborate above) *ST-TNG* engages in its own process of re-appropriation as it comments on gender and the media precisely by invoking those traits of reception that have been coded as feminine.

Thus, while I am interested in notions of reception, this book does not fall under the rubric of what has come to be known as "reception studies." That work—drawn from the subcultural and resistance models developed at the Centre for Contemporary Cultural Studies (CCCS) at the University of Birmingham, the theorization of the everyday appropriation of popular texts, American studies' ethnographic analyses of fan, reading, and/or viewing communities, and recent developments within communications and social sciences—also challenges the image of the television viewer as pure receiver, demonstrating the complex, multiple, and active ways in which people engage with cultural texts.[25] This range of research on reception (grouped together here, for the sake of convenience, simply as "cultural studies") has been extremely valuable: by detailing the productive processes by which social subjects (who are located in specific historical formations, watching under particular conditions of reception, and "reading" according to varied codes of relevancy and interpretation) create meanings, identifications, and pleasures, some of which might even be seen as empowering to the audience groups involved, cultural studies scholarship has struck a fatal blow to the image of the totally passive and pacified viewer.[26]

Yet it is as important to analyze the connections and contradictions within televisual discourses—the positions inscribed for spectators and for TV itself—as it is to analyze the ways in which these constructions might be activated by specific populations—how these positions might be taken up and/or rejected. Television may allow for a diversity of uses, but to concentrate only on these while ignoring "the subject of representation" (in both senses of the term) may actually lead us away from focusing on particular differences (the specific strategies of depiction and address that mediate notions of culture and identity) to amassing an indifferent collection of varieties of sameness (Mellencamp, *Logics* 5). As Mimi White has written,

> Television proposes modes of subjectivity that can be conceptualized as fluid and provisional, and yet simultaneously refer to conventional and fixed positions in terms of class, gender, and race. It is this simultaneous bind that is so difficult to grasp in any form except its local operation— through particular programs or moments of viewing. (*Tele-Advising* 20–21)

My attention here to 1980s U.S. network television (and its solicitation of both viewer and critical identifications) certainly does not claim to capture all that might have appeared on our sets, let alone all of the modes of relating or meanings attributed to this output. Yet given the need to ground analysis in specific instances, cases, and signifying situations, such a textual attention is nonetheless crucial, operating, I believe, as a necessary complement to audience research.[27] Furthermore, because television is already quite self-conscious about addressing viewers, already "encoding" presumptions about viewer "decodings" within the text itself, discussions of television textuality are significant to—and indeed, just as significant as—discussions of television viewing (with the reverse holding true as well).

Of course, many people have noted the difficulty of even defining what the television text is (an episode, with or without "interrupting" commercials? the complete history of a series? a whole night's line-up? the entire range of TV options?), thus making, some would claim, any attempt to study it an already flawed if not impossible endeavor. According to this argument, textual analyses of television are bound to be either fragmentary and irrational in their selectivity, or abstract and totalizing in their generalizations. Yet descriptions of the seductions of irrational fragmentation (or conversely, dismay at TV's unruly flow) resonate with exactly those gendered images of television that I am attempting to analyze, and while I agree with critiques of the dangers of totalized accounts, ethnographic and empirical studies which purport to dispel essentialized models by concentrating instead on the varieties of reception often just displace those problems to another level. Rather than attaining some register of "the real" outside of a critic's own abstracted view of what constitutes the text, the empirical researcher simply demarcates another text—this time of viewer responses and reading formations—which then must also be analyzed with no guarantee that this interpretation will be any more "authentic" than the one available through textual analysis.[28]

Furthermore, while audience studies attempt to distinguish the differential readings produced by individuals variously situated within the social field, as these readings accumulate, the differences tend to get diffused onto a general notion of "the people" as a whole, thereby establishing a reified (and often fetishized) collective subject that is just as abstract as notions of the spectating subject derived from the text. Demonstrating the ways in which people are able to decode the most dominant texts in subversive ways (for, in all cases, some viewers who "poach" illegitimate meanings from hegemonic holdings can always be found), cultural studies runs the risk of losing its critical edge. That is, by inverting the usual condemnations of mass culture to emphasize instead the seemingly unlimited power of viewer creativity, it may inadvertently signal its own irrelevancy while bolstering the claims of TV itself: if the people are able to produce such clever readings on their own, there seems to be little need either for changes in media institutions or for cultural critique. While the goal may be one of empowering subordinated populations (or calling attention to the subtle and sophisticated ways in which subcultural and audience groups empower themselves), cultural studies may then end up reiterating the same celebratory rhetoric expounded by commercial television interests—a rhetoric of demography rather than democracy (that is, the false democracy of the marketplace alone). In this way, even if the evaluation of the television viewer is reversed (the audience now considered good even if television texts themselves are seen as bad), this approach to TV studies may maintain the very discursive conventions that I critique above (the assumption that reception is universal, all providing, and even nurturant as it offers endless possibilities to all of its consumers).[29]

It is thus not surprising that aspects of this work have been critiqued from a feminist perspective. For in addition to perpetuating some of the same figurations of reception mentioned above—but now turning this "hypostasized model of sexuality into the grounds of resistance"—ethnographic, subcultural, and audience analyses have proven to be particularly problematic in their treatment of actual women (Probyn 156). Since the days of research into radio soap opera listeners, traditional empirical investigations have paid especially close attention to the viewing (and consuming) behavior of women, pathologizing femininity through an emphasis on woman as problem and object of concern.[30] On the other hand, the method of subcultural study developed at Birmingham's CCCS tends to overlook the specificity of gender, thus contributing to the opposite, but equally disturbing, problem: the neglect rather than the supervisory scrutinization of female subjects.[31] Because of both its emphasis on public modes of resistance and its insistence on the primacy of class, this work has paradoxically excluded a consideration of women and girls even though the cultural products shown to have been appropriated by male working-class youth cultures are precisely those objects that have been condemned by "official" arbiters of tradition, taste, and value as feminizing in their glossy seductions.[32]

Also paradoxical is the way in which some feminist work on television (explicitly committed to countering the "othering" tendencies found within the approaches noted above) has tended unwittingly to reiterate the same problematic. As Charlotte Brunsdon has explained, due to its recognition that the place of the researcher is not a neutral one and its emphasis on the political nature of personal experience, feminist criticism has validated the use of autobiographical data in its focus on issues of concern to "us women" without always clearly articulating either the inclusionary bounds of, or the critics' relationship to, this viewing category. Thus maintaining an investigative look at an audience group (women) posed as an objectifiable and given entity, feminist interventions may "reproduce exactly the existing structure" of audience research (Brunsdon, "Television" 68). It then seems crucial to step back and interrogate the assumptions behind reception studies before we investigate the way in which "actual women" really do receive TV.[33] In other words, though much significant scholarship has emerged which takes the figure of the female viewer as a starting point for empirical work, this very premise of female receptivity demands its own demystification.

My Generation: Critical and Cultural Encounters

The caution expressed above is in no way meant to call into question the enormous contribution that research on female audiences has made to feminist, cultural, and television studies, let alone to dispute the existence of "real" women viewers—indeed, I am one of those "actual" viewers. This might seem to state the obvious, but it is nonetheless important to acknowledge my own investment in television even as I want to investigate that "preoccupation." For despite Brunsdon's salient warning about the possible implications of relying on autobiographical data, current debates over the text and audience have made the intellectual's relationship to television a point of contention, thus demanding that critics place themselves in regard to their objects of study.[34] As an avid viewer, I would still argue against simply grounding readings in an unexamined call to experience (considered as a full and immediate presence); however, it probably comes as no surprise that my engagement with these issues grew out of my own cultural encounters.[35] Specifically, this research initially emerged from an interest in the intersection of two phenomena: (1) critical debates on mass culture, gender, and postmodernism; and (2) popular television texts airing in the late 1980s which made use of what have become known as postmodern representational devices. In other words, what had started off as two separate proceedings—on the one hand, an intellectual concern with critical and cultural theory, and on the other, my own television viewing—came to seem more and more intertwined.

To some degree, this is symptomatic of the "nature" of U.S. commercial television, whose commodified time flow and institutionalized textual structure (perpetual and continuous yet segmented and "interruptible") encourage a spillage from TV to the texts of "daily life" (even, or perhaps especially, if these include theoretical texts). But the intersections that appeared through these cultural meetings are not only symptomatic of TV itself. They also seemed to indicate something about the particular period in both television and American history (including the history of cultural criticism): namely, that at this time of upheaval (as in other times of change or unrest), both televisual and theoretical texts tended to displace anxieties around difference onto the figure of femininity. That is, in all of the previously mentioned tensions perceived in the 1980s—between the past and the future, modernism and postmodernism, feminism and postfeminism, and even TV's own shift from the unification of a national family of networks and viewers to the diffusion of global technological penetration—woman's place became both an issue and stake in the struggles. My discussion of the way in which the figure of femininity circulates in both television's own representations and representations of the medium is thus an attempt to account for and critically analyze this place.

While this book then references various theories—postmodern theory, psychoanalysis, film theory—these are not employed as master doctrines, as complete explanatory systems which uniformly anchor my reading of television. Rather, they are presented as discourses which must also be read, as interpretative frameworks that often make use of the same gendered imagery, and thus participate in the same sexual/textual dynamics, as TV itself. Indeed, postmodernist discourse is sometimes discussed in ways that suggest it is virtually an outgrowth (rather than a meta-mapping) of television: reproducing TV's own terms, many accounts of postmodernism almost read as descriptions of viewing experiences, and some critics have traced the rise of postmodern theory to the cultural changes brought on by mass-mediated life (see Poster). Similarly, in its use of therapeutic and confessional strategies, television itself both references and defines psychoanalytic understandings, taking Freudianism out of the restricted sphere of academic and psychotherapeutic practices and implicating it in daily media consciousness (see White, *Tele-Advising*). As formations of cultural knowledge that concern themselves with subjectivity, representation, and exchange, psychoanalysis and postmodern theory may then be played off of television, analyzed for the intersections and contradictions that emerge in their encounters with another discursive system (TV) involved in these same spheres.

Finally, my use of films and film theory (particularly, feminist film theory) is not designed to provide an absolute standard of media value nor an essentialized description of textual difference. In other words, it is not simply a foreign overlay, idiosyncratic application, or yardstick with which to measure television or television studies. Rather, the comparison to film is introduced in order to indicate both popular and academic modes of cultural appraisal, common ways of thinking through and making sense of everyday evaluation. Thus, in examining how film and television get posed in relation to one another, I am attempting to investigate the ways in which viewers and critics produce, reproduce, and come to understand cultural distinctions, particularly interrogating the role that gender plays in constructing and maintaining these divisions (see Petro). The theoretical apparatuses referred to in this book should then be considered objects of analysis as much as the television apparatus is: by reading these various ways of seeing against one another, exploring the conjunctions and disjunctions between their figurations of gender and reception, we can better understand the discursive context of 1980s mediated culture.

This discursive context has been of interest to other critics as well, many of whom have provided fascinating accounts of the terms through which television has been (or continues to be) placed in American life. For example, in her analysis of representations of television from the 1940s to the present in fiction, journalism, advertising, and cartoons, Cecelia Tichi documents the competing discourses of fear and desire, exploration and control that have mediated the American public's response to television and its understanding of TV's relationship to cherished national imagery and values. Yet while I share this concern with how TV is both figured and perceived, this book has a different scope: rather than detailing the ways in which TV is portrayed in other popular media forms (magazines, novels, et cetera), I look at the representation of television in primarily evaluative and scholarly works and then compare this to television's own representations, thus incorporating analyses of TV's portrayals. I also concentrate specifically on one recent period in the histories of television and critical theory and on one particular (and particularly important) register—that of gender—which (because of factors like TV's position in the home, the industry's marketing and scheduling strategies, the historical way in which gender is taken up as both symbolic stake and reassuring object, and so on) has, as I will elaborate in future chapters, a privileged relationship to both television and this period in time.

In various ways, this particular relationship has also been very productively explored by other scholars. For instance, in *Make Room for TV: Television and the Family Ideal in Postwar America*, Lynn Spigel focuses on precisely that aspect of historical discourses on television that Tichi skims over: the inscription of familial power dynamics in a culture divided by generation and gender. In *High Anxiety: Catastrophe, Scandal, Age, and Comedy*, Patricia Mellencamp explores these same power dynamics and struggles as they have been articulated within television texts themselves, noting that our nation's "domestic policy" of "containment" referred as much to women's positions in the suburbs and home (and to the sometimes bizarre permutations of this in television's simulations) as to cold war rhetoric. Shedding light on television's pretensions toward healing these rifts is Mimi White's *Tele-Advising: Therapeutic Discourse in American Television*, an analysis of television's deployment of a discursive system and confessional mode that, while not limited to women, has historically been associated with (and had significant repercussions for) female subjects. Lastly, in addition to these (and other) discussions of the (sexed) strategies that pervade both televisual discourses and discourses about television, there have been numerous studies of particular texts and genres of special interest to women, soap opera being the most obvious but certainly not the only example.[36]

These studies of women and TV have been very influential for my own thoughts on gender and representation. Yet in addition to my interest in texts, genres, and issues marked as relevant to women is my concern with the ways in which sexual difference appears even in work (televisual and academic) not explicitly tied to gender—the unacknowledged stakes, figurations, and power dynamics in the multiple "discourses of television" (that is, the discourses both on and about TV). For gender is not simply a potential *subject matter* for television—it is a classificatory strategy, a structuring system, a very significant *matter for subjects* constituted through its terms of enunciation and address. This book will thus focus on the articulations of gender in televisual discourses and on the way in which these discourses, textual formations, and social apparatuses themselves engender and articulate social and sexual subjects.

Neither these apparatuses nor these subjects, however, are constant and stable. In the chapters to follow, I examine some of the tensions and contradictions that emerge in television's articulations of gender, demonstrating how TV's address to gendered subjects is not fully unified even though its multiplications are certainly not benign in their (market, rather than democratic) pluralizations. Yet even if television's postmodern construction of split and/or multiple subject positions is promoted solely for its profit-making potential, its discourses (and the discourses around it) may nonetheless reformulate our notions of identity and difference, both extending and negating conventional terms. Indeed, as one can expect from any analysis of commercial television (which prides itself on its constant "newness"), this book traces the contours of a discursive environment that may have already begun to change.

As mentioned above, the system of commercial broadcasting that forms the backdrop for my analysis of 1980s U.S. television is quickly mutating: modifications in technology, programming, and marketing have led to even more demographic segmentations and a proliferation of TV's strategies of address. Rather than centralization under the reign of the networks—with their unifying logics and relatively stable set of codes—there is a multiplication of minor distinctions. Furthermore, these changes in television's conception of difference seem to be part of a larger historical shift. For example, just when postfeminism announced that we finally knew what it is that women want, the "culture wars" began to force Americans to confront and acknowledge, even if only negatively and defensively, other interlocking questions of difference and its discontents (the heated debates over multiculturalism and cultural diversity). No longer able simply to project difference onto the binary figure of sexual division, both popular and scholarly discourses now represent difference(s) in more plural terms.

As with the case of gender examined in this book, the critical and televisual scenes again seem to parallel one another in regard to these notions of cultural differences. That is, scholarly debates about postmodernism, consumer society, and mass-mediated life have shifted toward concerns about cultural diversity and populism in and through mass culture even as television itself is undergoing a similar transformation. New marketing strategies have redefined the notion of "innovative" or "quality" television from those texts of the 1980s which examined the possibilities and / or limitations of their own media norms (*Max Headroom, Miami Vice, Moonlighting,* et cetera) to texts which attempt to examine the possibilities and / or limitations of social, cultural, and historical norms (*Brooklyn Bridge, Home Front, I'll Fly Away, Northern Exposure,* and in a different way, *Quantum Leap* and *Star Trek: The Next Generation*).

Yet while recent television programs may have shifted from an emphasis on the movement within and across texts to the movement within and across populations and history, as the return to my initial example of *Star Trek: The Next Generation* implies, TV's terms of reception and (gendered) address have not necessarily "progressed" at all, intimating that the notion of cultural specificity may itself be turned into an item for sexed subjects to consume. This indicates that an analysis of television's deployment of cultural distinction—and the ways in which this mirrors television studies' deployment of the same—might help us interrogate the stakes and implications of the Academy's own discourses on diversity, just as an examination of its figurations of gender sheds light on theoretical constructions of sexual difference. It also suggests that this "new generation" of television shows has not simply surpassed the enunciative and discursive codes, terms of incorporation and exclusion, and representational and rhetorical strategies of the old. Television might once again claim to be exploring new terrain, but its promise to go where no one has gone before—or, perhaps even more revealing, where "no man" has gone before—may still seem awfully familiar to women at home.

Roseanne Conner watching television on *Roseanne*.

Frisco Jones immersed in the soaps on *General Hospital*.

II

GOOD RECEPTION?
TELEVISION, GENDER, AND THE CRITICAL VIEW

The Treatment of Television

In an article discussing American viewing habits and the popular reception of TV in the mid-1980s, a journalist for *TV Guide* unwittingly summed up the state of television studies during this embattled era:

> Like death and taxes, there are two things that are certain about television audiences. One, they'll complain that a lot of the programs are trivial and/or stupid, and two, they'll spend more and more time watching them. (Hickey 40)

This statement is interesting in several respects. Not only does the author discuss television by way of an analogy to death and money, hinting at television's relationship to the economy as well as the supposed passivity of its viewers, but he points out what is both known and yet strangely disavowed in much contemporary criticism: the enormous significance of television for American culture. Despite the fact that television receives a tremendous amount of popular interest, serious attention to television is still frequently treated with condescending amusement (if not scorn), and TV criticism is relegated to the margins of film or communication studies if, indeed, it enters into academia at all.[1] Outside of a handful of television scholars, few intellectuals want to admit that they watch TV, and even "quality" television shows are devalued in comparison to the more respected arts of theater, literature, and even film.

Yet many criticisms of television have little to do with actual analyses of television programs—instead, it is often the technology, economy, or audience that is the hidden target of attacks. Since recent information technology has created the market, forms, and practices of media culture, a reaction against the ways in which this technology is organized is often conflated with a rejection of "mass art" itself. This rejection is rarely offered on behalf of the "masses" who bear its name: anxieties and defenses surrounding the reorganization of capital, consumer culture, and class divisions are evident within the debates over "high" and "low" forms. Television quite clearly breaks down the traditional relation between textual production and an educated cultural elite who appreciates the finished product (the art object).[2] Further, because the conditions of TV spectatorship are incompatible with classical notions of aesthetic contemplation and instruction, some critics are led to think of the viewers themselves as the problem: The typical viewer is imagined as passive, lazy, vulgar, or stupid—a bored housewife or lethargic child. Behind many critiques of the medium as exploitative, sensational, trivial, and inane lies an unacknowledged disdain for an audience that is deemed infantile and feminine.

Nonetheless, as the recent increase of television scholars indicates, television demands to be studied and analyzed in detail. Not only has it transformed the social, political, and economic organization of our society, TV has begun to alter our very ways of seeing and knowing. Framed by the discourses of television, contemporary formations of knowledge, identity, and reality have shifted in ways that radically alter the epistemological, aesthetic, and ideological space of American culture. Clearly, this has serious consequences for all aspects of our society—including (but not limited to) constructions of sexual difference. In analyzing the specific place of television in American culture, this question of sexual difference arises with an urgency. While, as noted above, the evaluative standards by which TV is decried are perhaps most centrally defined by divisions of class (assumptions concerning taste, value, critical judgment, and so on), it is precisely because class is already an avowed referent of the attempts to map out a high vs. low cultural distinction that it is crucial to recognize the way in which this distinction is also marked by a difference, that of gender, no less significant yet further veiled. As I argue, the inscription of gender, though often masked, is key to the reception of television—the positioning of the TV viewer as well as television's critical reception—and crucial to the industry's own strategies of production and distribution. Historically, mass culture has often been figured as feminine and denigrated for its supposed threat to the stability of the (masculine) dominant order of high art.[3] Though television is clearly fundamental to the maintenance of contemporary American society, it too has been figured as feminine and thus has been slighted by popular and academic critics alike.

Perhaps symptomatically, then, traditional discourses of evaluation (which are already implicated in the polarized divisions interrogated here) cannot account for TV's specific impact on American culture. It is precisely because television shifts the terms of these discourses that they are inadequate both to the analysis of television's difference and to the interrogation of their own powerful yet unacknowledged assumptions regarding sexual difference. Indeed, it is not surprising that among the programming most disparaged by such criticism, most likely to be attacked for their "feminine" or "childish" associations—daytime TV and music videos, for example—are texts that accept these assumptions and address themselves largely to an audience of women or youths. It is my contention, however, that because of this positioning, these forms are in many ways the most telling, revealing in a particularly clear manner the specific textual conventions, discursive configurations, and dynamics of viewing and consuming invoked by the television apparatus. Far from being trivial diversions, such texts compose the cultural language that surrounds us, articulating the reality of American life.

Thus, rather than disparaging U.S. television for its disordered aesthetic, its narratives for their lack of development and resolution, and its viewers for their effeminate and infantile passivity, we need to understand how television constructs the relations between the audience, text, and culture in new and significant ways. Television requires a theory that will analyze it in all its complexity: as a technological form, as an economic and political institution, as a specific collection of narrative and textual strategies, and as an ideological apparatus that is interwoven with the language of culture as well as unconscious desire. Many of these questions have already been posed within the burgeoning field of television studies. However, in reviewing the specificity of the televisual text—a specificity that is related to the technology of the mass media, the economic and ideological locus in which the media function, and the processes of spectating / consuming that ensue from this interaction—few analyses of television review their own language of criticism. While I am interested in the relationship between television specificity and television spectatorship, I am also interested in the ways in which this relationship (particularly as it has been articulated in television, film, and critical theory) intersects with other discourses on gender and consumer culture. Why, for example, are the distinctive narrative strategies of TV belittled in ways that implicate a presumed female audience? What *are* the relations between the specific textual flow of TV (often dismissed as disordered and fragmented in comparison to other cultural forms), the position constructed for the spectator, and the familial, sexual, and economic structures of our society?

By tracing the terms in which television has been figured in popular and critical discourses as somehow "feminine" and then considering some of the ways in which TV has both employed and defended itself against the "threat" of a feminized world, the tensions in constructing a sexed and commodified viewer might be exposed. Although it is impossible to locate any singularly representative televisual text of the period on which I focus—indeed, the very omnipresence and multiplicity of discourses on and about TV contribute to the portrayal of television as *the* diffuse and enveloping medium of this (and our) time—a brief survey of some depictions of television to be read in relation to subsequent analyses of TV's own depictions might help to clarify the contradictions involved in television spectatorship and, more generally, in postmodern consumer culture as a whole. That is, by discussing television's critical reception and then a number of television programs themselves (programs which are not necessarily exemplary of 1980s television, but which do reveal some of its characteristic concerns), I hope finally to suggest new modes of intervention demanded by this particular cultural form and delineate a criticism which goes beyond either the uncritical celebration of TV's "femininity" or the nostalgic call for a return to more traditional forms.

The Emergence of a Critical Discourse on Television

Many of the strands of recent American television criticism were inaugurated by the popular culture debates that spanned the decades from the 1930s to the 1960s, reaching their peak in the 1950s.[4] For instance, in his famous 1953 essay, "A Theory of Mass Culture," Dwight MacDonald laid out the arguments that continue to influence much cultural analysis. In this article, MacDonald describes mass culture as a parasite, a "cancerous growth" that feeds on both high and folk cultures as it substitutes standardized and predigested formulae in place of "genuine art" (59, 61). Although mass art theorists often disagreed on the historical or political roots of this "problem," such critics as Clement Greenberg, Ernest van den Haag, Jose Ortega y Gasset, and many others agreed with MacDonald in the conclusion that the mass media promote a "debased, trivial culture" by exploiting our aesthetic and intellectual needs (72). Basing their critiques on traditional standards of aesthetic value, these theorists could only reject the popular culture that is incompatible with such standards. This is clear in the case of television. Lacking the individual expression and personal vision of a unique author or artist, and perhaps more importantly, lacking even a unified and bounded aesthetic object, television texts necessarily defy the terms of a humanist aesthetic discourse.[5]

Unacknowledged in the criticism that came out of the "Great Debate" is the fact that these accepted norms reflect not simply aesthetic values, but ontological, epistemological, and ethical concerns as well; furthermore, these concerns were often articulated across the lines of cultural, class, and sexual difference(s). Claiming that it is art's responsibility to instruct, uplift, unify, and order, both liberal and conservative critics assumed the universality of such criteria as well as the clear and agreed-upon meaning of these rules. Within much of the debate, artistic quality was described as a property which is both timeless and inherent (excellence simply exists in the work to be contemplated) rather than recognized as a socially determined category. That is, aesthetic worth was considered both self-evident and self-realizing: a work's value is immanent to its existence alone. Mass culture, on the other hand, is based upon exchange. By leveling traditional standards and making all works comparable through the medium of money, the mass media dismantle the very categories of analysis brought to bear upon them by their critics.

Collapsing the standards of traditional criticism, television cannot be adequately analyzed in these terms. Although MacDonald remained loyal to traditional aesthetic models, he did suggest television's power to subvert these norms:

> Mass Culture is a dynamic revolutionary force, breaking down the old barriers of class, tradition, taste, and dissolving all cultural distinctions. It mixes and scrambles everything together, producing what might be called homogenized culture.... It thus destroys all values, since value judgements imply discrimination. (62)

Indeed, a culture so "mixed and scrambled" is, for MacDonald, no culture at all. In other words, MacDonald equates the "difference" of mass art—its position outside of traditional cultural and aesthetic categories—with the vacuum of no difference whatsoever, the charge of a lack of distinction.

Within his framework (as well as that of several other critics), this absence of form, the 'nothing to see' of mass culture, is intimately tied to the notion of a female public and a feminized media: MacDonald defines mass culture as "a tepid, flaccid Middlebrow Culture that threatens to engulf everything in its spreading ooze" (63–64).[6] The aesthetic disorder he discerns in mass culture is therefore related to a particular spectator position. Remarking on the masses' lack of "cultural equipment," Mac-Donald associates mass culture with a childish, weak, and impotent viewer, condemning the media for encouraging overstimulation yet passivity, infantile regression, sentimentalism, and what he calls "Momism" (66). Yet MacDonald fails to analyze the significance of his own critical terms. Trapped within the very discursive formations that television dismantles, MacDonald cannot address the specificity of mass-mediated texts and their consumption, let alone the implications of his critique for theories of gender and culture. Rather than trying to fit mass art into an already disintegrating canon, what is needed is a theory of representation that includes an analysis of the place of gender within cultural production and reception.

Offering the promise of such a theory, Marxist critics, most notably those of the Frankfurt School, also participated in the popular culture debates. By examining the relations between industrial rationalization, social consciousness, and mass culture, theorists T. W. Adorno, Max Horkheimer, and Herbert Marcuse outlined a sophisticated theory of the mass media in terms of ideological hegemony.[7] Yet despite a political framework which offered possibilities for a complex analysis of gender and class relations, the position detailed by members of the Frankfurt School was still largely determined by traditional notions of aesthetic value which again were often figured in gendered terms. In other words, the politics of mass culture were more closely examined than the critics' own politics of interpretation, which were more likely to justify the hostility commonly directed at mass-produced texts and their supposedly feminine audience than to counter it.

This justification once more depends on a comparison between mass culture and genuine art: the rise of the mass media under capitalism is shown to signify the triumph of instrumentalization and commodification over the nonpracticality, play, and negativity inherent in true art, particularly in modernist experimentation. According to the Frankfurt theorists, the mass media lose the independent critical potential of artistic texts as they are restructured along the lines of efficiency and rationalization. Lacking the immanent value of art, media products are reduced to commodities having value only as they can be used to attain consumer satisfaction. Through this promise of fulfillment, mass culture successfully channels desire into a commodity structure, manipulates our sense of needs, homogenizes pleasure, and freezes our critical capacities; like a drug that keeps its audience happy but immobilized, mass culture acts as a seductive but illusory sedative. Exemplifying this process, television has been described by Adorno (borrowing a phrase from Leo Lowenthal) as "psychoanalysis in reverse"—rather than revealing and clarifying our desires, TV exploits and mystifies them in order to further ensnare us in its power. Individual resistance is destroyed as all viewers become consumers fused into conformity, exhibiting *en masse* a passive acceptance of the status quo.

Yet such regrets over the death of the autonomous individual at the hands of consumer culture fail to question the ways in which "the individual" described is always already presumed to be male. Thus, Adorno too associates the rise of mass culture and the death of a virile and authorial modernism with the threat of femininity and infantilization. In his essay "Television and the Patterns of Mass Culture," he claims that the TV viewer has become "other-directed" rather than attuned to inner conflicts (477) and that with television, the "longing for 'feeling on safe ground'—reflecting an infantile need for protection, rather than his desire for a thrill—is catered to" (476). Rather than the masculine spectator stimulated by the negativity inherent in modernist art, television creates an effeminate viewer, passive and gullible, in need of comfort and support. Within this discourse, TV's mystification becomes almost a castration.

Discourses of Social Science

The concern expressed by Marxist theorists over television's power of mystification and indoctrination was taken up by American social scientists, although they moved away from the Frankfurt School's emphasis on critical social theory.[8] Turning from the interrogation of social and cultural processes—what Paul Lazarsfeld termed "cultural criticism"—to what was known as "administrative research," mainstream television studies aligned itself with communications research in the pursuit of empirical data and in the application of such data to a cultural model.

Two general areas of research took shape: there were initial attempts to determine the persuasive power and effects of television, followed by audience and use-based studies of the needs gratified by television viewing. Each of these models relied upon quantitative content analysis in order to gauge exactly what TV involved: the manifest material of television's output was monitored to determine either how the content of TV's messages affected the audience or how individual audience members made use of these messages in order to actively fulfill their needs (for information, aesthetic experience, stability, reassurance, contact with others, leisure, or escape). Much of this research was valuable, particularly the work that called attention to the limited representations of subordinated groups, demonstrating that the media produce particular constructions of the world rather than "measuring up" to a presupposed reality. Nonetheless, these empirical studies as well as their bases in content analysis tended to be narrowly conceived, and they could not adequately address the question of television's relation to American culture.[9] Even the most politically engaged research on women in the media, for example, has been critiqued for its failure to fully analyze the problem of gender and the gendered subject.[10]

For one, these studies isolate abstract variables from the overall viewing experience, disregarding the complexity of television's relation to American culture as a whole, the processes by which behaviors, attitudes, and identities (including those of sexual and/or familial positions) are constructed and assumed, and the multiple contexts in which television (as well as gender) is experienced. Rather than investigating practices of viewing and the ways in which these might intersect with other practices and interpretative frames, most empirical studies maintain an image derived from communications research of an individual viewer in one-to-one contact with a message sender, therefore ignoring the textual, institutional, and "situational" specificity of broadcast television.

Furthermore, while the content of the message is quantified and counted, there is no explanation of the particular ways in which this "content" is structured and composed; a specious distinction between "form" and "content" is both presupposed and reinforced rather than being subjected to needed interrogation. Ironically, although radio and television (unlike previous communication technologies or aesthetic forms) were systems devised as means of distribution—as abstract processes of transmission and reception with little or no articulation of intended output, and production considered merely as a requirement for the goal of distribution—these studies assume that observation of manifest content alone provides a sufficient understanding of the televised text (Raymond Williams 25). The presumptions about communication inherent in much empirical work thus reverse the medium's own historical hierarchy of technology and form over content: television communication is construed as a simple and direct process of transporting messages through a neutral media channel which exists outside of history and the active processes through which meaning is made.

Despite the value of empirical research, conceptualizing projects in this way actually impeded the analysis of television's meanings as cultural constructs; indeed, the methodological requirements of effects research inhibited the treatment of television and gender as interlocking signifying systems, while effects research itself is unable to account for the complex negotiations by which viewers relate to these representations. Instead, the viewer is often portrayed as a test subject who is summarily "injected" with an overt message which then either takes effect or fails—the reason why some effects research has been characterized as the "hypodermic needle model" of media influence. In the popular and scientific imaginations, this needle is certainly not a sanitized one: what the viewer is pricked with is considered neither pure nor healthy. As both Jane Root and David Morley have pointed out, undergirding the concern with television effects is the notion that the "junk" that viewers are fed (or, to reiterate the more alarmist image of media "addiction," injected) has the power to transform them into either hypnotized and glassy-eyed zombies or, conversely, hyperstimulated automatons incited to violence and/or consumer frenzy (Root 7–20; Morley, "Changing" 16). Yet both the narcoticized dupes and their counterparts, the overactive hotheads in the supermarkets and the streets, are always *other* viewers: effects research tends to demonstrate a patronizing concern for groups posed as more vulnerable than "us."

Not surprisingly, these "others," the subjects of studies on media effects, are frequently women and children, precisely those populations who most lack access to control over both television production and its reception (the selection of what, when, and how to watch, determined by what Morley, following Sean Cubitt, calls "the politics of the living room" [Morley 37; Cubitt 48]).[11] Therefore, although empirical research moved away from cultural critique in its depiction of a viewer isolated from all other social stimuli, the discourse of social science maintained mass culture criticism's denigrating image of its audience. Even if the viewer was considered to be, at least potentially, one of "us" (not, that is, one of the already powerless "others"), he was figured as nonetheless still in danger of TV's feminizing and infantilizing influence.

In a widely cited study on the harmful effects of television on the American character, for example, Dr. Eugene David Glynn produced some extraordinary generalizations.[12] Remarking upon the "structure inherent in the very medium of television" itself, he warns us of TV's chief dangers: the creation of receptive, smothered, and conformist men in whom "the passive dependent oral character traits [have] become fixed" (179). After listing cases of mental illness that correspond to these problems (illnesses that are, in his opinion, easily incited by television's power), Glynn notes that such are "the traits which children, exposed to television from childhood (infancy, really!), and all through the character forming years, may be expected to develop" (177). He continues:

> [These traits] all demonstrate quite clearly the special set of needs television satisfies, needs centering around the wish for someone to care, to nurse, to give comfort and solace. . . . These infantile longings can be satisfied only symbolically, and how readily the television set fills in. Warmth, sound, constancy, availability, a steady giving without ever a demand in return, the encouragement to complete passive surrender and envelopment—all this and active fantasy besides. Watching these adults, one is deeply impressed by their acting out with the television set of their unconscious longings to be infants in mother's lap.[13] (178)

Reinforcing enormous but unexamined cultural assumptions—assumptions concerning the nature of TV's effects as well as the value of qualities culturally coded as feminine—even such "clinical" research promotes the image of an "unmanly" viewer, passive and helpless before the onslaught of TV.

The "uses and gratification" school of social science depicts the viewer

as active in relation to the message and therefore more "manly," appropriating television for his or her own purposes. Nonetheless, there are
problems with this approach as well. The television text still tends to be
portrayed as simple and univocal, the viewer as outside history, and the
contact between the two as direct and individual. In their attempts to
outline the correlations between human needs and the televised message,
many uses and gratification researchers have assumed that the urges they
describe are universal, timeless, and immediately apparent to viewers
who consciously pursue their fulfillment. Disregarding the historical and
political realities of social and cultural influences, most researchers make
no attempt to analyze the relations between television and the spectator in
terms of the social order, let alone unconscious desire. For this methodological reason alone, their ability to analyze gender (and the gendered
assumptions of their own and other TV research) is severely limited.

The emphasis in this type of work is on successful communication, and
any breakdown is considered a dysfunction, thereby promoting a mecha-
nistic model of spectatorship which is not attuned to the social and familial
dynamics that determine viewing "choices." This instrumentalized view
reverses the "hypodermic needle" problem: here, the question of television's ideological effectivity withers away. The notion of television's
influence—the political interests of the media—is displaced onto that of
individual motivation, the personal interests of the (undifferentiated)
viewing public. Given this construction, it may come as no surprise that
uses and gratifications studies are apt to echo the rhetoric of consumer
culture itself. Indeed, the models guiding both effects and uses and
gratifications research are often fully compatible with the goals of broadcasting institutions (as well as frequently funded by them), helping advertisers determine how to best influence their audiences (and assuring them
that TV messages do have a clear effect) and promoting an image of
television as a beneficent educator that meets our various needs for
information, communication, and enjoyment.

Early work on public policy, taste, and cultural value within the humanities often appropriated the frameworks devised by communication
researchers, thereby inheriting many of the problems of these accounts.[14]
Dominated by functionalist models which divorce television's meanings
from their textual, cultural, and institutional determinants, this work
describes the world portrayed by television and how audiences respond,
employ, or enjoy this world. Reiterating the rhetoric of "democratic"
consumer culture, the emphasis is on choice, free flow of information, and
the individual's prerogative to make what he or she chooses from what is
seen. Not only did this model fail to challenge the notion that television is
simply a window on the world, it failed to analyze the social forces that
interact with this world, cloud the transparent window, and create individual (not to mention institutionalized) preferences.

More recent work within cultural studies has certainly refined these
efforts, often combining empirical research with textual and cultural
analysis in order to better understand the specifically social contexts in

which television (in addition to other media and leisure activities) is used.[15] While interviewing audiences about both their practices of mass culture consumption and their patterns of interpretation, this scholarship treats viewer/reader responses themselves as texts to be read and interpreted, producing fascinating accounts of the multiple meanings that television forms and figures hold for viewing populations. Yet it too may veer toward an instrumentalized vision of the media as it valorizes the ways in which various cultural, subcultural, and "taste" groups use television texts to consolidate identities already partly determined by mass culture itself.

These identifications are used to define not only individuals and communities; they also regulate and order the ways in which these same communities conceptualize media forms. Commenting on the appropriation of "Americana" within British culture, for instance, both Dick Hebdige and David Morley suggest how American television programming, with its promotion of "soft" disposable commodities and its connotations of passivity and domesticity, has authorized ways to interrogate "traditional British values" even as it has been condemned for its enervation of "the authentic muscle and masculinity of the British industrial working class" (Morley, "Changing" 32–33; Hebdige, *Hiding* 45–76). Pointing toward the contradictions of television's cultural location, the challenge that American television may pose in this context to dominant norms is both advanced (in regard to discourses of nation) and yet dismissed (in terms of discourses of gender). In order to account for such complexities of meaning, value, and emotion surrounding television and television viewing, the circularities of functionalist models must be replaced with more nuanced understandings of power—those that locate it neither simply on the side of media effects nor on that of receivers' "rights."

History/Authority/Reality

From its inception, television history has attempted to provide this nuanced view, exposing the fallacies in many of the assumptions plaguing empirical research. From early work by Erik Barnouw, Todd Gitlin, and Raymond Williams to more recent work by (among many others) William Boddy and Lynn Spigel, historical scholarship has demonstrated that far from being a neutral instrument or transparent conduit of information, television (video technology, the broadcasting industry, and the commodity forms of both programming and TV sets) has been organized in particular ways, with particular intentions, and with particular effects on the television "message."[16] The social relations of ownership and control behind this "neutral" medium very much define what is presented on TV, how it is presented and received, and therefore, what "reality" is produced. This reality then has important consequences for the representation of gender as well as the specific uses and meanings surrounding TV. Yet histories of television are not immune from the gendered rhetoric that plagues other commentary and analysis—a point apparent even from the title of Barnouw's well-known book, *Tube of Plenty*, which, like much scholarship, implies that television functions as a maternal substitute, offering its own comforting abundance. In fact, some "historical" analyses of mass culture have contributed to, rather than mitigated, the misconceptions surrounding the supposed feminization of American culture under the mass media's sway, and while these arguments now seem outdated and sorely lacking in substantiation, their presumptions nonetheless set the terms that continue to haunt popular and critical accounts of TV.

For example, Gilbert Seldes—a critic who attacked mass culture for both its "teenage standard[s]" and its appeal to wives who "play" rather than "keep" house (evident primarily in their refusal to accept the traditional role of motherhood)—demonstrates typical (il)logic in his account of the roots of our impoverished mass art (74):

> The [American] writers and the painters longed for European recognition, and many of them went to Europe; the gap between the intellectual and the people widened. The thin and sentimental novels, the stiff pretty paintings, had nothing to say to men who may have been, as Lewis Mumford has said, brutalized by their "rape of a continent"; the men left the arts to the women, and another American tradition took root. . . . It was an unfortunate division of interest, . . . encouraging men to keep their active life away from their women and women to keep the life of the mind and the spirit away from their husbands; encouraging also the artist to address himself chiefly to women, to be precious and flattering and dandified. (76–77)

Forced to respond to such contemptible tastes—tastes that Seldes sees as intrinsically female, preexisting the actual production of mass art—American artists lowered the standards for centuries to come. While social and material power (not to mention control over the emerging media industries) lay in the hands of American men, in Seldes's account, they played no part in its rise: "the men who were too busy conquering a wilderness to pay much attention to the arts were less to blame for the isolation of the intellectuals than the intellectuals themselves"—and, of course, the women with whom they were isolated (77). Within this scenario, it is *man* who is the victim, plagued not only by his own virile deeds (the rape and conquering to which Seldes refers) but by the women and effete artists who conspired to feminize his world—indeed, given the language of sexual violence in this passage, to emasculate brutally his very identity.

A similar, if slightly less melodramatic, argument is made by the literary historian Ann Douglas in what the *New York Times* calls her "indispensable" book, *The Feminization of American Culture*.[17] Like Seldes, Douglas traces the rise of mass culture to an alliance forged between nineteenth-century women and disenfranchised intellectuals, in this case, the Protestant clergy. Provoking "the split between elite and mass culture so familiar today," the unholy union of women and church pushed

American interest toward the trivial and narcissistic concerns of "feminine purity [and] the sanctity of the childish heart" and away from the greatness of genuine art. Tragically lost were those authentic American artists who "wrote dramas of the forest, the sea, the city"; authors who "sought to bring their readers into direct confrontation with the more brutal facts of America's explosive development" through stories "about men, not girls and children, . . . men engaged in economically and ecologically significant activities" (4). In Douglas's view, the sentimentalism and self-flattery inherent in those new cultural forms preferred by female readers laid the groundwork for the style of advertising and TV soap opera that still prevails today.[18]

Because Douglas's book is a self-proclaimed feminist analysis of the historical roots of mass culture, the contradictions in her argument are even more pronounced than those of Seldes. Douglas explicitly states that "Northeastern clergymen and middle-class literary women lacked power of any crudely tangible kind, and they were careful not to lay claim to it." Yet she goes on to grant them an almost indomitable potency to control the future of the emerging culture industry: the alliance of women and clergy exerted an "influence" that was "discreetly omnipresent and omnipotent" (8). Rather than exposing the motivations (economic, ideological, and psychological) behind the widespread disparagement of mass culture as feminine, then, Douglas assumes the truth of this charge and takes on the task of proving that the accusations against women are, in fact, quite justified. While she condemns other historians for shying away from the study of women and culture because of their "fear of contamination" (6) and goes on to assure us that "our current allegiance to the comforts of our televisions is not altogether a matter for embarrassment or shame" (399), her own research can only encourage this fear and shame. Failing to treat the discursive connection between mass art and femininity as just that—a discursive construction—she promotes the view that nineteenth-century consumer culture and its popular narratives, as well as their legacy in TV today, are inherently feminine in both cause and effect.

Because of the obvious problems in such assertions, more recent work within television and cultural studies has both explicitly and implicitly subjected these claims to interrogation, investigating the complex relations between audience, industry, and text, between televisual and other social meanings and practices.[19] Yet in the arena of popular judgment, the terms and values of the early mass culture debates seem to have had a surprising longevity, and the gendered rhetoric of traditional standards of evaluation are apt to go unchallenged. Television may still be condemned for its failure to conform to accepted criteria of art or slightly modified criteria of "positive" media images, for its inability to rise above what is posed as its sentimentality, triviality, and disordered flow to provide viewers with unified, ordered visions yielding, at best, genuine insight or, at least, informative portrayals of reality. Some viewers and/or critics have attempted to rescue television from its place of low esteem by arguing that television can and does meet these aesthetic standards, pointing, for example, to possible instances of television auteurs even where they might be least expected (Gene Roddenberry of *Star Trek* and *Star Trek: The Next Generation*, Paul Henning of *The Beverly Hillbillies* and *Green Acres*).[20] In this way, one might try to indicate an elevating vision and coherent aesthetic behind the television text and so salvage a sense of "masculine" authority lying just beneath the amorphous surface of what is then only ostensibly a "feminine" form.

Feminist art and literary theorists have questioned the assumptions undergirding these aesthetic principles of order and reflection, noting the ways in which such principles may reproduce hierarchies of sexual, and other, divisions.[21] Yet while academic feminist criticism has largely moved away from early approaches to "images of women" that concentrated on television's failure to portray female characters positively or realistically (that is, with historical accuracy and/or the goal of intervening in history and producing new realities), a demand for the unmediated real may be even more strongly asserted by the viewing public today than ever before.[22] Certainly, misleading stereotypes and media distortion remain important areas of concern. Yet these same concerns may also blur the discursive connections between mass culture and femininity, promoting the notion that research can accurately reflect the position of women in television just as TV should accurately reflect the position of women in society. Not only do such arguments neglect television's specific signifying system (suggesting that there might indeed be such a thing as unmanipulated representation), but they also fail to analyze the implications of the language of television theory itself. The problem of gender and television reception—TV's popular as well as critical acceptance—thus remains an open question.

New Cultural Configurations, New Discursive Frameworks

The reception of television is further complicated by its privileged place within debates on (mediatized) postmodernism. Many of the perspectives I've discussed are based on a traditional set of assumptions concerning the nature of art, reality, and communication and therefore exhibit a nostalgic faith in the possibility of "authentic" expression. Television, however, is often seen as a sign—perhaps *the* sign—of the futility of such longings, as the mark of the encroachment of the "hyperreal" into all aspects of daily existence.[23] Undermining the determinate order of history through its explosion of images and implosion of meaning, television—taken as token of the hyperreal—threatens to rupture the discourses on which the very notion of referentiality is based.

While previous (and, indeed, much continuing) work in cultural criticism operates within the terms of the discourses discussed above, many scholars have begun to explore this terrain of the hyperreal.[24] Focusing on the changing economic, ideological, and cultural practices produced by the mass media and by information society as a whole, these theorists propose that such new cultural configurations produce and demand new discursive and critical frameworks. As many critics stress, we are no longer in the epistemological and interpretative order of the earlier aesthetic debates. Emphasizing this point, for example, Donna Haraway writes that "post-modernism is not an option, a style among others, but a cultural dominant requiring radical reinvention [of politics, interpretation, and criticism]. . . . One cannot be for or against post-modernism, an essentially moralist move" ("Manifesto" 69). One can only, she suggests, attempt to understand how its discursive system subverts accepted ways of seeing, refiguring (among other things) conventional terms of analysis and traditional standards of value. For as Haraway reminds us, social reality, lived relations, and historical agencies are never simply referential; they always exist as cultural fictions. As the dominance of cultural forms shifts, so do the fictions (and vice versa). In postindustrial America, television, video games, and computer networks make up our imaginary and symbolic systems, and as the narratives and conceptual frames that construct our experiences and our society change, so too must the discourses of criticism applied to these fictions. This demands a shift in the critical analyses applied to television and other media.

Though writing in the context of both modernism and the mass culture debates, Marxist critic Walter Benjamin prefigured many of the concerns of postmodern theory in his contribution to the Frankfurt School's critique, providing an analysis which began to revise aesthetic standards of evaluation in the light of the technological and cultural changes of the twentieth century. In his essay "The Work of Art in the Age of Mechanical Reproduction," Benjamin explains that though in principle a work of art has always been reproducible, the rise of technical means of reproduction and mass marketing has caused a profound change in the meaning and impact of aesthetic production. With the multiplications of mass art and the media, the aesthetic object loses its unique presence and thus its claim to autonomous existence, historical testimony, and cultural tradition. Because "the presence of the original is the prerequisite to the concept of authenticity," writes Benjamin, "the whole sphere of authenticity is outside technical— and of course, not only technical—reproducibility" (220). As the concept of authenticity loses meaning, an entire set of traditional concepts and values surrounding art, as well as reality, collapses.

This collapse is further theorized by Jean Baudrillard in his musings on "hyperreality."[25] Moving from Benjamin's analysis of mechanical reproduction to a discussion of today's characteristic forms—electronic and computer simulation—Baudrillard explains that the existential hierarchy of production and reproduction has at last reversed its claims. Not only are objects and texts reproduced, but their very production is governed by demands of reproducibility; the media have become merely a set of codes and operations applied to models which have no independent life, which exist as pure simulacra— "copies" without originals.

With the breakdown of the binary opposition *original/copy* comes the breakdown of other such polarities and, according to Baudrillard, the subversion of binary thought entirely. For as mass culture abolishes notions of authenticity and high technology blurs the boundaries separating science and art and man and machine, firm distinctions between true and false, reality and fabrication, fiction and nonfiction (distinctions which, of course, are always slippery and tenuous no matter how anxiously defended) become even further threatened: culture seems to lose its stable ground in history, and tradition as referential logic is jeopardized. Our reality, he claims, becomes as mobile as the media upon which it is based, making it impossible to define an instance of control: "For manipulation is a floating causality where positivity and negativity engender and overlap with one another, where there is no longer any active or passive . . . , a system where linear continuity and dialectical polarity no longer exist, in a field *unhinged by simulation*" (30–31).

Within this field of media-infused reality, television ceases to stand out as a theatrical or spectacular form, becoming instead much more banal. In Baudrillard's vision—one perhaps borne out by the camcorder boom and the ensuing explosion of "reality shows" (whose very designation indicates the conflation of previously opposing poles)—we can no longer resolutely distinguish between seeing and being seen. Given this assessment, he questions modes of media analysis which are based upon these customary oppositions—not, I would argue, because the oppositions have in fact disappeared (if they ever existed in definitive form to begin with), but because in the discourse of postmodern theory, television has come to mark the very fragility of these divisions.[26] In other words, although visual, epistemological, and even ontological categories may always have been flexible, television brings this to the fore, celebrating the reversibility of positions rather than guarding against their collapse. Baudrillard thus cautions against any description of TV based upon "the perspective, deterministic mode, the 'active,' critical mode, the analytic mode—the distinction between cause and effect, between active and passive, between subject and object, between ends and means" (55). Television scrambles these categories and makes us all both active and passive, subject and object.

Certainly, the material divisions defining television production and consumption continue to exist; despite Baudrillard's idealist vision, the institutional structure of the broadcasting industry has hardly been "unhinged." Yet as his statements demonstrate, "television" as a signifier within popular and critical discourse has come to suggest something quite different, demanding an analysis that can come to terms with the cultural reconfiguration that TV represents and through which it is, in turn, represented. Earlier criticism had evaluated television (and other cultural forms) on the basis of the binary terms noted above, prioritizing one pole (truth on the side of the active subject) and relegating the other to a position of low esteem (the passive object, often figured as feminine and duplicitous). According to this theory, however, TV scholars must admit that we are all tainted by the "otherness" of the subordinate position— television viewers (and television critics) are refused the security and unity of the traditional (masculine) subject, possessor of the active gaze and master of history and reference.

Representation and Sexual Difference

Feminist theory and criticism provides a framework for understanding the significance of this discursive break in constructions of both knowledge and spectatorship; indeed, it alerts us to what is at stake in even conceptualizing change in terms of such divisions. Employing psychoanalytic and/or deconstructive theory, feminist theorists have shown that traditional discourses governing patriarchal capitalism support a scapegoat logic which dichotomizes culture in order to repress difference and reproduce dominant relations of power.[27] Those groups or related attributes marked as lacking are denied recognition even as they are made to reflect and maintain dominant culture through their own effacement. Through the imposition of hierarchized categories—presence vs. absence, culture vs. nature, mind vs. body, subject vs. object, white vs. black, man vs. woman—difference is subsumed under a binary opposition which tames its dissonance. As one pole of the duality is valorized, the subordinate pole is relegated to a position of otherness, situated as the negative image, the reflective counterpart of the one recognized principle.

Woman, in this system, is man's opposite—a similar yet deficient being who is defined only in relation to the single standard of value which is Man (figured as a universal ideal yet nonetheless marked by attributes of middle-class, white heterosexuality). While the logic appears to recognize two separate entities, difference is actually made to uphold unity and sameness. Distinctions and disparities—not only those between men and women, but those among and within women (and men) themselves—are effaced, reducing complex and overlapping sexual differences into a univocal sexual division. The projection of all lack and instability onto the Woman (figured, indeed, as the eternal feminine) assures Man of his own unity and rationality; as complement to the subject, Woman guarantees his position as subject of mastery.

Film theory has shown how this logic has been produced and reproduced in Hollywood films with particular ideological effects. In the classical narrative film, the actual means of film production (camera, lights, microphones) are hidden from the spectator's view, yielding a sense of the world seamlessly unfolding before our eyes. The spectator, identifying with the camera's power of the gaze, is thus positioned as an ideal subject, freed from material constraints and offered a flattering illusion of power.[28] Yet this effect is based upon an opposition established between subject and object of the look even as critical awareness of this opposition is impeded by the denial of the intervening presence of the apparatus. Feminist film theory goes on to demonstrate how the conventions of film neatly combine spectacle and narrative so as to reinforce the sexual coding of this subject/object opposition.[29]

In perhaps the most influential article in feminist film theory, "Visual Pleasure and Narrative Cinema," Laura Mulvey uses psychoanalytic theory to explain how film spectatorship is structured along gender lines. According to Mulvey, pleasure in looking involves both sexual drives and ego identification—we take others as objects of the sexual gaze and also identify with screen surrogates in a (mis)recognition of the self. Yet Mulvey argues that the careful balance of the contradictory aims of ego and libido is securely achieved only for (some) male spectators: in classical film, as "in a world ordered by sexual imbalance, pleasure in looking has been split between active/male and passive/female" (11). The male spectator (at least one that assumes the dominant position of white hetero-masculinity) can, through secondary identification, align himself with the active male protagonist, who in turn looks at the female characters within the story. The coincidence of these looks grants potency to the man while the woman, framed for the gaze of both male characters and viewers, simply connotes "to-be-looked-at-ness." Further problems posed by the female figure (because of the threat of sexual difference and the castration anxiety this evokes) are handled through the mechanisms of fetishism and voyeurism, making the female form assure rather than undercut hetero-masculine mastery.

Mulvey summarizes the implications of her analysis in an oft-quoted passage:

> Woman then stands in patriarchal culture as a signifier for the male other, bound by a symbolic order in which man can live out his phantasies and obsessions through linguistic command by imposing them on the silent image of woman still tied to her place as bearer of meaning, not maker of meaning. (7)

Articulating the subject/object opposition inherent in film spectatorship along the lines of sexual polarity, the cinema reinforces a particular social hierarchy, inscribing power relations through its very visual and narrative codes. Situated through these signifying strategies, the film spectator is necessarily (even if unconsciously) implicated in these relations. Of course, since Mulvey's famous article appeared, volumes have been written which modify and/or complicate her argument, considering desires, identifications, readings, and viewers not adequately addressed (if addressed at all) within "Visual Pleasure and Narrative Cinema." Yet while feminist film theory has certainly subjected its understanding of cinematic and psychic formations to a number of "re-visions," the Mulvian model has itself informed much of this attention, suggesting its continued importance for discussions of film.[30]

Television, however, involves a different set of codes and signifying strategies, thereby constructing a different viewer-text relation. Indeed, the very status and parameters of the text with which viewers engage may be questioned. Because of this, the social and ideological dynamics of television diverge from those of film so that while U.S. television clearly reinforces American culture's dominant gender and economic system, the spectator is positioned as a sexed and consumerized subject in a slightly different way.[31] As I've indicated, television can be (and has been) seen as a threat to the linear logic of both film and other classical narrative forms. In disrupting accepted categories of authenticity, knowledge, and mastery as well as further confounding the bases of history and origins (which in turn form the bases of traditional notions of the individual), television weakens the oppositions that maintain the stability of the sexed gaze. This is not at all to say that television in fact subverts conventional alignments of power (although this occasionally may be the case with particular texts, or much more frequently, with particular readings); it is to consider how television has been positioned within the discourses of both mass culture and mass-cultural critique and, further, how this intersects with the gendered, raced, and classed positions offered to and imagined for its viewers.

This may be clarified by returning to a previous example: in discussing the new discursive configurations that television employs, Baudrillard suggests precisely the possibility of such subversion (a subversion he treats with some ambivalence) by remarking that television cannot be considered a spectacular medium. Penetrating reality to the point of abolishing a stable referent, television also collapses the distance between subject and object—a distance that is crucial to the construction of spectacle and the mechanisms of voyeurism and fetishism that uphold a sexual opposition in looking. To demonstrate how this operates in Baudrillard's discourse, let me quote him at length:

> The eye of TV is no longer the source of an absolute gaze, and the ideal of control is no longer that of transparency. The latter still presupposes an objective space (that of the Renaissance) and the omnipotence of a despotic gaze . . . in a position of exteriority, playing on the opposition between seeing and being seen. . . . It is entirely different [with TV] where the distinction between active and passive is abolished. Such is the slope of a hyperrealist sociality, where the real is confused with the model. . . . A turnabout of affairs by which it becomes impossible to locate an instance of the model of power, of the gaze, of the medium itself, since *you* are always already on the other side . . . and hence, the *very abolition of the spectacular*. (*Simulations* 52–55)

While television may not be as "entirely different" as Baudrillard claims—its sense of immediacy and democracy are also based upon specular illusion—its specific logic marks its illusions in quite particular ways. Appearing to abolish spectatorial distance as it disturbs binary categories, television involves the viewer in a very different relation to the screen.

It is because of the ostensible absence of viewer distance from the image as well as the weakening of the oppositions *passive/active* and *subject/object* that television spectatorship has been linked, in serious discussions as well as in offhand remarks, to figures of femininity. As I suggested in chapter 1 and will further elaborate in the next chapter, tropes of "nearness," "proximity," and "overpresence" (related to the more conventional notion of "feminine empathy") have been used in both popular and scholarly accounts to describe the position of the female subject in regard to the object, the image, and her body—a position ensuing, according to psychoanalytic and many feminist theorists, from the woman's lack of a firm subject/object dichotomy.[32] Lacking the gap required for mastery of both signification and sexuality that is provided for men by the phallic signifier (representing the possibility of loss), women are assumed to be too close to the original (lost maternal) object.

As Mary Ann Doane demonstrates, such assumptions enter into both film theory and popular conceptions of the female film viewer: women are represented as overinvested viewers, exhibiting "too close" a relationship to the screen, and they are thus apt to manufacture a distance from the image through an act of masquerade (flaunting "womanliness" to fore-ground it *as* an image, involving, Doane states, "a realignment of feminin-ity, the recovery, or more accurately, *simulation*, of the missing gap" [em-phasis added]).[33] This convolution of spatial and subjective locations (that is, acting as a receptacle, exhibiting spectatorship)—whether valorized for marking off a space for women or condemned for making any such space untenable—has then been associated not only with a female identity (or the lack thereof) in general but with what seems to be posed as a feminine viewing identity in particular.[34] There are certainly problems in assuming any such singular identity (for both women and/or viewers). Yet whatever the difficulties are in defining a "feminine viewing subject" (and these problems are massive), television as a whole has been seen as replicating precisely the conditions that yield this formation. Because television is marked by similar convolutions in spatial, spectatorial, and subjective relations—indeed, by a comparable mode of simulation—it is attacked (or applauded, depending on the view of the critic) for putting all spectators into a "feminized" position.[35] These unexamined tropes of femininity inscribed into the language of mass culture, film, and television theory then contribute to the widespread disparagement of TV and its viewers.

Television and the "Feminine" Viewer-Consumer

Yet simply because television has been associated in both the popular and critical imagination with femininity is no reason for feminist theorists to embrace TV uncritically (if, indeed, at all). The common-sense under-standing of female identification in terms of empathy, proximity, or "wo-man's intuition," as well as theoretical attempts to define "the feminine" in terms of a breakdown in classical logic (as that which escapes binary oppositions), are also discursive and cultural constructions of femininity on par with the assumed feminization of the TV audience. This "feminiza-tion" is thus not a natural occurrence, but a socially constituted one—and one that is beneficial to the dominant socio-economic structures of the United States in general and the TV industry specifically—even if it alludes to a subjectivity seen by some critics as descriptive of women's position in culture. Although TV's confusion of oppositional categories and apparent neglect of classical form may provide some possibilities for a radical intervention, television as it is currently organized gears its specific textuality and viewer/text engagement toward a goal quite consonant with capitalist patriarchy—the encouragement of consumption.

It comes as no surprise that a medium which has been seen as "feminine" is also a medium which is intimately tied to consumerism. Not only do we "consume" television texts themselves, we are encouraged to consume the products advertised as well as the "lifestyle" images promoted by both. The "feminization" of the TV viewer thus relates to women's role as primary consumer in our society as much (or moreso) as it is derived from the particular dynamics of television spectatorship (which, of course, need not be coded as either feminine or masculine outside of cultural mappings that stake out such positions). For the television industry, the construction of the viewer as consumer is certainly of much greater import than any gender connotations attached to this status; institutionally, that is, the connection between consumerism and femininity may be purely instrumental if it is acknowledged at all. Given the economic imperatives of late capitalism, broadcasters and advertisers are first and foremost concerned with increasing ratings and sales rather than with promoting particular social and sexual relations, but it is impossible (and I believe counterproductive) to map causality in any unilateral direction. TV producers may be trying to reach "consumers" more than they are trying to address "feminine" (or "feminized") viewers, but they assume that the heaviest consumers are most likely to be women on the basis of historical, social, and ideological constructions that mass culture (including television) has itself enforced.

While the material conditions linking femininity and consumerism are then historically determined, the discursive connections are mutually sustaining. Indeed, the very lack of distance involved in TV spectatorship that has led to the tropes I've discussed also yields the psychology of the perfect consumer: an overidentification with the image, or as Benjamin writes, "the desire . . . to bring things 'closer' . . . the urge . . . to get hold of an object at very close range" that is symptomatic of mass (consumer) culture (223).[36] The instability that television evokes and plays upon—an instability fostered by the dissolution of traditional categories, the breakdown of polar logic, the abolition of a fixed referent, and the subversion of unified subjectivity—is thus related to its promotion of consumption. The role of consumer is the sole identity that remains stable in this field of fluid signs; left anxious, bored, or distracted by the continuous barrage of messages, images, and positions, the television viewer may cling to consumption as the only certain value.

In fact, among the open-ended texts of much American television, the commercials notably stand out as offering clear resolution: while prime-time characters and situations never progress (the same faults are exposed in new comical situations each week; no lesson is ever learned), and soap operas stifle any hope for closure, the commercials give us mini-dramas in which progress, knowledge, and resolution *are* possible—merely through a simple purchase.[37] Assuredly, not all television commercials work by providing punctuation in precisely this way: some, indeed, mimic the continuing narrative forms of the surrounding television texts (the Energizer bunny that, since 1989, "keeps going and going," or even more indebted to the soap operas which it "interrupts," the ongoing saga of the romantic couple in the Taster's Choice coffee ads initiated in 1990). Yet these commercials employ such clever narrative strategies in order to stand out from the rest of television's flow, therefore also supplying a type of punctuation, one which depends on presenting themselves as exceptions to the rule.

But perhaps these cases are not quite so exceptional after all; U.S. television is so intertwined with consumerism that the relation of programming to advertising goes well beyond the obvious role of the TV show as frame for the commercial and enticement for a particular (commodified) way of life.[38] Some current television forms collapse the distinctions between product, text, and ad entirely; the unambiguously named "infomercial" clearly signals the interpenetration of information technologies and commercial interests. Music videos provide another example of such a hybridization (one that has been further mixed into a number of television programs and genres): videos can be described as texts which are commercials for themselves. In both their consumer appeal and their address to an audience of youths, a viewer who is not yet considered a man, music videos are in many ways exemplary, occupying a privileged place in both television history and the "televisual imaginary."[39] As such, they demonstrate the gender contradictions that may arise in a medium that is considered "feminine" by many critics but is itself committed to appealing to the public at large. The combination of genres and modes of address employed by the infomercial (particularly those that attempt to appeal equally to men and women) reveals similar pressures.[40]

Of course, these very contradictions—the multitude of differences within what's been dismissed as television's vast sea of indifference—prevents us from selecting any one case as *the* representative one. Nonetheless, some texts seem to me to be particularly instructive in considering television's relationship to discourses of gender (both on TV and about it). As I stated above, it is my belief that the forms most disparaged by cultural critics are frequently the most revealing—while one can't quite claim that they're "characteristic" of television and its specific textual economy (since this economy is distinguished precisely by its lack of unified and stable terms), they certainly adhere most closely to the image of a feminized and/or consumption-driven viewer.

By exploring a textual form that has been scorned for precisely this reason, the next chapter investigates this image—and what it means for television and postmodernism—in detail. Specifically, I turn to a consideration of melodrama, a genre historically associated with a female audience and intimately linked to the demands of consumer culture. Yet all of the television programs addressed here, as well as the criticism surrounding their popular and critical attention, are mediated by discourses of gender and consumer pleasure. By examining the meanings of television and the tensions thereby provoked, I hope both to expose the processes at work in television textuality and television theory and to open up a space for alternative readings and/or practices. While TV's "feminine" viewer is also America's primary consumer, television's "feminine difference" (its distinct logic, diffraction of the gaze, confusion of polarities) also shifts the terms of dominant cultural discourses, perhaps providing new positions from which to critique, intervene, and reformulate the media. Through an analysis of television, postmodern culture, and the unexamined discourses of gender and consumption, I hope finally to promote just such an intervention.

Cary Scott framed by television in *All That Heaven Allows*.

Maria Santos-Grey framed by television on *All My Children*.

III

ALL THAT TELEVISION ALLOWS
TV MELODRAMA, POSTMODERNISM,
AND CONSUMER CULTURE

Drama at Our Fingertips

In an emotionally charged scene in Douglas Sirk's 1955 film melodrama *All That Heaven Allows*, the protagonist (Jane Wyman) receives a TV set as a gift. Wyman plays Cary Scott, a white, middle-aged, and upper-middle-class widow in love with a man who is not only younger than she, but of a lower social class—she first meets Ron Kirby (Rock Hudson) when he's pruning her trees. In the course of the narrative, Cary faces increasing social and familial opposition to the romance and is forced to leave Ron. She receives the present from her two grown children who offer it as an affirmation of her continued bourgeois status (her decision not to marry "down" and leave the family home) and as a substitution for the love she has renounced. She is, in other words, given a typical "media fix" to the problems inherent in her gender, race, and class position—consumer compensation in exchange for an active pursuit of her desire. As the TV salesman explains that "all you have to do is turn that dial and you have all the company you want right there on the screen—drama, comedy, life's parade at your fingertips," there is an image of Cary's face, framed and reflected in the TV screen as she realizes the futility of her actions and the impossibility of her situation. Figured as the ultimate passive spectator, so tangled in the web of bourgeois culture that she is literally collapsed onto the picture of her misery, Cary's very subjectivity is incorporated into television.

In an article detailing the path of melodrama ". . . from its birth in the crowded city streets to its death in the television dominated home," Laura Mulvey refers to this same cinematic scene ("Melodrama" 82). In the 1950s, television erupted in the American home and placed itself firmly within the realm of family, domesticity, and consumerism—the very ground of the movie melodrama. Noting Hollywood's response to this invasion, Mulvey writes, "It is as though, at the moment of defeat, Hollywood could afford to point out the seeds of decay in its victorious rival's own chosen breeding ground" (82). Yet these seeds of decay were not enough to overthrow the new medium or its familial base. Instead, the consolidated family, with TV as its tool, seemed to triumph over critical melodramas. Mulvey concludes that the swing to political conservatism and the repositioning of women in the home gave order to the oppositions *public/private, production/reproduction,* and *inside/outside,* whose tensions had propelled melodrama and allowed it a political dimension.[1] According to her, the birth of television therefore displaced, and seemingly even resolved, the genre's animating force. As TV brought popular entertainment into the home, national consensus triumphed over a potentially oppositional melodrama.

But has melodrama died? Or has it been subsumed into television, engulfing the medium as it engulfs its spectators and precluding its location as a separate category? This possibility is strikingly figured in *All That Heaven Allows* as the TV screen takes over the cinematic frame, enclosing Cary and the entire melodramatic *mise-en-scène* in a haze of consumerism, impotent spectatorship, and televisual hyperreality. These are the terms of postmodern U.S. culture in which history, subjectivity, and reality seem to flatten out into a TV image, and we are left searching for signs of meaning within an endless flow of images—a situation leading to both nostalgia for past traditions and a related backlash against women's social and political gains.[2] In this historical scenario, television draws us all, women and men, into a shared bond of consumer overpresence and powerless spectatorship as melodrama becomes the preferred form for TV, the postmodern medium *par excellence.*[3]

In other words, rather than eclipsing melodrama, television incorporates it so as to bring the strands of passivity and domesticity associated with both melodrama and TV together in a simulated plenitude, thereby positioning all viewers as susceptible consumers. To continue a thread begun in chapter 1, one might say that television is "occupied" by (or "preoccupied" with) melodrama and vice-versa. At the same time, the "feminine" connotations traditionally attached to melodrama—and to both consumerism and television viewing—are diffused onto a general audience, opening up contradictions of spectatorship and sexual difference(s) in the TV melodrama which invite further investigation. In the previous chapter, I traced the ways in which television has been figured as feminine in both popular and scholarly discourses on media and mass culture and indicated that such discursive trends may be exacerbated, rather than eclipsed, by the conditions of postmodernity. In this chapter, I will investigate American broadcast television's relationship to gender—how it has taken up these associations, positioning itself and its viewers in ambivalent ways—by turning to TV melodrama and to several television texts from the 1980s which, even if not labeled as such, might usefully be considered "melodramatic." Because melodrama is a form which has been historically associated with a female audience, the rise of the TV melodrama raises questions of gender and genre as well as that of television's place within American life.[4] By offering an initial exploration into such issues, I will attempt to map out the discursive connections forged between television, melodrama, and postmodern consumer culture, focusing on the problems of gender constituted within this field.

Television: The Melodramatic Screen

With a broadening appeal to a general audience of viewer-consumers, melodrama moves to television and so dominates its discourses that it is difficult to locate as a separate TV genre. Of course, there are some television forms that are clearly marked as melodrama. Both the daytime and prime-time soap opera, for example, seem to employ many of the characteristic devices of the film melodrama.[5] The use of music to convey emotional effects defines the basic attribute of melodrama in all its forms, and this same trait distinguishes the soap opera. Music orchestrates the emotional ups and downs and underscores a particular rhythm of experience. This rhythm, in film melodrama and the TV soap opera, is one of exaggerated fluctuations, marking the discontinuities of emotional experience as the plots slowly build, amid much delay, to dramatic moments of outbreak and collision before sudden reversals of fortune begin the movement again.

Dramatic intensification is also heightened by concentrated visual metaphors and gestural codes—the repetition of configurations of actors from one scene to the next, for example, to indicate similar or contrasting emotional relations, the references to visibly different styles of dress or color of hair to signify opposing positions within the programs' familial schemes, or the externalization of affect onto representative objects that act as stand-ins for missing human contact. The meaning of everyday action, ordinary gesture, and standard decor is thus intensified so that the psychic strains, breaks, and escalations of feeling are made manifest. Like the film melodrama, television soap opera expresses what are primarily ideological and social conflicts in emotional terms. Action then largely takes place within the context of the home or in sites at the intersection of public and private space that are central to personal concerns (the hospital room, a hotel, the private office available for intimate conversations, et cetera). The intensification of the significance of mundane objects and locations—the doorbells and telephones, doctors' offices and bedrooms so charged with connotations in the soap opera—works to displace the emphasis from social relations to material objects even as they express an anxiety about the uncertainties of daily life.[6]

While such patterns drawn from the cinematic conventions of the family melodrama seem appropriate to the typically domestic interiors of the soap opera, in the 1980s soap opera expanded to include broader and more diverse settings while extending melodramatic conventions to a wider scope.[7] Soap opera increasingly combined with other genres: police, crime, and spy dramas became popular on *General Hospital*, for example, and the world of big business was taken on by prime-time soaps such as *Dallas* (1979–1991), which also employed elements of the western, *Dynasty* (1981–1989), and *L.A. Law* (1986–1994). Soap opera even incorporated elements of science fiction, previously hailed as the last domain of wide open space,[8] in episodes of *One Life to Live* (whose stories included such things as time

warps, hidden underground cities, and a spaceship traveling to heaven)
and the 1987 finale of *The Colbys* (which wrapped up its broadcast run with
the UFO abduction of a major character [1985–1987]).

As these examples indicate, soap operas were able to move into realms
not usually associated with the melodrama, while at the same time, TV
forms not typically seen in this way became more and more melodramatic.
This is certainly not to imply that other genres—the comedy, to take one
crucial example—failed to maintain a strong presence on network schedules and to exert an influence on television programming in numerous
forms (variety and talk shows, situation and domestic comedies, et cetera).
Yet the development in the mid-to-late 1980s of programs such as
Hooperman (1987–1989), *Frank's Place* (1987–1988), and *The Days and Nights
of Molly Dodd* (1987–1988, subsequently picked up by the Lifetime cable
channel from 1989–1991) suggests that even what Jane Feuer has described
as television's "simplest and least cinematic genre," the situation comedy,
could incorporate some of film melodrama's conventions ("Narrative"
107). Termed "dramadies" to denote their combination of comedy and
serialized drama, usually within a half-hour format, these shows were
symptomatic, revealing that both U.S. television's and consumer culture's
specific demands tend to propel comic forms as well toward a focus on
character and affect and an emotional investment in the realm of personal
relations—the realm, that is, of the melodrama.[9] Of course, the term
dramady largely functioned as a marketing device; the programs mentioned above were innovative in certain ways, but as I elaborate in chapter
5, the label attached to them also acknowledged what was always already
true about comedy—its absolutely serious role.

Television texts taken to be explicitly serious, in fact, rely on quite
similar strategies. The made-for-TV movie, for example, is often marketed
as a form particularly suited for dealing with contemporary social issues.[10]
Like the 1950s film melodrama, however, it manages these issues by
inserting them into a domestic framework in which the family functions as
the sole referent.[11] Police and detective dramas also purportedly deal with
the social issues of crime, drugs, prostitution, and so on; yet even while
their emphasis on action seems to remove them from the domain of the
melodrama, they exhibit many of its characteristics. Although they are
able to act freely against the criminals, the heroes of TV cop shows are still
trapped within a confined world in which emotional pressure, familial
concerns, and gender or class position take on heightened importance.
Because of the economic and institutional demands of television, the good
guys are never fully allowed to conquer their enemies; instead they are
forced to repeat their actions week after week, trapping them within a
restricted world of perpetual victimization and thereby lessening the gap
between these dramas and the soap operas where perpetual suffering is
the rule.

As direct action proves futile, the emphases of even the crime series shift
to the more personal issues traditionally associated with the melodrama.
In many cop or detective shows, the audience's emotional involvement is

induced by a focus on the family in danger of dissolution. The officer or detective then must strive to save the family—either his own (*Heart of the City* [1986–1987], *Simon and Simon* [1981–1988]), those of his clients (*The Equalizer* [1985–1989], *Stingray* [1986–1987], and *Spenser: For Hire* [1985–1988], among many other shows, have featured such plots), or that of the police force itself (*Hill Street Blues* [1981–1987]). Very often the strains and tensions that exist between members of the police "family" are investigated, and the contrasts drawn between members of the team are used to explore issues of class, race, or gender dynamics. For example, *Spenser: For Hire* can be seen as mapping out relations (and exposing contradictions) of race and class in the contrasts made evident between Spenser and Hawk, his "street-smart" African American buddy who assists him with his cases. *In the Heat of the Night* (which premiered in 1988) is another such example. Gender, on the other hand, is made central on *Magnum, p.i.* (1980–1988), *Miami Vice* (1984–1989), and other shows in which, as I argue in chapter 4, the attempt to define masculinity is a crucial issue, often taking precedence over the specific crimes portrayed.[12] As the focus shifts from problems of crime to questions of identity within familial and social roles, these television series move into the realm of melodrama.

Crime and social crises are the mainstay of network news programming as well, yet these forms also turn to melodrama to handle such "stories." Peter Brooks concludes his influential study of the melodramatic imagination by noting its persistence in today's dramas of natural disasters and political personalities, the stuff of newscasts "homologous to the dramas played out every day on television screens" (203–204). Like cop and detective shows, news stories are often framed in personal terms as a way of avoiding the larger institutional, political, and ideological issues they raise. By employing conventions taken from narrative television (including a focus on the family—the news "family" and the families investigated), news programs achieve the emotional intensification and moral polarization associated with dramatic serials. The cast of newsworthy figures (presented by a network of reporters linked to one another as well as to the viewer by the anchor's paternal glance) are thus often characterized by a schematization which externalizes strife onto visibly polar forces, allowing television news to forego in-depth analysis.[13] As in the explicitly fictional melodrama, conflicts are brought to the surface and expressed through contrasts that rehearse and flatten out the issues.

Emotional release is likewise provoked by familiar dramatic and visual conventions—tight close-ups of grieving families or victims, an emphasis placed on symbolic objects (the American flag at half-mast, for example) or settings (news reporters dwarfed by the image of Capitol Hill or the White House even if these locations are not the actual sources of information), and the rise-and-fall patterns of narrative movement that organize both separate news stories and the composition of the segments in news programs as a whole. When the space shuttle *Challenger* exploded in January 1986, TV utilized all of these devices in repeated shots of the disaster intercut with close-ups of attending family members and small school children. Even the rhetoric used was drawn from the melodrama: this was not simply an accident, but a tragedy in which ordinary people sacrificed themselves for the future of our children and our nation. Interrupting the usual melodramas on the air, the soap operas, TV substituted this "real life" drama, obsessively replaying all the poignant moments. More recent examples—but equally symptomatic of the technological, political, and/or social anxieties of the Reagan-Bush era—would include the 1991 television coverage of the Persian Gulf War (a violent mobilization that was timed and staged for domestic viewing/consuming) and the Clarence Thomas–Anita Hill hearings (a public airing of a dispute over the boundaries of the personal and the professional).[14]

The interpenetration of the public and the private, politics and affect, that fueled these events—or, more specifically, their television coverage— is indicative of our mass-mediated culture; it also suggests the significance of TV's melodramatic mode which both exploits and manages this commixture.[15] In each of these cases, a representational "shorthand" was employed, turning extremely complex national, racial, and sexual "battles" into personalized contests of good vs. evil, right vs. wrong. The temporal extension of live coverage was combined with the emotional and even physical compression of the melodrama, thus defining "current affairs" as "domestic affairs" in quite striking ways.[16] Indeed, on a similar note, the affective content and form of the entire spate of sensational "current affair," "news-magazine," and reality-based "public service" shows (texts ranging from, for instance, *A Current Affair* and *Inside Edition* to *America's Most Wanted, Unsolved Mysteries,* and *Rescue 911*) reveals the pervasiveness of the melodramatic mode. In discussions of film and literary history, "realism" is often opposed to melodrama; TV's "reality programs," however, suggest that in televisual terms they may be one and the same.

Melodrama emerges not only in television's most "pedestrian" forms (as in these frequently imitated, low-budget shows), but equally within its most "experimental." In other words, even TV programs or genres that seem far removed both from one another and from the melodramas of the cinema employ devices that link them together. To turn to another example (one that might not be so different after all), in the late 1980s, the series *Max Headroom* (1987) was hailed as one of TV's most innovative shows because of its self-reflexive use of video and computer technology, imaginative sets and costumes, distorted visuals and unusual camera angles, fast-paced editing, and up-to-date language (dialogue that only a techno-whiz-kid could fully understand). While *Max Headroom's* televisual life (at least in *our* media reality) was quite short-lived, its appearance and commentary on the postmodern scene was not only historically significant but theoretically engaging. Yet even this "postmodern" program ultimately resorted to melodrama as it collapsed back into a standard representation of good versus evil.

The good guys were, of course, hard-working, independent men and women who cared about the common folk while the bad ones were associated with a powerful bureaucracy that fed off of human suffering. Such oppositions were made visible through contrasting clothing, styles, manners, and possessions: the wealthy villains were well-groomed smooth talkers in black suits who guarded their rare possessions while likable characters wore casual clothes, understood street talk, and treasured their old stuffed animals. In providing this typically melodramatic scenario even while attempting to remain informed and self-aware concerning television's power to construct identity, history, and reality, *Max Headroom* existed in the tension between modern and postmodern forms. As I will elaborate in chapter 6, the series solved this contradiction by splitting its protagonist into two—we were given both the tough and dedicated TV journalist Edison Carter and his video-generated alter-ego Max Headroom, who was created by a young computer genius while Carter battled crime. By so splitting the character, the program was able to displace all the cyborgian elements of postmodern subjectivity onto Max, leaving Carter free to play the role of hero who was nonetheless caught in a limited world—his actions, risks, and sacrifices could never really free society of its problems or contradictions.

This variety of cases demonstrates the extent to which U.S. television has continued to rely on melodrama, deploying its iconography and language in texts that range from the most "everyday" (such as the daily news) to those that have been lauded as TV's most "advanced" (*Max Headroom*). This last show's project may have "failed," but its strategies nonetheless suggest that we turn to melodrama to ward off the threat of a new form of culture, to buttress ourselves against a postmodern world in which even the distinction between video image and human identity becomes blurred (a situation apparent not only in futuristic drama but within our own "reality shows"). Despite Mulvey's claim that melodrama (or at least its potentially subversive mode) has died in the TV-dominated home, television melodrama stands strong. Its conventions are employed in a wide span of programs as television attempts to maintain the clarity that melodrama provides through its strongly marked oppositions and heightened moral register. Yet as it spreads out across a number of TV forms from the soaps to the police show, comedy to "reality," the news to the commercials, melodrama loses its specificity, becoming diffuse and ungrounded in its multiple deployments in the flow of TV.

Simulated Sentiment

It is not surprising that today's media-saturated society has been linked, in Mulvey's analysis for example, to the end of melodrama. As Fredric Jameson remarks, postmodernism is repeatedly marked by such "senses of the end of this or that . . . the hypothesis of some radical break or *coupure*, generally traced back to the end of the 1950s or the early 1960s," the death of melodrama in the TV-centered home being one more example of this phenomenon ("Postmodernism" 53). Yet melodrama's popularity has historically coincided with times of intense social and ideological crisis, and the postmodern age is certainly characterized by its many theorists as *the* age of crisis.[17] This is not to say that "our" crises are somehow more severe, more "meaningful" (or perhaps meaningless) than those of other eras (periods in which melodrama also flourished), but that postmodern life has indeed been thus represented, leading to a particular cultural (and televisual) landscape. Aligned with the rise of multinational and con-sumer capitalism, postmodernity threatens to replace determining ma-chines of production with weightless models of reproduction, dissolving any possible distinction between aesthetic and commodity production and proclaiming the end of meaning, the liquidation of the referential, and the dissolution of identity.

With this crisis in representation comes a crisis in power, authority, and legitimation as the traditional "master narratives" fail to obtain. It would then seem that postmodernity multiplies the contradictions that animate melodrama—contradictions between production and reproduction, aver-age and excess, topicality and timelessness, public and private, the Law and desire, masculine and feminine—further dissolving the ostensible stability of Western culture. Given this state, Jean-François Lyotard an-nounces that "[t]he narrative function is losing its functors, its great hero, its great dangers, its great voyages, its great goal. It is being dispersed in clouds of narrative language elements" (xxiv).[18] In other words, we face the death of the great white male story. As Lyotard claims, all is "dis-persed" in a cloud of dramatic fragments held together through only surface relations and tensions—a description corresponding remarkably well to both melodrama and network television.

Other critics have recognized the ties between contemporary media culture and melodramatic form. David Thorburn, for example, claims that "television melodrama has been our culture's most characteristic aesthetic form," and in his discussion of this broad category—encompassing the made-for-TV movie, the western, "all the lawyers, . . . cops and docs, the fugitives and adventurers," as well as the more easily recognized daytime and prime-time soap operas—Thorburn argues for the specific suitability of melodrama for television (628, 631).[19] Like television, melodrama is scorned for its moral simplification, reassuring fantasies, and immediate sensation in its effort to portray behavior "shocking" to its time (630). TV parallels melodrama in its form as well as content as it centers on familial space, a situation fostered by the (usual) size of the screen and its custom-ary location in the home. Together with the low visual intensity of the medium and the smaller budget of its productions, these factors encour-age television's reliance on background music, the close-up, confined interiors, and intimate gesture rather than action—elements that resonate with melodramatic conventions.

TV melodrama is then ideally suited to reveal the subtle strains of bourgeois culture with all of the contradictions it entails. Because televi-sion programs are market commodities structured according to rigid schedules and commercial interruptions, such strains include the tensions that emerge in the juxtaposition of the drama proper and the mini-melodramas seen in the commercials—stories which convey the hopeful sensibility of advertising (even as they disclose the daily problems of dirt and stress) and so potentially jar with the claustrophobic and often pessimistic worlds of prime-time serials (which nonetheless mask the labor required to maintain their luxury).[20] Yet Thorburn claims that such commercial limits are merely formal conventions guiding the genre (631–34). While he notes that as both aesthetic and commodity creations, TV melodramas may reveal the ambivalence of [post]industrial society, Thorburn does not fully explore the discord expressed by this form—frictions arising in consumer culture and tied to the shifting gender and class relations of postmodern America. In fact, Thorburn argues that television resolves melodrama's basic conflict: TV's ability to present intimate detail and intense emotion in a small and familiar space minimizes the tension between ordinary reality and the excessive emotionality brought together in the genre (638). Yet as the cultural form which perhaps best illustrates the fluctuating ground of a mediatized world, television cannot resolve the contradictions of postmodernity. It may evince a desperate attempt to evade these tensions by reclaiming meaning and tradition, but this attempt is doomed to failure and TV melodrama is forced endlessly to replay its contradictions—contradictions which must be investigated so as to open a space for renewed feminist analyses and politics.

As I noted in the previous chapter, according to Baudrillard, the discord of postmodern culture infects even the "certainties" of determinate history and coherent reality: no longer tied to origin, reference, or identity, our culture is ruled by what Plato called the "simulacrum"—"the identical copy for which no original has ever existed" (Jameson, "Postmodernism" 66). Just as the territory of the real is no longer mapped onto a representation but "the map . . . precedes the territory," events are already inscribed by the media in advance as television is diffracted into reality and the real is diffracted into TV (Baudrillard, *Simulations* 2; see also 3–7, 30–32).[21] Simulation has thus been seen as the ruin of representation, giving the lie to our faith that a sign can exchange for meaning since it only exchanges in itself—we find only more signs and images in a circuit without order or direction (10–11).[22] Of course, this description of postmodern culture may not in fact be "true"; ironically enough, however, it does seem to be "real," capturing a feeling prevalent in the 1980s (and beyond) that has had palpable effects. The fear that meaningful identity and rational expression have somehow escaped us—that we have lost all grounding in our culture and our lives—has led to a situation that national politicians, educational "canonists," and commercial investors have been happy to exploit.

Paradoxically, while capitalism was the first system to destroy the referential by establishing a law of equivalence in which all is exchangeable through the medium of money, it must now protect itself from the subversion of order inherent in the simulacrum. America has therefore hardened itself against its own hyperreality (43–44). As Baudrillard remarks, "a panic-stricken production of the real" and the referential today overtakes even the drive toward material production (13). We exhibit an obsession with signs of reality, tradition, and lived experience as nostalgia engulfs us in a hysterical attempt to find stakes of meaning. Thus we stockpile the past to guarantee authenticity, and we create imaginary fantasies (Disneyland is his example) to convince ourselves that a separate imaginary is possible—to assure ourselves, in other words, that the real exists apart, and is therefore distinguishable, from Disneyland. The production of such fictions of the real defines the role of TV in both its "realistic" (news, live television) and imaginary (narrative) forms—both provide the illusion of actuality and bolster our sense of the reality of the stakes.[23]

Melodrama might at first appear to be an odd form in which to search for social grounding and signs of the real. But as Peter Brooks has argued, the melodramatic mode, above all, expresses the desire to find sure stakes of meaning, morality, and truth. It thus emerges in times of doubt and uncertainty, employing signs which may seem overdetermined and excessive in order to mark out values left cloudy by a disintegrating sacred system. Combating the anxiety produced by a new order which can no longer assure us of the operation, or even existence, of fundamental social, moral, or "natural" truths, melodrama "arises to demonstrate that it is still possible to find and to show the operation of basic ethical imperatives, to define, in conflictual opposition, the space of their play. That they can be staged 'proves' that they exist" (200–201). That is, moral struggle is made visible, announcing itself as an indisputable force. By enacting irreducible imperatives, melodrama serves to reassure a doubting audience of essential truths while its "logic of the excluded middle" acts to focus feeling into pure and immediate knowledge (15).

The staging of melodrama's Manichaean conflicts as a strategy to counter the decentered consciousness arising in a society in which fundamental meaning and morality have been thrown into question, then, sounds strikingly like the strategies Baudrillard outlines for the postmodern world. Both may be seen, in other words, as desperate attempts to map out artificially a real which is in danger of being lost in the shift to a new social and discursive field. While Brooks calls melodrama "a peculiarly modern form" (14), it is also particularly suited to our postmodern sensibility. As the political, social, and aesthetic representations of modern society lose their legitimacy, we are forced once again to find new stakes of meaning, and melodrama is the form to which we turn. Promising to ease "the anxiety brought by a frightening new world in which the traditional patterns of moral order no longer provide the necessary social glue," melodrama strives "to find, to articulate, to demonstrate, to 'prove' the existence of a moral universe which, though put into question, . . . does exist and can be made to assert its presence . . ." (20). The way in which this description of the melodramatic impulse resonates with the rhetoric of a "New World Order" is telling: the Reagan and Bush administrations used precisely these (mediated) methods to bolster and substantiate their claims.[24] Perfecting the art of the "sound bite"—postmodernity's own expressive shorthand—these politicians exacerbated any "crisis" in representation even while complaining of a crisis in moral values. In a simulated society which typically stages reality in order to "prove" its existence, melodrama offers a way to assert the "actual" drama of life.

In order to find such meaning and make it universally legible, melodrama leaves nothing unsaid. Its hyperbole and emotional heightening correspond to the difficulty of naming the reality it strives to locate. But with the loss in traditional guarantees, meaning becomes sentimentalized and individual. As Brooks explains, "melodrama represents both the urge toward resacralization and the impossibility of conceiving sacralization other than in personal terms. . . . The decision to 'say all,' . . . is a measure of the personalization and inwardness of post-sacred ethics, the difficulty of their location and expression" (16). Personality becomes the new value and 'sole referent—a condition central to today's consumer culture in which TV takes the leading role. Personality is used to evaluate and judge (consider again the Hill-Thomas hearings, not to mention TV talk shows), and it is one of television's primary selling points, the basis of its performers' appeal. Producing a sense of intimate contact, "personality" on television is an effect of TV's fiction of presence. Unlike the enigmatic aura of the film star (who is desirable insofar as s/he is distant, absent, and mysterious), the television personality seems immediately available to us.[25] Personality is then constructed as an outer layer, readable to all and there for us to have—or, as the commercials imply, to buy. In this way, it becomes a key element in the marketing of almost all commodity goods.

Americans' preoccupation with personality in the form of emotional satisfaction, psychic health, and images of well-being is tied to the rise of a therapeutic discourse that is central to media culture and consumer society. Like the melodrama, this therapeutic ethos is "rooted in peculiarly modern emotional needs—above all the need to renew a sense of selfhood that had grown fragmented, diffuse, and somehow 'unreal'" (Lears, "From Salvation" 4). While the growth of the therapeutic ethos and a consumption-oriented secularism has been linked by T. J. Jackson Lears to a sense of weightlessness found in the late nineteenth and early twentieth centuries (see *No Place*),[26] these phenomena are today almost fully institutionalized, exerting, as Mimi White has shown, an enormous influence over American television. As she states, "the therapeutic mode may be most strongly associated with women's genres and female viewers, but it is also popularly associated with the medium [of television] as a whole, or at least with the full range of daytime programs and prime-time fiction"—an effect, I would argue, of the way in which melodrama has enveloped much of television's discourse (*Tele-Advising* 36).[27]

Yet rather than fulfilling the need for self-realization and the experience of "real life," the therapeutic prescriptions offered by TV narratives, advertising, and the "leisure industry" as a whole have exacerbated the problem, further enmeshing us in a web of consumer interdependence and ego diffusion. As consumers continue to search for the path to the "real" self, they are led in circles, a situation which reinforces rather than resolves this sense of weightlessness and the process of rationalization. The same sense of unreality that nourishes the melodramatic imagination then fosters a consumer culture bent on supplying a simulated image to make up for our sense of loss of place and identity confusion.

The Space and Time of Consumerism

While melodrama, like advertising, figures social turmoil in the private, emotional terms of self and experience, it rejects the psyche as a realm of inner depth. As both Brooks and Thomas Elsaesser point out, psychological conflicts are externalized so that they may be clear as fundamental forces. It is in the clash and play of their visible oppositions that melodrama's meaning becomes both legible and consumable. Elsaesser thus emphasizes the genre's "non-psychological conception of the *dramatis personae,* who figure less as autonomous individuals than to transmit the action and link the various locales within a total constellation" (2). Charting a relational field, melodrama may be seen as architectural rather than literary, "a combination of structural tensions and articulated parts" (13). It is through its connecting points, rather than the interior depth of its characters, that melodrama expresses a particular historical consciousness.

Television has also been criticized for its failure to portray fully rounded characters, and as a medium composed of disjointed parts that are only held together in overlapping networks of shared commercial time, TV creates a constellation of consumption. Postmodern culture in general has been linked to such a space—a hyperspace of "constant busyness" suppressing depth, or as Jameson puts it, a packed emptiness "without any of that distance that formerly enabled the perception of perspective or volume" ("Postmodernism" 82–83). Depth is replaced by multiple surfaces across which codes play and flow. In the words of Baudrillard, the psychological dimension has given way to the "forced extroversion of all interiority, this forced injection of exteriority" ("The Ecstasy" 132). Even the fiction of autonomous subjectivity vanishes as our sense of inner space collapses. Identity is instead caught up in the circuit of "connections, contact, contiguity, feedback and generalized interface that goes with the universe of communication. With the television image—the television being the ultimate and perfect object for this new era—our own body and the whole surrounding universe become a control screen" ("The Ecstasy" 137).

The spatial logic of postmodern culture has its counterpart in a weightless relation to time, history, and memory—a construction also found in television melodrama. As images and narratives become fragmented and spectatorship appears more and more dispersed, we are said to inhabit "the synchronic rather than the diachronic," leading to what has been described as a crisis in historicity. To paraphrase Jameson, our relationship to the past is one of "historicism effacing history"; as even the illusion of a full or authentic relation of lived experience to history dissolves, we seem left with merely a random collection of images to which we turn in a frantic effort to appropriate a collective past ("Postmodernism" 64–65). Responding to the same conditions as the cultural critics, the television industry both "mediates" and exacerbates this situation. In its endless replaying of yesterday's shows, nostalgic fondness for former styles, and obsessive announcements of its own historical weight, television contributes to both the dissolution of the aura of tradition and the attempt to reformulate a new historical connection. History is constantly invoked as a reassuring anchor, but as it is dispersed in a pastiche of partial testimony and resituated in the flux of media production, it is deflated and eclipsed in a frame of eternal "nowness."[28] TV narrative provides a present method of consuming the past.

Television melodrama in particular plays on this hollow sense of time— its artificially contrived plots vacillate between both the compression and extension of time as old plots and stereotypes are frequently recycled or rehearsed rather than being fully developed. By replaying its own formulas, television fosters a sense of living tradition, a continuously available history that appeals to the nostalgic mode of postmodern culture. With no sure transcendental value to be achieved, melodrama can offer no final closure, and thus its narratives—in both continuing serials and episodic series—are circular, repetitive and irresolvable.[29] This is clear in the case of melodramatic series—weekly doctor or detective dramas, for example— in which characters are doomed endlessly to re-enact the dilemmas propelling their shows. Daytime and prime-time soap operas, on the other hand, provide continuing stories that seem to demand a historical sense of time. Yet comparable to the series, soap operas ultimately reject the notion of progress, the belief in a visible difference between past and future. In a genre whose form has been described as "an indefinitely expandable middle" lacking beginning or end, the viewers as well as the characters are trapped in an eternally conflictual present (Porter 783).[30]

Such melodramatic serials thus create a strange sense of time as they run vaguely along "real" time, stretching it at some points—when a climactic diegetic moment fills up several episodes or time freezes to hold a tableau—while compressing it in others—when children leave for boarding school, for example, and return in a year or two as teenagers. Noting this "curious holding of memory and forgetfulness" that is specific to television narration, Rosalind Coward asks, "If these programmes require such feats of memory, how is it that they also require equally spectacular acts of forgetfulness?" ("Come Back" 172).[31] Invoking history and memory even as they refuse historical grounding, TV melodramas disrupt traditional notions of coherent time, position, and identity, manipulating the televisual past in order to encourage continued consumption. It is not uncommon, for example, for a soap opera to deny and/or rewrite its own past in order to justify its current plots, and such breaches in historical accuracy

often incur the outrage of viewers who, as reception studies have demonstrated, actively "collaborate" on readings with which to make sense of—
or indeed, critique and resist—such manipulations.[32]

As Coward asserts in her article, one way TV melodrama twists memory
and history is by substituting actors in the roles of continuing characters,
a situation leading to some curious (and often criticized) results. For
example, there was a period on the soap opera *One Life to Live* when the
actress Christine Jones played the character Victoria Buchanan, substituting for the regular actress Erika Slezak. After Slezak returned to the role, it
was only a short time before the soap introduced a new character, Pamela
Buchanan (the wife of Victoria's father-in-law), who was played by none
other than Christine Jones. Regular viewers of *One Life to Live* then had the
strange experience of watching the woman who used to *be* Victoria
Buchanan be introduced to Victoria Buchanan. According to the narrative,
the two women had been total strangers but were now "related" through
marriage. Yet in many viewers' minds, they were already oddly connected, providing ample opportunity for *One Life to Live* fans to engage in
comic and/or tragic speculations. Such unusual memory effects are not
uncommon on the soap operas where actor substitution is a standard
practice—a practice which has also been employed on prime-time soaps,
although with less success and even more audience resistance (as in the
case of the 1984 substitution of Donna Reed for Barbara Bel Geddes in the
role of *Dallas*'s Miss Ellie, leading to Bel Geddes's return in 1985 and
Reed's subsequent suit for breach of contract that was settled out of court)
(Alex McNeil 176).

Viewers' memories of actors may also be deployed when an actor moves
to a new show, an event that can work as a selling point for the program
even as it may occasionally lead to some jarring developments (for instance, when actors who once played siblings wind up playing lovers on
another soap).[33] It is, of course, routine within Hollywood's star system to
rely upon the popularity and cluster of connotations attached to certain
actors, but because of U.S. television's particular construction of and
location within domestic time and space, these associations become quite
pronounced, constituting the very core of the TV personality. Such associations are then available as elements for production and publicity units—as
well as viewers themselves—both to work with and "work over."

For example, in 1987, ads in *TV Guide* for the NBC soap opera *Days of Our
Lives* featured Genie Francis, an actress who achieved fame playing Laura,
the ultimate good girl on ABC's *General Hospital* when that show was at the
peak of its popularity (due largely to the well-known romance of Laura
and her reformed-lover-but-one-time-rapist, Luke). Making obvious reference to viewers' recollections of Francis's previous role, the ads asked,
"What do you do when you've had it with doctors in white, white hospital
walls, and a white wedding to end all weddings? . . . You switch to *Days of
Our Lives*." Here television played with viewers' knowledge of TV's past
history in order to instigate present viewing and consuming (a knowledge
and appeal that crossed network lines). A less ironic, if also more typical,

 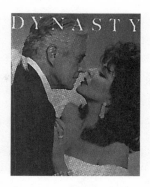

The dream ends on *Dallas*.

The dream continues on *Dynasty* (ad from *TV Guide*, January 1987).

campaign occurred when Francis returned to *General Hospital* (*GH*) in 1993. Both explaining and disavowing all the media attention, *GH* writer Claire Labine told *TV Guide* that she saw "the Luke-and-Laura partnership not as a show-biz phenomenon, but as 'two very old and dear friends whom we deeply loved but lost . . . coming home again'" (Logan 15).

One of the oddest cases of TV's deployment of history, memory, and time—infamous within the 1980s prime-time serial boom but still jokingly remembered (even used as a yardstick) today—was the 1986–1987 season premiere of *Dallas*. In this episode, the character Bobby Ewing, who had been hit by a car in the 1984–1985 season finale and lay dead and buried in 1985–1986, returned through an incredible rewriting of diegetic history.[34] The explanation tested even viewers accustomed to soap operas' ability to resurrect dead figures. In the "corrected" diegetic reality, Bobby's accident and death did not really happen—the fatal moments, along with all of the other episodes in the 1985–1986 season, were merely scenes in Pam Ewing's bad dream. Here the demands of demographics (Bobby was an extremely popular character) overruled any sense of rational history, and the *Dallas* spectator, not to mention the viewer of the *Dallas* spin-off *Knots Landing*, was left with some troubling but unanswered questions: Did Pam dream *all* of the events, involving all of the characters, in 1985–1986? Why didn't the characters in *Knots Landing* (who mourned Bobby in 1985 but never realized their mistake) awaken from Pam's dream? Whose dream is this anyhow?

If anything, it is the dream of postmodern culture in which consumer desires can alter history while providing current pleasures. In fact, "Pam's dream" was used to sell programs other than just *Dallas*—rival serials *Dynasty* and *The Colbys* ran ads in *TV Guide* in the fall of 1986 stating, "This is no dream" and "What we dream, they live" in an attempt to exploit the viewer's knowledge of events on *Dallas*. Parodying such melodramatic excess and artifice (while still using it to its own ends) was the brilliant final episode of the 1982–1990 situation comedy *Newhart*, in which Bob Newhart's character Dick Loudon is knocked unconscious by a stray golf ball and wakes up in bed—next to Emily Hartley, his wife from his previous sitcom *The Bob Newhart Show* (1972–1978), suggesting that the entire *Newhart* series had been nothing but his prior character's, Bob Hartley's, dream.

Consumer Closeness and Constructions of Femininity

Such cases may be amusing, yet the concern that history and memory are allowed to wander as emotion provides the only stake—a situation giving free rein to consumer fantasies—is a sobering one. With the elision of history comes the promotion of the image (of both the commodity and the self) which is now personal and self-referential. Space flattens out and history appears to dissipate, making it difficult to ground any unified position. It is then no surprise that melodrama, television, and post-modernism, which all share this particular construction of flattened space and weightless time, have been linked to the dissolution of a stable site of mastery, the ideal of masculinity. They are thus aligned with the threat of the feminine, the gender assigned to consumer passions.

The melodrama, for example, seems to disallow the achievement of a masculine ideal even as it reflects the loss of such mastery; not only is melodrama motivated by the anxiety of a decentered existence (as Brooks argues), but it lacks effectively powerful protagonists with whom to identify, thus situating the spectator in a fairly powerless position. As film theorists have noted, there is a split in the American cinema between those forms considered "feminine" in which a passive heroine or impotent hero suffers (the melodrama) and those deemed "masculine" (by both critics and audiences) which feature an active hero immune to suffering (typified by the western) (Newell-Smith, "Minnelli" 115). Placed on the side of femininity as its claustrophobic and implosive world precludes the direct action of a masterful ego, melodrama has been noted for its exploration of feminine subjectivity and its appeal to a female audience.[35]

Yet like Cary in *All That Heaven Allows*, the female viewer thus addressed is positioned as a "spectacle of the impotent spectator" (Pollock, "Report" 111).[36] While the spectator may have greater knowledge than any of the characters, she is still unable to determine the course of the narrative and is thus helpless, at least as far as the "official text" is concerned. It is very common for viewers to "write" their own plots, often speculating on what will happen through the aid of not only other viewers, but other "consumer services" as well (fan magazines, soap opera updates, telephone hotlines, computer subscription services). Yet however much pleasure or compensatory control these activities provide, they nonetheless fail to affect the unfolding of the broadcast drama itself (which, in its diegesis, often pedagogically narrates the futility of attempts at causal intervention). With no controlling protagonist to provide her with a lead, the spectator is at the mercy of the story and must wait (as is so common for the characters) for time to unfold. Indeed, according to Steve Neale, it is this relative powerlessness that drives melodrama's viewers to tears; we cry from the lack of coincidence dramatized on the screen, a lack we are unable to change—the gap between our knowledge and that of the characters, between what should happen and what actually does, between the "rightness" of a union and its delay. Invoked in these gaps are deep-rooted fantasies of fusion, of a perfect coincidence of both communication and desire—yearnings related, he suggests, to the nostalgic fantasy of union with the mother, the wish for maternal plenitude ("Melodrama" 11, 17, 19).

By engaging such wishes, melodrama is able to *move* the spectator, to manipulate affect to a degree that seems to many critics to go beyond aesthetic or rational justification. This assessment is conveyed even in the labels commonly applied to melodrama (especially in film): "weepies" and "tearjerkers," terms that imply the strength of the genre—powerful enough to shake emotions out of the viewer—even as they discredit the presumed female spectator. This spectator, overinvolved and displaying an excess of feeling, is figured as powerless to attain any distance from the sentimental fantasies portrayed. Though this image may infuriate melodrama fans, the woman viewer's relationship to the screen, as noted in the previous chapter, is commonly appraised as an overly close one—she is so bound to the drama, so susceptible to the image, that it evidently can even evoke a physical reaction in her tearful response.[37]

What the female spectator supposedly lacks is the distance necessary for "proper" viewing and judgment. As Mary Ann Doane has argued, while the cinema appears to offer a plenitude of sensory experience, it necessarily depends upon an absence and the ensuing irreducible distance between viewer and object. Yet the cultural place assigned to women as viewers works against the maintenance of such distance:

> A distance from the image is less negotiable for the female spectator than for the male because the woman is so forcefully linked with the iconic and spectacle or, in Mulvey's terms, "to-be-looked-at-ness." Voyeurism, the desire most fully exploited by the classical cinema, is the property of the masculine spectator. Fetishism—the ability to balance knowledge and belief and hence to maintain a distance from the lure of the image—is also inaccessible to the woman, who has no need of the fetish as a defense against a castration which has always already taken place. Female spectatorship, because it is conceived of temporally as immediacy . . . and spatially as proximity . . . can only be understood as the confounding of desire. (*The Desire* 12–13)

For "the female spectator" (as she is culturally conceived, even if not always experienced and lived), there is an overpresence of the image—she is supposed to *be* the image—and her desire is thus disavowed, regarded as trapped within the confines of either narcissism (as she becomes the object of desire) or masochism (as she overidentifies with the passive character). Unlike the man, whose voyeuristic and fetishistic distance allows him to master the image and whose cinematic counterparts control its flow through time, the female spectator is cast as too close to the image

to achieve such mastery, and melodrama, the genre most often addressing
female audiences, exploits this closeness through its tearful fantasies of
(maternal) union.

Much recent work in feminist film theory attempts to shift this disheart-
ening appraisal, refiguring viewers so as to realize more powerful or
pleasurable spectatorial identifications as well as more progressive readings of melodramatic (and other) texts. In discussing the female spectator
in terms of masochism, narcissism, and overpresence here, I am not
claiming (nor, in fact, is Doane) that these are the only or the essential
identifications available for women audiences.[38] Rather, I am focusing on
the *representation* of women in conceptions of spectatorship—the historically and culturally sanctioned positions for female viewers which are
quite limited (and limiting) even though alternative constructions of
pleasure are certainly possible, particularly for viewers who have been
positioned "differently" by other formations, including those of feminism
itself.

Yet some feminist discourses have contributed, perhaps unwittingly, to
common assumptions about female subjects. For the image of the overinvolved female spectator not only occurs in the popular imagination, but
can likewise be found in theoretical accounts of feminine desire; there is a
convergence, in other words, between mass cultural and scholarly discourses on femininity apparent, as I suggest in chapter 1, in shared notions
of female "reception." Tropes of proximity and overpresence have also
been taken up by feminist and psychoanalytic theorists to explore basic
constructions of feminine subjectivity and sexuality, particularly in relation to the maternal origin and object of desire. Just as some film theory has
posited the female spectator as "too close" to the cinematic image to
command the text adequately, psychoanalytic theory represents women as
too close to the maternal and their own bodies to claim the gap essential to
signification and desire—the liability of loss that is marked by the phallic
signifier and thus culturally available to men rather than women.

Within this discursive field (and aligned with popular representations
of femininity), women are seen as confounding the terms of a subject/
object dichotomy. Michèle Montrelay, for example, describes femininity as
"one chaotic intimacy . . . too present, too immediate—one continuous
expanse of proximity or unbearable plenitude. What [is] lacking [is] a lack,
an empty 'space' somewhere" (88, 91). Similarly, Luce Irigaray defines
female subjectivity as that which resists a separation of isolated moments
and locations, thereby allowing the woman a self-caressing eroticism in
which she can touch herself without mediation. Again the notion of an
overpresence that disallows mastery over objects and their linguistic,
economic, and/or sexual exchanges is suggested (even though Irigaray
offers her constructions in resistance to traditional psychoanalytic theories
of femininity): "Nearness so pronounced that it makes all discrimination
of identity, and thus all forms of property, impossible" (*This Sex* 31). In the
discourses of psychoanalysis and many of those of feminism as well,

woman (treated as a singular entity) is frequently figured as too close to the object to become a full subject.[39]

While, as this last example suggests, some feminist theorists may posit such a self-receptive nearness as a subversive alternative to a masculine model of identity, proximity is also bound to consumer desires. The same closeness that ruptures the boundary between subject and object, perhaps allowing women a multiplicity of identifications and a self-embracing eroticism, also makes the female subject susceptible to the lure of consumerism, which plays on this fluctuating position and the narcissism it implies. It is the focus on self-image that invites the consumer to attend to the images of advertised products, and the woman, whose role in our culture is to purchase in order to enhance her own status as valued item, becomes the prototypical consumer—the same overpresence that ties her to the image allows her to be situated as both the subject and the object of consumerism at once. As Mary Ann Doane writes, "the increasing appeal in the twentieth century to the woman's role as perfect consumer (of commodities as well as images) is indissociable from her positioning *as* a commodity and results in the blurring of the subject/object dichotomy" (*The Desire* 13). The proximity that defines femininity in psychoanalytic discourse then corresponds with women's social position under capitalism—women are assumed to be the perfect consumers, devouring objects, images, and narratives just as they have been said to "devour" their loved ones.

Yet the discursive link forged between consumerism and femininity, both related to an overidentification with the image or commodity object, affects the whole of Western culture. Not only are women presumed to be the best of consumers, but all consumers are figured as feminized—a situation yielding tension in a culture desperately trying to shore up conventional markers of difference even as its simulations destabilize such attempts. As the distance between subject and object threatens to diminish in the weightless space of postmodern culture, the risk of a gendered disempowerment as well as an all-encompassing consumerism hangs over everyone. In the previous chapter, I indicated the way in which the same tropes of proximity applied to women's viewing have been used to explain the rise of the mass media and the development of a consumer consciousness for all; "the desire of contemporary masses to bring things 'closer' spatially and humanly" that Walter Benjamin discusses in his famous work on mass culture resonates with the desires so familiar from analyses of female subjectivity (222–23). With mass reproduction now fully established and indissociable from consumerism, the discursive equation presumed between consumer and feminine subjectivity produces disturbing tendencies in the representations of and within our own mass-mediated world.

As I've argued, symptomatic of the ideological conflation of femininity and consumerism is the way in which both postmodernism, the cultural dominant of late capitalism, and television, so central to consumer culture, are themselves often figured as feminine. Just as melodrama is seen to collapse distance, particularly as it appeals to the female spectator, so television has been regarded in much the same way—both by critics expressly making this claim, and (as explained in the previous chapter and to be further detailed in the next) by critics who do not explicitly state this contention but nonetheless allow gendered imagery to creep into their analyses. According to such accounts, television's hypermediated field imperils us all, drawing each viewer-consumer into the vacuum of mass culture—an irrational and diffuse space coded as feminine.

It is for this reason that, as mentioned above, the "threat of feminization" seems to lurk over the whole of U.S. mediatized reality, posing serious problems for a society that was in the 1980s (and, as the current "culture wars" demonstrate, still today) furiously trying to retrieve and maintain traditional distinctions. Postmodernity decenters oppositions even as it attempts to resuscitate them (feminization "infects" everyone just as renewed efforts to define sexual difference are launched across the political spectrum), and in this swirling movement, strains and contradictions emerge in both media criticism and media texts. Such stress must then be managed, and the melodramatic mode is once again employed to ease these tensions.

Melodrama is therefore a privileged forum for U.S. television, promising the certainty of clearly marked conflict and legible meaning even as it plays on the closeness associated with a feminine spectator-consumer. Melodrama allows us both "nearness" and assurance through its appeal to a pre-linguistic system of gesture and tableaux that aims beyond language to immediate understanding.[40] In its attempt to render meaning visible and recapture the ineffable, melodrama emphasizes gestures, postures, frozen moments, and expressions. Television strengthens these conventions as it clearly directs attention to the revelations of facial expression, providing close-ups that disclose "what before . . . only a lover or a mother ever saw" (Porter 786). TV melodrama, like its precursors in the theater and cinema, then tends to deny the complex processes of signification and to collapse representation onto the real, assuring its audience of firm stakes of meaning.

This assurance, however, comes with a price. As I've indicated, melodrama has historically been associated with female audiences who are figured in popular and critical discourses as unsophisticated viewers. For, as Doane writes, "there is a certain naiveté assigned to women in relation to systems of signification—a tendency to deny the processes of representation, to collapse the opposition between the sign (the image) and the real" (*The Desire* 1). Still, the attractions of the melodramatic mode need not be judged so negatively, and the security it provides today appeals to men as well as women. Melodrama helps us place ourselves in a confusing world—its insistence on the validity of moral or experiential truths and its faith in the reality of the stakes create a space from which to act. The "naiveté" associated with a "feminized" spectator may in fact reflect melodrama's suspicion of linguistic and cultural codes, a suspicion that is well founded given postmodernity's flood of mobile signs and codes. While melodrama—and its presumed female viewer—has been seen as suspect, there is something offered in this stance. Melodrama's promise of universally legible meaning seems to be particularly compelling in the postmodern era, experienced by many as desperately in need of some kind of grounding. It is the panic provoked by this sense of weightlessness that adds to the mode's recent appeal—and yet this is a panic which may serve the political right and consumer capital as much as it might offer any cultural critique.

Envisioning "Another World" of TV Melodrama

Melodrama is thus an ideal form for postmodern culture and for television—a form which arises from a fragmented network of space and time yet still seems to offer a sense of wholeness, reality, and living history. Raising conflict to the level of fundamental ethical imperatives, melodrama provides a world into which we can fully immerse ourselves and evokes emotions with which we can immediately identify. In the struggles it presents, there is no doubt that real forces are at stake. As Ien Ang explains in connection to the prime-time melodrama *Dallas,*

> The melodramatic imagination is therefore the expression of a refusal, or inability, to accept insignificant everyday life as banal and meaningless, and is born of a vague, inarticulate dissatisfaction with existence here and now. . . . In a life in which every immanent meaning is constantly questioned and in which traditions no longer have a firm hold, a need exists for reassurance that life can in fact have meaning and therefore life is worth the trouble, in spite of all appearances to the contrary. (79–80)

While the apparent banality and meaninglessness of everyday life might historically be most pronounced for women (given the material conditions of their labor in the home and workplace), the frustration provoked by a shallow, ungrounded existence was not only shared among numerous people within the last decade but is one that is still quite common today.[41] Lacking a sense of tradition, place, and meaning in their own lives, many Americans turn to the media to find such values.

Making up for our want of these certainties is TV melodrama which plays on and profits from our feeling of shifting reality. But also profiting from this lack of stable ground are neo-conservative politics and multinational capitalism, each of which has been linked to postmodern culture. The rhetoric of both expansion and retrenchment, effective within 1980s national politics as well as within the ongoing academic "canon wars," has certainly demonstrated the deployment of precisely those melodramatic conventions which, ironically, are themselves apt to be critiqued for their subversion of traditional standards of value and taste. Merely because melodrama has been seen as emblematic of feminine subjectivity is no reason for feminists to applaud uncritically its rise and continued promi-

nence on American television. We are reminded by Thomas Elsaesser of
the "radical ambiguity attached to the melodrama" which may "function
either subversively or as escapism—categories which are always relative
to the given historical and social context" (4). It is often the status of
the "happy ending" which determines melodrama's political meaning—
whether a text's ending convincingly resolves all the problems and closes
the issues, or on the other hand, whether conflicts remain a bit open,
leaving the viewer to consider their import. As Jane Feuer has noted, this
ambiguity is even more apparent in regard to television melodramas—
lacking the "happy ending," in fact never really ending at all, TV melodramas may lack the ability to draw attention to unresolved contradictions
and excess, the key to film melodramas' subversive potential.[42] While
melodrama has at times functioned as a politically progressive form, it is
not clear that TV melodrama allows for this possibility.

Yet it is also not clear that TV melodrama has precluded this potential.
Peter Brooks remarks that melodrama has been such an enduringly popular form because it is both "frightening and enlivening" as it exists on the
"brink of the abyss," allowing us the comfort of belief in the importance of
our lives as well as the challenge this entails. As such, it may give a false
sense of strength, but it also "works to steel man for resistance, it keeps him
going in the face of threat" (205–206). As a feminist concerned with the
historical connections between women, melodrama, and consumerism, I
hope it may work to steel women for resistance too. Film melodrama has
been able to call attention to the contradictions in our class and gender
system through its use of formal conventions that stand as ironic commentaries on otherwise conventional narratives. By reading TV melodramas
against the grain—or playing out the multiple readings that already exist
within the polyvocal texts—and providing our own ironic commentaries,
feminist criticisms emerging not only from the Academy but from many
other locations as well (the kitchen, the workplace, the community center,
the computer forum) may continue to bring out the contradictions of our
society so that these issues do not get lost in the flow of media images. Such
work might then make more visible the sites of stress and contradiction in
postmodern culture, its construction and deconstruction of the terms of
gender and consumption, so that the boundaries thus drawn may be
stretched in new directions. To define these directions, we too may turn to
the melodramatic mode—but by recognizing the provisionality of these
heightened dramas even as we play them out, we open up the space for
both pleasure and resistance, activating melodrama's contradictions in
our struggle for new meanings.

Video side-splits: technological/sexological transformation in
Videodrome.

TV side-kicks: textual/sexual transactions in *Miami Vice*.

IV

THREATS FROM WITHIN
THE GATES
CRITICAL AND TEXTUAL HYPERMASCULINITY

Horrific Visions: Television's Textual and Sexual Arena

Television, as I've detailed in the previous chapters, has been an object of ridicule, scorn, concern, or even fear for many cultural critics. This is not solely because of the political and/or economic effects that U.S. television has had on our and many other societies; related to, indeed reciprocally constructing, the material practices surrounding the production and consumption of TV are discursive practices: the ways in which television has been portrayed in feminizing terms, represented as a medium capable of emasculating viewers posed as helpless before its onslaught. Further, apocalyptic accounts of mediatized, technologized, and consumerized life similarly present fearful visions of postmodernity, revealing how historical shifts within sexual and cultural formations intersect with concerns about mass art and, specifically in the past few decades, about TV.

In fact, the image of television as a feminizing force has quite literally been taken up as a horrific one. David Cronenberg's 1983 film *Videodrome*, for example, explicitly marks the place of gender within the discourses surrounding television and postmodernity. Its story of a cable TV station owner who is incapacitated—psychologically and physically transformed—by exposure to high doses of video signals vividly narrates anxieties over the ever-increasing "penetration" of television into our lives, giving graphic embodiment to notions (drawn from both the hypodermic needle model of social science research and humanist versions of cultural critique) of television's emasculating and addictive powers. In this horror film, video scans are used literally to open viewers to total control: exposure to the signals transforms the human body into a living VCR which can then be pierced and entered by videotapes, preventing the "programmed" subject from differentiating reality from televisual simulation. Not only does this illustrate the worst fears of mass culture critics (fears concerning the power of the media to seduce and rape the viewer), but it clearly—indeed, violently—marks the receptive TV body as feminine: the tapes are thrust into a gaping wound that slits the hero's stomach. *Videodrome* thus brings together the image of the "cyborg body"—a postmodern hybrid of human, animal, and machine—and the image of the "feminine body"—a body yielding to manipulation, too close to the image to evaluate it properly.[1]

Such conceptual ties between TV, postmodernism, and femininity (or, more accurately, the meanings our culture assigns to "femininity") are symptomatic of shifting gender relations in our technologically mediated culture. As I suggest throughout this study, television, today's cyborgian "machine-subject," can be seen as playing out these relations in all their contradictions, revealing a network of sexual and textual differences that we have only recently begun to explore.[2] These differences—the multiplicity of subjectivities, readings, desires, and identifications that televisual discourse deploys and evokes—exceed the binary conception of gender imposed by the classificatory practices of our culture's heterosexual imperative; while representations of and on television may work to order the meanings of both media and social formations, such "regulation" is bound to fail (and not simply because of institutional attempts at media "deregulation"). Situating television texts against texts marking TV's critical reception reveals the complex relationships forged between TV and postmodern culture, allowing us to examine the (veiled) references to sexual difference and the problematic of gender constituted within this field. Though noting the ways in which television has been figured as feminine in both film and mass culture criticism—a phenomenon exacerbated by the fluctuating ground of postmodernism—I argue that while such tropes of analysis are seductive, they are also potentially dangerous, encouraging critics to ignore the complexities and contradictions of gender inscription as well as the other fields of difference (race, class, sexuality, age, nation) which traverse the TV text and audience alike.

Further, to accept uncritically these figurations is not simply to risk overlooking the complexity of television's multiple address; it is also to deny the divisions of power that underlie the fearful visions of television's emasculating force. In fact, attending to the complex dynamics of gender within both television and TV criticism may lead us to a very different conclusion than that initially implied by *Videodrome*'s sexual imagery; despite the prevalence of such figures and images in accounts of TV, we cannot simply claim that television is itself either feminine or feminizing. Rather, this ontological premise recuperates the feminine—as well as the critical insights of feminism—within a new version of masculinity that inhabits television studies as well as television texts. In other words, the focus on TV as "feminine" masks a deeper cultural concern with masculinity—a concern that may express itself through the construction of a "hypermasculinity" which serves to render the presence of women within both TV representation and TV criticism unnecessary.

Tellingly, in *Videodrome*'s own narrative, the "invagination" of the protagonist is merely a method by which to actualize a complex plot involving violent pornography, multicorporate expansion, and militaristic action—the brutal stuff (indeed, in this plot, "snuff") of hypermacho aggression that produces and affects the simulated surface of a feminine form.[3] Embodied within the technology but expendable in fact, the female/

feminized subject is thus both visible and derealized at once. Of course, *Videodrome*'s futuristic fantasy is extreme, but its metamedia commentary is revealing—not solely for what it suggests about the place of television within the postmodern arena, but also for how it displays what Susan Jeffords has called the "remasculinization" of our culture within the last decades (*Remasculinization*). My interest in what I have termed "hyper-masculinity" can thus be seen as both "practical"—embedded within the practices of everyday life (including those of media consumption)—and "theoretical"—engaged with developments within cultural critique.

Specifically, while the figure of femininity has been quite productive (if, as I hope to show, very problematic) for cultural analysis, the figure of masculinity has recently become important for feminist analysis. Critical of the way in which the concept of "sexual difference" is simply projected onto women as *the* different sex (just as gays and lesbians alone are presumed to have "sexual preferences" and only African Americans are seen as raced—"white" and "heterosexual" comprising tacit norms), femi-nist theorists have interrogated the supposed unity of gender identity and attempted to dismantle the dualistic logic which underpins this assump-tion. The investigation of the construction and embodiment of the previously unmarked category of masculinity is part of this effort to emphasize the differences among and within (not simply between) definitions of *masculine* and *feminine, men* and *women, male* and *female*. Within film and television studies in particular, the consideration of masculinity as a position of spectatorship and/or spectacle has both enlivened discussions of viewing pleasures and further exposed the per-formative processes by which gender and sexuality are constituted and assumed.[4] Television's ostensible relationship to femininity should not therefore occlude an analysis of its equally significant relationship to con-structions of masculinity. Because of the tropes commonly used to de-scribe it, television might appear to many of its detractors as a feminine or feminizing form, but as feminist critics, we must question what meanings themselves are made to appear, what modes of power enacted, by the textual (and sexual) productions of this particular media ap-pearance.

"The Enemy Within"? Il-logics of Television

Several theorists have noted that consumer culture and the culpable masses blamed for its existence have often been figured as feminine. Tania Modleski examines this aspect of historical accounts and emphasizes the problems involved in either simply condemning or celebrating these feminine inscriptions ("Femininity"). Andreas Huyssen has also explored attacks on sentimental culture—slurs based on fears of the engulfing ooze of the mass which provoked the "reaction formation" of a virile and authorial modernism. Yet he concludes his analysis by claiming that such gendered rhetoric no longer works and has diminished with the decline of

modernism: "Mass culture and the masses as feminine threat—such notions belong to another age, Jean Baudrillard's recent ascription of
femininity to the masses notwithstanding" (62).[5] Nonetheless, despite
Huyssen's optimistic conclusion, such gendered imagery *can* still be seen
in many analyses of television. It is thus fitting that Huyssen cites Baudrillard's theory of hyperreality—which at times reads almost like a
dizzying description of TV viewing—as the one remaining account which
portrays mass culture in gendered terms. But Baudrillard is not the only
theorist of the postmodern age who has used sexual metaphors to describe
mass culture and the receptivity of the masses to its lure.

While, as Huyssen argues, the "great divide" between art and mass
culture may have narrowed (or even imploded) in the postmodern age,
this rupture does not necessarily extend to a generalized dissolution of
binary categories of analysis. Rather than living in an age in which bipolar
thinking is no longer operative, we exist in a transitional space in which
new dichotomies are erected as fast as the old ones break down. In fact, the
very rupture of traditional modes of thought provokes a panicked attempt
to create new divisions rather than working to dispel our society's felt
need for oppositions. Therefore, the kind of binary divisions used to
discount mass art by the modernist critics that Huyssen discusses continue
to exert an influence over critics associated with the rise of postmodern
theory in spite of their apparent reluctance to condemn all forms of mass
and subcultural production. In other words, distinctions of value seem to
hold sway within the realm of mass texts themselves even if the grand
opposition between high and low art can no longer describe today's
aesthetic theory or practice. As I've argued in the preceding chapters,
those commenting on television regularly define their object through such
polarities; by constructing a duality in which television is placed in
opposition to some other, more "respected" medium, these critics and
theorists articulate cultural and textual differences in terms that are remi-
niscent of what is still posed as the dominant binary of our culture—sexual
difference.

In *Understanding Media,* for example, Marshall McLuhan compares
today's media to the previously dominant system of print, arguing that the
new holistic and participatory modes promote a "global embrace" (19)
and the implosion of margin to center. Associating these media with the
"nonconform[ity]" of "the criminal . . . , the child, the cripple, the woman,
and the colored person," McLuhan distinguishes the heterogeneity of
television from the regularity of book culture (31). The "rational" form of
print, allied with "literate man," is uniform, linear, and isolated—it is, like
film, a "hot" medium based on exclusion. It thus creates the centralized,
autonomous subject motivated toward impersonal domination, expan-
sionism, and departmental organization. On the other hand, the "irrational" media of the electric age, particularly television, return us to the
mythical form of the icon in which distance—the distance between subjects as well as the distance between sign and referent—is abolished. The
mosaic of TV requires the involvement of all senses in a tactile, primitive

intimacy that produces, according to McLuhan, retribalization, organic interlacing, proximity, and empathy.

In addition to the imperialist and racist connotations of such descriptions, these qualities are clearly drawn from stereotypes of femininity, and while McLuhan values them, he nonetheless believes that what he terms the "threat" from "within the gates"—the new media—must be kept under control by the masculine logic of print (32). The phrase "threat from within the gates" comes from Hegel, who, in theorizing the disruption provoked by Woman, writes, "[The community] creates its enemy for itself within its own gates, creates it in what it suppresses, and what is at the same time essential to it—womankind in general. Womankind—the ever-lasting irony in the life of the community—changes by intrigue the universal purpose of government into a private end" (496). McLuhan's metaphor for the disruptive media then clearly genders television as feminine—intrinsically so since "the medium is the message." Any enthusiasm he expresses for the organic qualities of television thus evades important historical questions. For example, McLuhan's claim that TV is inherently decentralized allows him to ignore the fact that it is very much economically centralized and that its femininity consists more in the gender of its primary consumers than in its ontological or aesthetic nature. Ignoring the particular social construction of both television and femininity, McLuhan produces a celebratory reading of television in which sexual difference, once again polarized and essentialized, is made to uphold a historically specific mode of consumption.

Several other critics comparing television to earlier media similarly figure opposition in gendered terms. In *Reading Television,* for example, John Fiske and John Hartley use McLuhan to support their theory of television as our culture's bard, exploring the "oral logic" by which TV involves its viewers as it draws them into positions of cultural proximity.[6] Arguing that television is criticized merely because it fails to conform to the standards of Rational Man, they too employ unacknowleged gender codes in their evaluation of television as a 'separate but equal' medium. Once again described as immediate and illogical, TV is contrasted to the linear, abstract, and universal codes of print which alone can support the individualism and Cartesian philosophy upheld in novelistic realism. While Fiske and Hartley do not recognize these oppositions as gendered ones, their description of television as an intimate medium—personal, familiar, and working to bond all viewers in an inclusive world—repeats the same sexual stereotypes found in McLuhan's *Understanding Media* (and, in fact, mirrors the distinction between "feminine" and "masculine" narrative forms that Fiske himself makes in his later book, *Television Culture*).[7] Furthermore, it is in the space between TV's irrational "feminine" mode and the "masculine" logic of print that the viewer can position him/herself so as to decode cultural practices in alternative ways. Through tacit metaphors of sexual difference, then, Fiske and Hartley construct a theory of television's difference, echoing a position frequently found in contemporary literary theory which has also aligned textual difference

and ideological subversion with figures of the Woman.[8] The cultural
denigration of television is thus related to the marginality of an unnamed
femininity—as Fiske and Hartley claim, TV is scorned merely for being
TV: nonlinear, illogical, and unmasculine.

Similarly, in *Visible Fictions*, John Ellis compares television to the cinema,
arguing that in our historical era the culturally respectable has become
equated with the cinematic (116, 122, 146). According to Ellis, the cinema's
visual form and mode of narration incite voyeuristic fascination, granting
the spectator power over the image and centering the look on the female
body as film both provokes and fulfills inquiring expectations. TV, on the
other hand, has little narration in the cinematic sense and the narrative
enigma is usually incidental. Instead there is open-ended repetition which
defies closure—the "continuity with difference" theorized as "flow" by
Raymond Williams (Ellis 123; Williams, *Television*). Lacking what Ellis
(after Roland Barthes) calls the "photo-effect"—the present absence of the
cinema that creates desire in its spectators—television offers itself as an
immediate presence, failing, he suggests, to produce a sufficiently voyeuristic position for its viewers (see 57–61, 135–39, 141–44, and 160–71).[9]
Attempting to call back the attention of a viewer who merely casts a "lazy
eye over [its] precedings" (137), TV can only invite what Ellis calls "the
glance"—"a look without power" (163)—rather than cinema's more intense gaze. Divested of this potent look, the TV viewer must delegate his /
her "eye" (as well as "I") to television itself, forging a sense of intimacy as
events are shared rather than witnessed (164–71).[10] In other words, the
glance of the TV viewer is a domestic, distracted, and powerless look that
implies both complicity and continuous co-presence—a "feminine" look
that is too close to the object to maintain the gap essential to desire and full
subjectivity.

As this brief survey shows, the use of feminine imagery to describe our
"lowest" cultural form (in opposition to whatever is held up as more
respectable and "masculine"—print or film) has not faded away with the
passing of modernism.[11] In fact, such gender coding takes on new meanings and implications in the postmodern age as the threat of fluctuating
signs, unstable distinctions, and fractured identities provokes a retreat
toward nostalgia for firm foundations of meaning. As the "'natural'
grounding principle" once seemingly offered by sexual difference erodes
under the weight of these forces—including, importantly, the forces of
various feminisms (Doane and Hodges 8)[12]—new anxieties are created
which are then often projected onto television (a medium which has been
taken as the ultimate in fluctuating signs even as it tries to remain a bastion
of family values).

Therefore, far from being an exception to the (historical) rule as Huyssen
suggests, Baudrillard simply reiterates the terms of these accounts of
"feminized" media and attaches them to his analysis of the postmodern
condition. Claiming, for example, that "we must imagine TV on the DNA
model" as the code that 'programs' our culture (rather than a reflection
of pre-existent reality), he explicitly associates television's 'immediate,'

'overpresent,' and 'illogical' mode with the very chaos of postmodern simulation that makes distance and contemplation impossible:

> [T]he opposing poles of determination vanish according to a nuclear contraction . . . of the old polar schema which has always maintained a minimal distance between a cause and an effect, between the subject and an object. (*Simulations* 56)[13]

In the circular logic of simulation, classical reason threatens to vanish, and separate positions merge. In Baudrillard's oft-cited words, "positivity and negativity engender and overlap . . . there is no longer any active or passive . . . linear continuity and dialectical polarity no longer exist" (30–31). As dialectics collapse, the oppositions that maintain a binary structure of sexual difference and the ostensible stability of the sexed gaze seem to shift, if not fully disappear.

This collapse of the very oppositions which have upheld the primacy of the heterosexual masculine subject is further suggested in Baudrillard's description of television as he discards what much film theory has taken to be the terms of sexual difference: "TV is no longer the source of an absolute gaze, . . . no longer . . . a system of scrutiny . . . playing on the opposition between seeing and being seen . . ." (52). In rejecting the applicability of the categories *subject/object*, *active/passive*, and *seeing/being seen*, Baudrillard rejects the divisions that have been considered by many feminist film critics as constitutive of the male spectatorial ideal.[14] In other words, for Baudrillard, postmodernism—and television in particular—seems to disallow the security and mastery of the masculine position, and as this stable site disappears, we are all left floating in a diffuse, irrational space—a space traditionally coded as feminine.[15]

In the essay "In the Shadow of the Silent Majorities," Baudrillard describes the masses as soft and sticky, lacking form and reference. They are like a black hole that engulfs all meaning in an implosion of the social—an overpresence that collapses inward, producing a lack of distance, defining feature, or visible attribute—and through this account, the masses are figured through clichés of femininity. But like women, the masses have access to a certain excess—they overconform and overconsume, reduplicating the logic of the media. Referring, like McLuhan, to Hegel's analysis of "womankind," Baudrillard writes that this "destructive hyper-simulation" is "akin to the eternal irony of femininity of which Hegel speaks—the irony of false fidelity, of an excessive fidelity to the law, an ultimately impenetrable simulation of passivity and obedience . . . which annuls . . . the law governing them" (33). This theorization of subversive hyperconformity is very familiar. It mimics both Luce Irigaray's analysis of feminine mimicry—a playful repetition in which women resubmit themselves to a masculine discourse in order to demonstrate their existence "elsewhere"—and the notion of feminine masquerade, drawn from Joan Riviere and elaborated by such theorists as Mary Ann Doane, Mary Russo, and Sue Ellen Case, in which women flaunt their femininity in order to hold it at a distance.[16]

Yet unlike feminist and/or queer theorists, Baudrillard is not advocating acts of *political* resistance; he assumes the position of the feminine in order to stress the vacuum of the enveloping mass rather than the possible differences that may be constituted within it. In an implosive system of deterrence and pacification, "the depoliticised masses," claims Baudrillard, "would not be this side of the political, but beyond it" (*In the Shadow* 39). He thus argues against those theorists who would,

> out of the involutive sphere which is opposed to all revolution, . . . like to make a new source of revolutionary energy (in particular in its sexual and desire version). They would like to . . . reinstate it in its very banality, as historical negativity. Exaltations of micro-desires, small differences, unconscious practices, anonymous marginalities . . . and . . . transfer it back to political reason. (40–41)

For Baudrillard, this goal is an impossible one. Substituting the fear of an all-consuming mass for the older notion of an all-controlling industry, he insists upon the anonymity of the feminized masses who are neither subject nor object, without determinate position or critical distinction.[17] In rejecting any theory of subjectivity that might valorize the deconstruction of identity in a play of differences as politically progressive, Baudrillard sentences the political (and political resistance) to annihilation. Nonetheless, as "a direct defiance of the political," the masses' feminine hyperconformity is still a show of strength, a mode of resistance escaping control (39). Through their ironic excess, the masses neutralize all attempts to bring them into the realm of meaning, destroying as well the possibility of knowledge (a possibility which is crucial for any kind of activist stance). In this way, Baudrillard employs the concept of the feminine, adopting its guise in his theoretical masquerade, but deprives it of the progressive force suggested by some feminist critics; instead, he merely recasts the division between mass culture and high culture in terms of a routine gender dichotomy.

Positions Of/In Difference

Baudrillard is not the first male theorist to cite the position of Woman as a way to signify ironic strength (whether deemed political or not). His analysis of hyperaffirmation recalls Jacques Derrida's discussion of the feminine in *Spurs* (part of which occurs, interestingly, in a section entitled "Simulations"). Considering Nietzsche's "affirmative woman" (67), Derrida writes, "she plays at dissimulation, at ornamentation, deceit, artifice, at an artist's philosophy. Hers is an affirmative power" (57). Woman is thus an indeterminable identity, "a non-figure, a simulacrum" (49). It is the very breakdown in logic that dismays readers of Baudrillard's *Simulations* that delights Derrida here, and the creation of a space between the self and the image through an exaggeration of this breakdown, the hypersimulation associated with feminine irony, is the only "hopeful" possibility that even Baudrillard seems to offer.

Yet feminists must approach a hope figured as feminine salvation with suspicion. As Modleski points out, figuring both the masses and their subversive mode as feminine does not necessarily give feminists concerned with the historical and cultural position of women any cause for celebration. Noting the (masculine) socio-sexual indifference that arises when the position of feminine difference is claimed by everyone, Modleski insists that the ascription of femininity to the anonymous mass glosses over crucial distinctions ("Femininity" 50–51). Attending similarly to Nancy Miller's warning, we must not lose sight of the ways in which a theoretical position that deems the question "Who speaks?" irrelevant can also maintain the institutional silencing of women. As Miller states, "Only those who have it can play with not having it" ("Text's" 53).[18]

Not only must we be leery of theorists playing with the demise of a social and political representation that we have never had, but we must not obscure the disparities that do exist for men and women within the realm of mass culture. Let me return to a statement I cited above—Andreas Huyssen's claim that images of a feminized mass culture no longer apply to the postmodern world—and continue this point:

> If anything, a kind of reverse statement would make more sense: certain forms of mass culture, with their obsession with gendered violence, are more of a threat to women than to men. After all, it has always been men rather than women who have had real control over the productions of mass culture. (205)

In other words, while television spectatorship may be figured as generically feminine, two crucial differences that exist for its socially situated, gendered viewers are overlooked: first, the power disparities created by the historical and sexual split between consumption and production (in which women are the primary consumers while men largely control television production); and second, television's reaction against the feminine through the construction of a violent hypermasculinity (a situation often found in TV action/adventure and police/detective dramas—texts that I will take up shortly).[19]

Exploring this first question of television's institutional practices and its gendered consumption, many television scholars have considered the material conditions of female consumption, women's viewing practices, and advertisers' address to this audience.[20] As I've indicated in previous chapters, one can also trace the discursive connections forged between constructions of femininity and the consumer subject, revealing how theoretical accounts of femininity accord in many ways with popular notions of women in relation to looking and buying. In the popular imagination, the woman is so bound to the scene of her desire (be this a screen or a shop window), so driven to possess whatever meets her eye (or as the pun suggests, her "I") that an almost tangible contact exists between her and the image that "tugs out" her response (intimated, for example, by a label commonly applied to genres aimed at female audiences—"tearjerkers").

Consequently, although some feminist theorists have taken up tropes of empathy, contact, and connection in opposition to a masculine model of identity which they wish to critique, the very notion of a "subject-in-proximity" offered as a subversive or hopeful alternative to dominant formations is itself implicated in the dynamics of consumerism and commodity culture.[21] It is precisely by inciting the viewer's overidentification with a purchasable "look" that consumerism operates, and advertisements which invite the would-be buyer to focus on a commodified self-image attempt to initiate the same subject/object implosion that has been marked as specifically "feminine" by many of the theorists treated in this study.[22] One of TV's most devalued genres, the soap opera, clearly exposes this intersection of cultural notions of femininity and consumerism: within a form seen by many critics as emblematic of female subjectivity, there are almost twice as many commercials as on prime-time TV. In fact, television theorists have suggested a relationship between serial form—a continuously disrupted present which refuses closure—and the effectivity of its commercials, which, rather than truly interrupting the serial, continue its narrative patterns while offering "oases" of narrative closure (Flitterman, "Real" 84, 93–94).[23]

As suggested in the previous chapter, however, the conditions that link consumerism and femininity define all of postmodern U.S. culture—men today must also attend to self-image and their value of exchange, similarly losing the distinction between subject and object that has characterized the prototypical "female consumer." Thus, while TV's market appeal does not stop with women, its consumers have been belittled in such terms in the critical and popular imagination alike, provoking contemptuous assessments of genres in addition to those traditionally associated with female audiences. Music television, for example—a form which also addresses a culturally devalued but economically desirable audience, here a "juvenile" one—further plays out the relations between a fractured Oedipal logic, postmodern form, and commodification: in a circularity of simulation, music videos dissolve the distinction between program, product, and ad by serving, as noted earlier, as their own commercials.[24] TV soap operas and music videos, among the programs most decried, are thus also among TV's most revealing, displaying the dynamics of continuity and difference, presence and interruption, viewing and consuming invoked by the television apparatus. In other words, the forms that have been cited by both defenders and detractors as particularly illustrative of U.S. television also exhibit a consumerism tied to an address to an audience deemed infantile or feminine, a spectator not fully a man.

Nonetheless, as the "feminine" connotations attached to television and consumer closeness are diffused onto a general audience, contradictions of gender and spectatorship emerge, and television is placed in a precarious position as it attempts to induce consumer overpresence even as it tries to attain cultural status by mimicking the more respectable (that is, "manly") cinema. This leaves television in a curious bind—a situation perhaps most evident in many prime-time programs which, in order to achieve social validation and appeal to male viewers, strive to elevate the infantile and deny the feminine conventionally associated with television. Turning then to the second point mentioned above, a common strategy of much of television is to react against this feminine inscription through the construction of a violent hypermasculinity—an excess of "maleness" that acts as a shield. In this way, television's defense against the feminine may be seen as corresponding with television theory's attempts to dispense with the same; by either resisting the feminine position (as many TV texts do) or else incorporating and hence speaking *for* it (as occurs in some recuperative critical texts), the real presence of women within both these particular televisual and critical discourses is deemed unnecessary.

Masculinity and Its Discontents

Within the realm of TV itself, there are a number of possible methods of defense against a supposed "feminization." By aiming for the status of "quality" television (producing texts that can function under the name of an author), creating "proper" spectator distance by mimicking cinematic conventions, or obsessively re-marking the masculinity of their thematics, some programs attempt to evade TV's "unmanly" connotations. Yet attempts at denial and male masquerade may produce problems which emerge on the surface of "masculine" texts.[25] Faced with the contradictions created by the imperative to inscribe order in a medium that disallows resolution and the demand to be "manly" in the "feminized" world of TV, these texts yield a realm of masculine excess that demonstrates their fragile position within both television's hyperreality and a "hypermasculinity" that is its defense.

The desire to construct a powerful masculinity (one which is free from feminizing influences) and the problems that this entails are both apparent in what is perhaps the most common, but also the most troubled, strategy that TV employs: its attempt to visibly establish an acceptable terrain of masculinity through exhibitions of male potency and prowess. As John Fiske argues in a chapter of *Television Culture* on "masculine" drama (a vexed term by which he refers to such programs as *Starsky and Hutch* [1975–1979], *The A-Team* [1983–1987], and *Miami Vice* [1984–1989]), because cultural ideals of masculinity are contradictory and unstable, involving demands that cannot be unified or easily met, television constantly redefines masculinity, attempting to make good on men's lack of its gains (198–223).[26] In other words, since men can rarely live up to cultural expectations of what it means to "be a man," the goal of virile performance must instead be satisfied through exaggerated and compensatory display—something that television programs (as well as other male leisure activities) regularly offer (see in particular 198–202 and 209–212). This is because of both the ideological contradictions within the notion of masculinity and the gap between social experience and ideological norms. Given that the demands of the workplace and the home not only tie most men to the binds of family and society (rather than allowing them to be fully independent and dominant), but also make masculinity socially and psychologically insecure (as it seems to involve opposing images of freedom and constraint, authority and compliance, uncontrolled sexuality and lawful maturity), the lines of ideologically approved male behavior are difficult to draw.

Television texts may deal with these tensions in a number of ways. Various aspects and positions of "manhood" may be distributed among different characters, as occurs, for example, in the 1980–1988 series *Magnum, p.i.*, in which Thomas Magnum's (Tom Selleck's) rugged but relaxed style of masculinity contrasts with the more "proper" demeanor of Jonathan Quayle Higgins III (former sergeant major in the British Army, now majordomo for the estate on which the disarming Magnum lives rent-free) and the more singular skills of Magnum's wartime buddies, T. C. and Rick (the strong helicopter pilot and smooth nighclub owner, respectively) who help with his cases. The distribution of models of masculine prowess is even more apparent on *The A-Team*, a series about the adventures of four Vietnam veterans who right wrongs (for those who can afford their services) while evading the U.S. Army which is pursuing them as outlaws. Among the team, some characters are marked as "childlike" (the comically unstable "Howling Mad" Murdoch and the strongman and ace mechanic "B. A." Baracus) and others as "adult" (the suave Templeton "Face" Peck and the patriarchal leader, John "Hannibal" Smith); some conquer by physical force and others by brains or social skills—and the fact that the physical and mechanical muscle on both *Magnum, p.i.* and *The A-Team* is provided by African American men (Roger Mosley and Mr. T) is surely no coincidence.[27] Employing another strategy common for programs whose premise involves a hero or hero team working outside of and often in opposition to the law, *The A-Team* (among many other shows) narrativizes the struggle between social authority and raw male power, often coding these in ambivalent ways according to race, class, ethnicity, and/or nationality.

The very impossibility of these "occupational" demands (the question not only of how to "get the job done," but how to occupy the position of masculinity in any satisfying way) might itself be narrated. This is what Scott Benjamin King suggests in his analysis of *Miami Vice* as a text which enacts a crisis of male work, the sphere in which men have traditionally been called upon to prove their accomplishments and "masculinity" itself (see especially 286). As men's once secure position within the arena of male labor is upset, the emphasis shifts to the other side of our culture's production/consumption polarity, leading the text to focus on "the look" of both the show and the commodities it showcases. What have been seen as *Miami Vice*'s failed narratives (its scant and incoherent plots) are thus, King suggests, actually narratives of failure (stories of men forced, one might say, to "labor in vain" as they are put on the image marketplace as products rather than producers). On the other hand, the split between action and image may be taken up in an attempt to manage, rather than embody, the competing demands of masculinity; for instance, some aspects of masculinity may be valorized within programs themselves while others are left to extratextual imagery. This is the way in which the conflict between the ideal of male independence and the ideological requirement of heterosexual romance is usually handled: in the narratives of the action shows, the heroes shun romantic involvement in order to "do their duty," while secondary texts (fan publications, talk shows, entertainment magazines) emphasize the stars' sex appeal and glorify their love lives.

Yet as this recourse to increasing fragmentation (indeed, fetishization) might suggest, dissonance and disavowals remain within U.S. cultural constructions of heteromasculinity despite efforts to mediate its terms, necessitating the spiraling of male performance and display, the endless struggle to prove and reprove the myths. Unable to resolve the contradictions that plague both representations and social formations of masculinity, television can only replay moments of its glory, attempting to reinforce the masculine ideal by repeated moments of visible achievement—a repetition which only signals the uneasiness of such attempts at resolution (see Fiske 212). While the media's fantasy compensations for the failures of masculinity may then solve some of the problems haunting men today, television's strategy of recurrent male display yields several other tensions. Having noted precisely the "strain" often manifest in male pin-ups, star imagery, virile performances, and other such enactments, Richard Dyer alludes as well to the historical dilemma which the media now face: "the values of masculine physicality are harder to maintain straightfacedly and unproblematically in an age of microchips and a large scale growth (in the USA) of women in traditionally male occupations" (*Heavenly* 12).[28] Not only does Dyer here point to some of the historical crises in constructions of masculinity within the postmodern, post–women's movement (and, I would add, post–civil rights and post-Vietnam) age, but his subtle reference to the difficulty of maintaining a "straight" image of masculinity also hints at the (homo)sexual panic played out within mass texts.[29] In other words, given the social and sexual codes of looking in our culture, the creation of male spectacle violates the same gender alignments that television narratives strive to uphold.

This "violation" is suggested by one of the first sustained considerations of the question of male display, Steve Neale's well-known article "Masculinity as Spectacle." In it, Neale takes the terms of film analysis made famous by Laura Mulvey and applies them to an exploration of "spectacular" genres aimed at men (the western, the combat film, the epic, the adventure).[30] As such, his work may be subject to the same critiques as hers, particularly concerning the difficulties that the psychoanalytic model poses for historical as well as televisual analysis; nonetheless, his discussion of the psychosexual dynamics and dilemmas of the heterosexual imperative provides a fruitful starting point for a consideration of masculinity and representation within postmodernity. Addressing the deployment of male spectacle in a number of films, Neale recalls that, in our culture, if the look at the male body is openly professed, that body appears feminized; yet avoiding both this "feminization" and the sexual/affective implications of the male-to-male gaze requires repressing the libidinous urges found in any form of looking. In these films, appealing images of masculinity must be present in order to provide viewers with standards of emulation, but this does not prevent them from also provoking transgressive desires (for men as well as women, heterosexuals as well as lesbians and gays).

In fact, even heterosexually normative identifications necessarily involve sexual undertones. In addition to the narcissistic gratification afforded the male viewer by identifying with a more perfect model of manliness, the construction of an ego ideal also evokes masochistic feelings, unleashing a homoerotic element as the spectator succumbs to the image, recognizing his own inadequacy in the face of that ideal. There is thus an oscillation between empowerment and submission, "between that image as a source of identification and as an other, a source of contemplation" (Neale 8; see also Rodowick). Furthermore (and related to the contradictory meanings of masculinity), narcissistic identification itself may be split: on the one hand, there is the wish to accede to masculinity as the Law, as the paternal embodiment of social authority, while on the other, there is the nostalgic fantasy of masculinity as a refusal of the Law, as a realm that excludes women through its celebration of phallic omnipotence. Although these conflicting urges may be managed by dividing the hero function in two (a device found, for example, in those westerns which offer both the civilizing figure of the sheriff and an outlaw gang of men), such strategies also express a homosexual subtext as they provide a vision of male bonding free from the constraints of femininity and heterosexual romance; in Eve Sedgwick's terminology, the homosocial in these cases veers as much toward the homoerotic as the homophobic.[31]

Thus, for male spectators the pleasures of looking are more contradictory than we might first assume—the processes of desire and identification are multiple and fractured despite mass culture's repeated efforts to regulate them into proper gender channels. In fact, this very repetition can yield its own instability, revealing the practices of impersonation and reiteration through which sexual identity is assumed. The seductions of simulation are not, as Baudrillard implies, the essential "property" of women; sex itself may be formed through simulation. For as Judith Butler argues in her provocative theory of performativity, the citations by which gender is demarcated produce the very effects that they purport to name (in this case, "manliness") (*Gender Troubles* and *Bodies*).[32] Far from establishing the priority of the heteromasculine ideal, rehearsals of this model (be these media celebrations or camp performances, mass cultural machismo or parodic drag) are copies with no originals, "proper" to neither sex, but (theoretically) available to all. Indeed, heterosexuality may be seen as derivative of homosexuality rather than the other way around: as the opposite against which to secure a notion of the "same," it is homosexuality which gives meaning to the heterosexual "standard," the exclusion of "the other" that establishes the compulsory status of the one. While heterosexual masculinity is then often presumed as the cinema's unquestioned norm (both within the text and beyond, in the spectator/image relations), even (or especially) the most "manly" of films fails to fully contain all the tensions evoked. As Neale writes, "male homosexuality is constantly present as an undercurrent, as a potentially troubling aspect . . . but one that is dealt with obliquely, symptomatically, and that has to be repressed" (15).

In order to suppress these socially forbidden erotics, the male-to-male gaze deployed by such genres as the western, crime, or war film must be attributed to something other than a curiosity to see, often through a narrative movement that both motivates the viewer's look and rejects desire as out of bounds. We might be offered the spectacle of male bodies, but neither their status as erotic objects nor the spectator's fascinated gaze are acknowledged as such: "we see male bodies stylised and fragmented by close-ups, but our look is not direct, it is heavily mediated by the looks of the characters involved. And those looks are marked not by desire, but rather by fear, or hatred, or aggression" (14). Never having to acknowledge his own interest in the virile form that is displayed, the heterosexual male viewer is protected from the implications of his look. Furthermore, instead of being openly glorified as overvalued objects of the gaze, the figures exposed are often wounded and abused, "marks both of the repression involved and of a means by which the male body may be disqualified, so to speak, as an object of erotic contemplation and desire" (8).

In this way, the targeted viewer is able to disavow his scopic drive, denying his attraction to the image and justifying his attention in the name of following the plot. Indeed, although scenes of male competition or combat engage both fetishistic and voyeuristic fantasies (as ritualized spectacle and narrative struggles intertwine), these two forms of looking almost act as alibis for one another, effecting a negation by balancing the terms:

> The shoot-outs are moments of spectacle, points at which the narrative hesitates, comes to a momentary halt, but they are also points at which the drama is finally resolved, a suspense in the culmination of the narrative drive. They thus involve an imbrication of *both* forms of looking, their intertwining designed to minimize and displace the eroticism they each tend to involve, to disavow any explicitly erotic look at the male body. (14)

Allowing the spectator to revel in a narcissistic image of male glory at the moment of its loss (particulary evident in scenes of slow motion violence [10]), these extended "climaxes" nonetheless provide a built-in defense: anticipating closure, they can justify the image, assure the viewer of his command over both spectacle and story, and promise to put all narrative and spectatorial tensions to rest.[33]

Yet however much films are able to manage all these strains by ostensibly resolving them within a narrative movement that leads to closure and control, television texts have no such final guarantees. Unable to suspend

time as the cinema does, television can only remain within its ongoing
flow, yielding ever more spectacle, posing, and display. That is, given the
specific constraints of U.S. network television (which requires that the
heroes return weekly and that the narrative enigmas remain open to more
plots), order can never be ultimately restored—there is no final solution
arising through successful male action. This results not only in the turn to
television melodrama (as explored in chapter 3), but also in the repetition
of a male masquerade: the attempt to establish clear lines of identification
and social/sexual difference can be achieved only through the surface
manifestations derived through masculine display. Of course, this reiteration—the exhibition and production of masculinity through constant
refiguration—exacerbates the very "gender trouble" that television tries
so hard to avoid.[34] Caught in a bind in which only repeated evidence of
performance can suffice, television's (and postmodernity's) construction
of masculinity becomes dependent on its "look," making it recall the same
feminine connotations of spectacle and image that it wishes to combat.

Racial and Sexual Simulation: A Masquerade
of (Hyper)Masculinity

Investigating a specific kind of mediated "combat" in an article on
televised sports, Margaret Morse notes that despite cultural inhibition,
"the gaze at 'maleness' would seem necessary to the construction and . . .
replenishment of a shared . . . ideal of masculinity"—an ideal rocked by
historical shocks and consumer demands and so particularly in need of
replenishing ("Sport" 45). Morse thus examines TV's discourse on sport as
"a place of 'autonomous masculinity,' freed even from dependence on
woman-as-other to anchor identity" (44). Yet as my comments above
suggest, sport is not the only televisual arena in which the male body is
displayed; the aforementioned programs (*Magnum, p.i.*, *The A-Team*) and
many others (*The Fall Guy* [1981–1986], *Matt Houston* [1982–1985], *Knight
Rider* [1982–1986], *Spenser: For Hire* [1985–1988], *MacGyver* [1985–1992],
and *Wiseguy* [1987–1990]) variously mobilize male spectacle and point
toward the historical significance of this practice.

For example, a television guide book describes the premise of the series
MacGyver thus: a "rugged, handsome hero who preferred to use paper
clips and candy bars than more conventional weapons. . . . MacGyver
could work wonders with the contents of a lady's handbag!" (Brooks and
Marsh 535). This celebration of the TV hero's ability to turn even a
woman's purse into the means of male prowess is not only comical but
symptomatic, suggesting the multifarious ubiquity of this textual (and
sexual) strategy—one found in programs that valorize "ingenuity rather
than brute force" just as in those that emphasize bodily exhibition alone.[35]
As this description also reveals, such displays do not necessarily establish
a masculinity free from relation to the feminine, despite their location
within the (generally) all-male preserves of sport and the cop/detective

show. They can instead be seen as an attempt to save masculinity even in the "feminized" world of TV, even in the vacuum of a crisis-ridden postmodernism. As suggested by many crime and action series (*Magnum, p.i.* and *The A-Team* again being two examples), this includes the crisis of Vietnam—a crisis in masculinity which has been treated explicitly in several programs, and which may also be partially responsible for the popularity of the genre in general.[36]

Yet perhaps even more than these other texts, *Miami Vice* is a show of male excess and display which may be analyzed as a hysterical response to a feminine contagion. *Vice* too dealt with the trauma of Vietnam— lead character Sonny Crockett, an undercover detective (played by Don Johnson), and police lieutenant Martin Castillo (Edward James Olmos) were both Vietnam veterans, and many episodes touched on this theme. Its characterizations and plots, however, received less attention than the show's look and sound. Typical in many ways of television's construction and concerns, *Miami Vice* was also lauded for its aesthetic and consumer innovations (the emphasis on *mise-en-scène* demonstrated by its pastel color scheme, fashion coordination, and artful use of Florida locations; its pulsating theme and score; its appropriation of music video form; and the commodification and marketing of all these devices). As suggested by the phrase "MTV cops"—the two-word notation made by then NBC entertainment president Brandon Tartikoff that supposedly engendered the show—*Miami Vice* was meant both to exploit and to stand out from the flow of television on the strength of its "arresting" visual and sonic style (Alex McNeil 496).

In his insightful analysis, Jeremy Butler reveals the ways in which *Miami Vice* capitalized on this style, aspiring to the cultural position of the cinema through its use of specifically *film noir* conventions (see especially "*Miami Vice*" 129–30, 132–33). Yet *Vice* differs from *film noir* in some important ways. In place of the duplicitous woman, the trouble that sets the cinematic plot in motion, the motivating forces in *Miami Vice* are all men. Women may be visible as background detail or decor, but in a world in which male criminals are the primary enigmas and objects of voyeurism, the woman is divested of all potency, including and most importantly, her power of masquerade, her ability to manipulate her femininity and hence unsettle the image in which she's contained. Here, the power of masquerade, the ironic potential of seduction, belongs to men, most frequently to Crockett and his partner, Ricardo Tubbs (Philip Michael Thomas), who display themselves as criminals in order to lure their prey into captivity. This display can also be seen in the ways in which the images of Crockett and Tubbs were taken up by the discourses of advertising and fashion— again, it is the male image which is the focus, the men who masquerade. While *film noir* investigates female identity and masquerade, *Miami Vice*'s central dilemma then revolves around the identity of *Vice* vs. vice and the possibility of differentiating between the cops and the crooks, the men and their roles.[37] Clearly at stake here is a question of masculinity in a world in which all stable distinctions have dissolved, in which the feminized object of the look and trouble of the text constitutes a position shared by every-one. This is a crucial question for postmodern, post-Vietnam America as well as an issue for television—the "consuming" and "feminine" form of this time.

One episode entitled "Duty and Honor"[38] (an episode confronting Vietnam) exemplifies the textual disturbances provoked by such displays of manliness. The narrative traces the paths of two characters. The first is an African American Vietnam veteran, called only "the Savage," who is responsible for a series of prostitute murders, each victim marked by the words *VC Whore* despite the fact that most of them are *not* Vietnamese (a bizarre enactment of the terms of simulation that reveals its deadly stakes). Interwoven with this narrative is the story of a Vietnamese police officer, a former friend of Lieutenant Castillo who comes to Miami to solve the murder cases that have haunted the two since their introduction years ago in Vietnam. As demonstrated by the way in which the victims are selected, the women are easily replaceable objects, chosen simply for their long, dark hair. One could say, however, that the killer makes much more of an impression. From our first sight of the Savage preparing for attack, he is marked as an object of the gaze as he appears before a mirror, eyeing himself and rehearsing a pose. He is thus constituted as spectacle—the spectacle of a perfect machine, a cyborg weapon of war, as well as that of a feminized icon demanding to be seen. Played out across the body of a black man—a man marked in our culture's racist discourses as little more than body—are thus the interlocking issues of race and sex, empire and nation, civilization and violence, identity and masquerade.

Discussing the spectacle of the cyborg body as well as the aesthetic of slow motion in her article on sport, Morse analyzes the athlete in terms of the cultural fantasy of the perfect machine body, a body moved by an "inner logic" beyond space and time, at one with nature and "unimpeded by acts of the ego" (44). In the ritualized experience of this unified "flow," she writes, "man can overcome his separateness from nature, God, other men and his own body and achieve grace, signified by slow motion" (56). In other words, as a cyborg body, an object displayed for the fascinated gaze, the male athlete or performer can ritually experience a subjectivity usually coded as feminine. This analysis of slow motion also applies to the visual style of *Miami Vice*, and particularly here, to the cyborg character, the Savage, who is positioned as both a (feminized) visual object and a perfect machine of death. His status as image is constantly emphasized as we see him primp in a black leather coat, repeating a gesture of smoothing his hair. In one scene, he even competes with a televised display of male bodybuilding as he yells at his landlady for watching too much TV and failing to look at him when they speak.

As both spectacle and object of the investigatory gaze, the Savage is assigned the role traditionally aligned with femininity. In fact, as the narrative progresses, we learn that he is literally feminized: he has been castrated in Vietnam, which is the reason for his hatred of Vietnamese women and their simulated stand-ins. Hypermasculinity as a response to

Rehearsal: "the Savage" in front of a mirror in "Duty and Honor."

Retribution: the murder scene.

such feminization, which I would argue is the underlying logic of texts of male spectacle, is then made manifest in the episode's central murder scene. The scene is marked by a flattened pictorial space fully dominated by the Savage. Staring into the camera, he is posed against a stark wall, apparently naked, with an enormous knife emerging from the bottom of the frame. Sharing the prostitute's point of view, we see the Savage approach and almost leap into the camera, returning the look of the spectator with a violent retribution that obscures our vision and concretizes the excess of his status as spectacle as well as the discord of such hyperphallic aggression, a reaction to castration.

It is, of course, overdetermined that this deadly conflation of excess and lack, threatening femininity and superabundant masculinity, would be projected onto an African American male, one who is socially positioned as both inside (in relation to black women) and outside (in relation to white men) of a privileged patriarchal realm. But it is in (imagined) relation to the white woman that this conflation appears at its most alarming; it is because the myth of the hypervirile black male rapist (used historically to justify lynch laws) that the symbolic castration of African American men became all too often realized in fact. The character of the Savage recalls (even as he reverses) this mythical trajectory, moving from castration to aggression and so embodying at once both stereotypes that govern mass cultural representations of African American men. For, as Robyn Wiegman has written, "it is in the oscillation between feminization (buffoonish Uncle Tom) and hypermasculinization (well-endowed rapist) that the contradictory social positioning of the black male has been negotiated, providing the means for disavowing his sameness to [the white masculine ideal] on the one hand, while marking his masculinity as racially produced excess on the other" ("Feminism" 180).[39]

In his work on racist and colonial discourses, Homi Bhabha also examines the oscillation between similarity and difference, recognition and disavowal, noting the ambivalent structure of the fetish in stereotypes and racial masquerade (apparent in the Savage's own violent fetishization of "Vietnamese" women) ("Other"). This ambivalence—the "almost the same but not quite"—maintains the racial/colonial subject in a contradictory position, shifting between "resemblance" and "menace" ("Of Mimicry" 127, 132; see also Fanon). Indeed the "not quite/not white" other is menacing precisely because of the aspects of resemblance, the very repetition which destabilizes claims of racial and cultural priority. The reiterative operations of stereotype and mimicry thus continually produce their own slippages and excesses. Not surprisingly, this slippage is apparent within the visual and narrative trajectory of "Duty and Honor"; the overabundance/lack that marks the Savage (and defines the parameters of black male stereotypical representation) cannot be contained.

In fact, in the logic of the episode, his castration is infectious: after the introductory, pre-credit flashback to the initial crime in Vietnam, "Duty and Honor" begins as Sonny Crockett is interrupted at the height of a sexual encounter by news of the latest homocide. As noted above, Sonny is also a Vietnam vet, and with the suspension of the hetersexual union, there is an odd mirroring established between two new "couples": Sonny and the Savage, and Castillo and Nguyen Van Trang, Castillo's former partner in the prostitute murder cases. In both couples, each "partner" has immediate knowledge of the other which goes beyond language but is distorted by masquerade. Sonny mirrors the Savage in two scenes as shots of his search for the killer are intercut with shots of the Savage looking for women. Finally, Sonny exhibits the contagion of feminization by smoothing his hair in the characteristic gesture of his prey moments before the Savage arrives and is instantly recognized through the crowd—even though Sonny has never seen him before—while making the same gesture.

Repetition: Sonny mirrors the Savage.

Threatening to disrupt the narrative and ideological order that the show tries to enforce, the textual connections that link these two men (and, similarly, Castillo and Trang) must somehow be controlled. Associating the characters not only with the menace of feminization but also with the forbidden possibility of homosexual desire, all hints of an affinity must be actively denied. It is thus important to note that within these "pairs," the conventional terms of sexual difference are displaced onto racial difference, a situation also key to *Miami Vice*'s primary partnership—that of Crockett and Tubbs. As a symptom of the tensions plaguing "masculine" texts, such racially / ethnically mixed hero-pairs have a long history in both literature and mass culture (Natty Bumppo and Chingachgook, Ishmael and Queequeg, Huck Finn and Jim, the Lone Ranger and Tonto—the examples go on).

Discussing the regressive fantasies that are part of so many American "classics" which might more accurately be described as "boys' books" (fantasies which are also commonly found in television shows marketed for a male audience), Leslie Fiedler relates the prevalence of such mixed hero-pairs to the United States' repression of homosexual desire. Arguing that the acknowledgement of homosexuality contradicts a national myth of masculine love—a myth intimately intertwined with popular representations of the black or "colored" man—he analyzes dominant culture's wish to maintain a belief in the possibility of a relationship immune to any lust:

> The nineteenth-century myth of the Immaculate Young Girl has failed to survive in any *felt* way into our time. Rather, in the dirty jokes shared among men . . . , there is a common male revenge against women for having flagrantly betrayed that myth; and under the revenge, the rather smug assumption of the chastity of the revenging group, in so far as it is a purely male society. (143)[40]

In order to maintain the vengeful belief in the purity of man, the texts disavow desire and instead promote a troubling vision of a different kind of love—the "innocent" camaraderie that unites all kinds of men.

Nonetheless, because close relationships between male characters suggest both an element of homoerotic desire and the danger of neutralizing hierarchical distinction, some discrimination must be made between male "soulmates" to assure readers / viewers that difference (and the attraction between "opposites") continues to exist. While its members might then work together (even preferring one another's company to that of women), literature's male pairs and TV's hero-teams are always differentially and hierarchically arranged. In this way, as Andrew Ross notes, although only men are joined through these bonds, the union between them "expresses the myth of complementarity that governs compulsive heterosexuality in our culture. . . . [The] men are *heteros* . . . since each 'naturally' supplies what the other lacks" (153). Creating a division to take up the place of gender by imposing racial ranks, *Miami Vice* attempts to establish lines of power that maintain our culture's norms.

Given the specificity of *Vice*'s *mise-en-scène*, these conventional divisions themselves are often masked. Located in a city connoting permeable borders (through which not only drugs but also immigrants might flow), *Miami Vice* seems to embrace a multicultural and polyracial solidarity. Yet even though several members of the squad are either African American or Latino—including their respected but aloof vice force chief—very rarely are these characters made the focus of the show (in fact, in this regard, the episode "Duty and Honor," which revolves to a large degree around Lieutenant Castillo, is an atypical example). In other words, while Castillo may be *institutionally* empowered as the leader of the team, he is *textually* disempowered, associated primarily with the bureaucratic hassles that TV's "real" heroes always try to avoid. As the many discourses (interviews, ads, fashion shoots) which circulated around *Miami Vice* ensured, the individual whose authority and, more importantly, masculine superiority really counted was star-signifier Don Johnson—the sole figure who needed no institutional backing in order to be "right" (visually, even if not legally or morally). The program's African Americans and Latinos (and women of any race and ethnicity) gained credibility primarily by tagging along, by associating themselves with this central figure of masculine appeal.

Racial and ethnic divisions may also be seen within the various forms of spectacle that exhibit male "virility." As Richard Dyer points out in his analysis of male pin-ups, while white men are most often displayed in terms of leisure time or sports (both revolving around a middle-class conception of the work/leisure split), black men are often placed "outside" of class and "given a physicality that is inextricably linked to notions of 'the jungle,' and hence 'savagery'" ("Don't" 68). The way in which these connotations are fully exploited, indeed literalized, in the image of the Savage—who is associated not only with the "primitiveness" that our society attributes to African Americans but also with the jungles of an "untamed" Vietnam—perhaps needs no further explanation. Suffice it to reiterate that it is no accident that the contradictions created by *Miami Vice*'s hypermasculine response emerge on the body of the Savage—the man who, given the United States' racial divisions, is most likely to evince the strains that this provokes. While not as explicitly marked, even the otherwise heroic Nguyen Van Trang is presented as possessing a "savage" side. Rather than exercising the (assumed) prerogatives of Law, he ultimately flings a knife through the white man revealed at the end of the episode as the "true" villain, a military bureaucrat who has hired the Savage for political assassinations (the prostitute murders merely being unfortunate but tangential casualties). Thus, though the narrative of "Duty and Honor" hints at the deep bonds uniting the male couples Sonny and Savage and Castillo and Trang (two familiar heroes and their "others"), the need to establish terms of difference is crucial to this text. In order both to deny the homoerotics that the text itself suggests and to inflect the heroes' power with even more cultural authority, any bonds that are implied must somehow also be repressed.

While the chase scene then locates Sonny and the Savage as (literally) moving down "parallel roads," the successful joining of Castillo and Trang is located in the hope for an impossible future world. It is only after Trang has saved Castillo from attack, tenderly examined his wound, and quickly disappeared that Castillo reads of his friend's masquerade—*Trang* is an alias, assumed for undercover work in South Vietnam and Miami. While he remains unnamed, his voice-over explains his real status as a colonel in the Army of the Republic of Vietnam, his new understanding of the Savage as victim (of the true savages in both their countries who nurture war), and his appreciation of Castillo's care despite the masquerade. He ends his letter asking for friendship: "I dream of a more perfect world in which we could also be comrades." The dream of male bonding, occurring against a backdrop in which it is impossible to distinguish opposing sides, to assert right or wrong, or to secure masculinity apart from a violent defense, is here played out in all its excess and contradiction.

The Playground of Style, The Battleground of Gender

While this (at least superficially) progressive "message" of cross-cultural, suprapolitical solidarity is striking in relation to the usual fare of TV cop shows, "Duty and Honor" exposes the problematic of which I am speaking in chillingly clear terms, embodying the hypermasculine defense against a feminization associated with TV and postmodernity (particularly, with post–civil rights, post-Vietnam, and post–women's movement America). As such, it reveals TV's masquerade of masculinity—a masquerade which may be seen as a violent response to the feminine connotations attached to television and its receptive viewers. Scholarly and popular accounts might "mediate" television through tropes of femininity, but we must not blind ourselves either to its deep concern for masculinity or to the contradictions this involves—contradictions which are often expressed in terms of race, nation, or class and which result in disavowals that further complicate textual and spectatorial relations.

In the case of *Miami Vice,* as well as in other shows of male spectacle, the very attempt to solve the problem of an (historically and psychically) impaired masculinity through exhibitions of manly display may provoke more ruptures than it is able to resolve, increasing the pressure placed on mass culture and gender formations. For, as made evident in the *Vice* episode "Duty and Honor," the art of the pose is most often considered a feminine ruse in spite of its presence in television programs that revolve around masculinity in both their address to a male audience and their narrative concerns. Associated by psychoanalysts with the construction of femininity, masquerade is a strategy by which the subject hides a lack— that lack of being that is represented in our culture through the sign of castration.[41] Standing as a literal embodiment of this Oedipal fear (and thus positioned, just like the woman, as one who *is*, rather than one who *has*, the phallus), it is not surprising that the character referred to as the

Savage attempts to assert his masculinity through such "feminine" tactics as spectacle and masquerade, posing as an object to assert himself as subject.[42]

Yet psychoanalytic theory emphasizes that each of us, male and female, poses in relation to the phallus. Going beyond any actual physical loss (such as that suffered by the Savage), castration ultimately signifies the price paid by all subjects upon formative entrance into culture as they are fundamentally severed from a "nature" which is itself retrospectively created as fantasy. Constituted by a law that exceeds any "purely biological" division, sexual identity is not pregiven; it is *ordered* as "sex" comes to be figured by, rather than simply enacting, anatomical difference. Because this organization is necessarily precarious, each subject can only take up a position which, though determining, is too but a pose. As theorists from Joan Riviere to Judith Butler have implied, all assumptions of a sexual and gendered identity may thus be analyzed as masquerade. Nonetheless, while "all human subjects [men as well as women] are subject to castration, . . . in a discourse that privileges the phallus, only women have been diagnosed as such" (Owens 15). Therefore, although TV's models of "manly" behavior are forced to operate by way of "artistic" impostures (as do all incarnations of gender), the feminine connotations of the pose and masquerade yield a number of contradictions for those television programs that attempt to erect a satisfying image of masculinity; as Jacques Lacan writes, "the fact that femininity takes refuge in the mask . . . has the strange consequence that, in the human being, virile display itself appears as feminine" (*Feminine* 85).

According to some critics, the instability that this provokes helps disrupt oppressive social and sexual norms, allowing television to escape the rigid binds of gender that the cinema upholds. For example, in a discussion of *Miami Vice*'s reliance on the trappings of surface appearance in its creation of male ideals, John Fiske argues that this posed construction of masculinity brings in a "potentially contradictory, potentially 'softening' dimension" which modifies traditional meanings of gender by opening up the program to the postmodern pleasures of spectacle and style (*Television* 221). While he notes other changes in the cop/crime show genre (such as the rise of male/female teams with their accommodation to women and "feminine values"), he reserves his highest praise for *Vice*'s emphasis on masculine display: "*Miami Vice*'s challenge to the meanings of masculinity may be the most insidious and politically effective, because it occurs not at the level of *what* is represented, but *how* it is represented. The other shows may represent women performing 'masculine' roles, but *Miami Vice* encodes masculinity differently" (222). Providing pleasures of image and sensation that go beyond those usually offered by the cop show, *Miami Vice*, in Fiske's opinion, can barely contain the anarchic delights that disrupt the genre's structural imperative to maintain ideological and narrative control. Even its title sequence, a dizzying montage of Florida's "playground," ignores the conventional shots of leading characters and fails to stitch the viewer into a coherent diegesis (261), offering instead only the disorienting impression of speed and surface blur (in addition to the close-ups of women's breasts, which Fiske fails to note).

For Fiske, this focus on physical sensation, the materiality of the body, and the signifier divorced from the tyranny of referential meaning recalls the resistant pleasures that theorists have associated with the carnivalesque, a mode that is revived in the excess, inversions, and "bad taste" of television's own "low" vernacular (*Television* 241). But even more than television itself, "in the postmodern world, style performs many of the functions of carnival" (249), and through shows like *Miami Vice* (television's "first postmodern cop show" [254]), TV has concerned itself more and more with what Fiske considers the "essentially liberating" language of style (249).[43] Claiming that the participatory nature of style (and postmodernism in general) is empowering for the subordinated, Fiske concludes that television texts based on such pleasures pose a serious threat to the dominant order and offer more to the disenfranchised viewer than mere fun. In fact, an attention to style defines, in his estimation, "the ultimate political act" as it invites the viewer-consumer to construct his/her own image, permits us the pleasure of making spectacles of ourselves as we toy with new meanings, and rejects all traditional categories and the judgments they contain (254).

In opposition to those who critique the vacuum of simulation and the consumerism it entails, Fiske thus celebrates postmodernism's "oppositional" and "disruptive" force (249):

> [Postmodernism] refuses sense, refuses the notion of subjectivity as a site where sense is made. . . . [S]ense, common sense, is the prime agency where the social machine enters and destroys the individual, so, in rejecting sense, postmodernism is rejecting the social machine and its power to regulate our lives and thinking. (254)

This understanding of illogic may seem paradoxical, but it is suggestive of many popular and critical trends (from the anti-intellectualism apparent within the raging "culture wars" to the more encouraging emphasis on style and performance in queer politics and theory). Yet as queer theorists/activists make clear, while style can be a powerful tool of parody and critique—a tool with which to reformulate, not simply reject, knowledge and sense—"putting it on" does not mean that one can simply choose to take an image off and change identities at will, a notion more attuned to commercial appeals than political action.[44] The "individual" is constructed only through society and not outside of it as Fiske implies, able to be "enter[ed]" by "the social machine" (shades of *Videodrome*) or else fabricating subjectivity for one's self. Minimizing the multiple and dispersed ways in which consumerism operates, Fiske denies the very real financial/corporate sense that this refusal makes, valorizing television texts based on a postmodern spectacle of style without interrogating the implications of their imagery.

Comparing, for example, the spectacular music video–like segments found in *Miami Vice* to the song and dance numbers of the classical

Hollywood musical, Fiske suggests that these narrative interruptions break the self-enclosure of the text, opening up the space for interrogative and resistant readings. By disrupting the ideological flow of action that works to stabilize the program, these moments of self-conscious artifice fracture the otherwise institutional and value-laden meanings that the text tries to enforce. Elaborating this theory in an analysis of a *Vice* episode which contains such a musical segment (involving extreme close-ups of a bankroll, credit cards, men's clothing, car, and gun—edited to match the beat of the soundtrack), Fiske claims that because the fragments don't "advance the narrative, . . . increase our understanding of the characters, plot, or setting, or provide any clues to the solving of the enigmas . . . , it is fair to assume that their function is *purely pleasurable*" (255, emphasis added). Yet it is precisely the "purity" of this pleasure that is open to question; if *Miami Vice* seduces the viewer into a carnival of postmodern play, then exactly whose playground does this seem to be?[45] Certainly the objects portrayed in this segment, however stylized, are loaded with cultural connotations and ideological significance, suggesting not only the traditional prerogatives of masculinity (the car, the gun) but also the 'virtues' of an affluent life. Here, the "pleasure" of consuming becomes an integral part of TV's "new" image of man, even as masculinity retains all of its stature and established terrain.

Referring to Ross's analysis of this program, Fiske states that the "vice" in *Miami Vice* (drugs, prostitution, pornography, and so on) consists simply of "bad" consumerism: as the flip side of "proper capitalism," these expenditures flaunt their lack of use-value and therefore crack the alibi of the commodity system. However much the narratives align viewer sympathy with the cops who police such consumption, the "voluptuous visuals" provide this very thrill, positioning the spectator as the ultimate consumer who, in Fiske's opinion, merely enjoys the "non-ideological" sensuality of the items on display (*Television* 258, 261). Of course, we can no more distance commodities from the social and economic systems in which they circulate than we can ignore the power differences articulated across gender, race, and class found in the "vices" named above. Nonetheless, Fiske claims that by shedding the realist signifieds which bind the image to the diegetic world, one can also shed the market function of the "goods" that are paraded before our desiring eyes. In *Miami Vice*, "the meanings of commodities are moved out of their original economic domain into the more pleasurable one of style" (259), and:

> [d]enying the narrative domain of these objects dislocates them from the ideological one as well. The pleasure here is not in resisting ideology, nor in challenging it with a "better" one, but in evading it, in liberating oneself from it. (260)

The problem with this view lies not only in its reductive notion of ideology as a force which can simply be evaded or separated from pleasure and the formation of identity, but also in its misreading of the marketplace. Neglecting the fact that style and pleasure cannot be divorced from the economic and ideological realms of late capitalism because they are exactly what tend to get sold, Fiske can only reduplicate the logic of consumerism, trapping himself within the same snare of hypersimulation that he tries to defend.[46]

Thus, like other critics who valorize the "feminine" irony of male masquerade, Fiske ends up voicing an indifference toward the very differences that he wishes to set free. Recalling and uniting the two issues that, as noted earlier, are often overlooked—the social and power relations that define current modes of consumption and a backlash against women through TV's hypermasculine defense—Fiske strives to redress the problems of gender and commodity culture by simply embracing current norms. Arguing, for example, for the radical, playful, and "essentially democratic" nature of a postmodern, commodified spectacle and style (*Television* 260), he writes:

> The distinctive and the personalized (that is, the *stylish* construction of the individual) is achieved through a creative bricolage of the commodities in the marketplace. The self is a shifting transient identity, literally self-created . . . , and in this spectacle, the gaze is neither masculine nor feminine, for it is not the gaze of a stable subject upon a stable object: both subject and object construct themselves out of the traditional signs and positions of either gender. This culture signals the death of authenticity, of any underlying "true" meaning of gender or of anything else. (259)

While Fiske is celebrating the utopian ability to fashion new appearances, his own imagery here bears an uncanny resemblance to that of previous claims, particularly those of Baudrillard, whose musings on the amorphous space of mass culture, death of the social, and seductions of the masses that already appeared (at least to Huyssen, in the remark with which I began) retrogressive and stale. Like the posings they each describe, such uncanny repetitions have themselves been seen as symptomatic of castration anxiety, displaying the desire to cover over lack (see Freud, "'Uncanny'").

The same may be true of television's own repeated male displays: far from marking the end of gender and power divisions, TV's masquerades—a response to the discursive constructions that put television and its viewing subjects in their (feminized) place—contribute to these very disparities; indeed, the primary thing often masked in such male masquerades is the desire to be rid of femininity itself. This may be even more evident in more recent cases of television's hypermasculinity; after their apparent peak in the mid-1980s, action and crime dramas slightly waned in popularity in the early 1990s, only to be replaced by the ever-expanding (and notoriously male-dominated) field of televised sports as well as the most alarming show of strength of all: the timed-for-TV Gulf War spectacle, itself covered very much like a sporting event.[47] The militaristic fervor exhibited—with its troubling deployment of discourses of nation and ethnicity, gender and family, and its structuring absence of discussion of postindustrial economics—more than demonstrates the menace of

The Gulf War troops watching Super Bowl XXV.

hypermasculinization; it certainly puts a new slant on the words "creates its enemy for itself . . . chang[ing] by intrigue the universal purpose of government into a private end," spoken by Hegel of femininity, brought by McLuhan into his account of TV.

In other words, while theoretical and popular discourses alike may figure television in terms of "the feminine," we should not accept such views uncritically, failing then to notice other crucial differences which run through television—differences related to nation, class, and race, for example—as well as the contradictions of gender that do exist within TV's multiple address. While the gender inscriptions of American broadcast television are complex, intertwined, and unstable, it is important to note that even the temporary securities offered in these shows require the punishment, neutralization, or absence of women (while still disavowing any overt homosexual eroticism). As I detail in the next chapter, the family offered is a family of man, and the gender positions cast are significant for both the men and women watching. In a cultural form so invested in domestic space (within the texts' diegeses as well as in the television industry's and advertisers' construction of the audience), this is the final irony that cannot yet be explained by current theories of sexual and textual difference—the masculine threat that lurks "within the gates" of a medium deemed feminine.

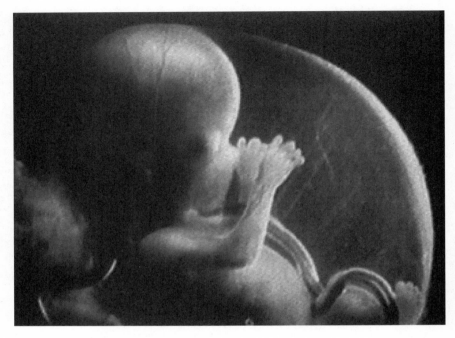

A fetus in the womb in *The Miracle of Life*.

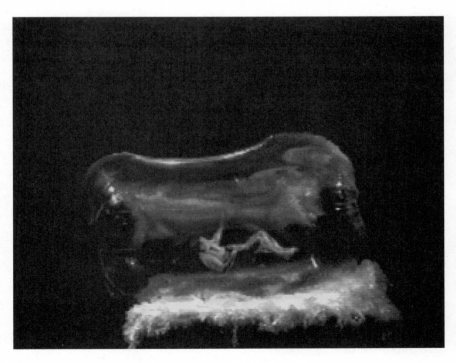

Bruce Willis in the womb on *Moonlighting*.

V

TUBE TIED
TELEVISION, REPRODUCTIVE POLITICS,
AND *MOONLIGHTING'S* FAMILY PRACTICE

TV's Family Affair: The Union of
Technical and Sexual Reproduction

On the eve of the 1980s, Roland Barthes observed that "television condemns us to the Family, whose household utensil it has become"; throughout the next decade in television history, this observation certainly seemed to ring true (as, in fact, it still does today) ("Upon" 2). However, just what the family is or should be, how it is to be constituted, and who has the power to determine this have become matters of heated debate within American culture. The resurgence of legislative battles around the issue of abortion, the development of controversial forms of birth control, and the advent of new reproductive technologies—not to mention social factors like growing divorce rates, "alternative" living arrangements, and single-parent households—have led to a general state of confusion about the family and its regeneration. As reproduction is increasingly divorced from sexuality, as sexuality detaches itself from the nuclear family, and as both appear to disclaim "biological destiny," anxieties and conflicts over these changes reach explosive proportions.

The conflicts became particularly pointed in the 1980s when shifts within "conceptions" of life and death—wrought by such phenomena as the rise of AIDS; the growing fields of fetology and immunology; and medical and legal disputes over parenting, childbirth, and physical and moral "care"—were met with a reductive "pro-family" agenda that merely exacerbated the tensions. Supposedly designed to protect "the family" (a family figured as devoid of sexually active adolescents, homo- and/or bisexuals of any age, and women capable of making independent decisions about the concrete circumstances of their lives), the policies enforced by the Reagan and Bush administrations did little to protect family members at risk. Their effect was rather to promote silences around the topics of AIDS, safe sex, and reproductive options; indeed, abortion was literally silenced when the 1991 Supreme Court, loaded with Reagan and Bush appointees, upheld the "gag rule," the 1987 ban that prohibited discussion of abortion under any circumstances in federally funded family-planning clinics. At precisely a time when society was placing an increasing emphasis on women's individual responsibility to families and "children" (inter-

preted as an inclusive category comprising those both born and "unborn"), information, resources, and services that might have assisted
women were being restricted and cut.[1]

Given the patriarchal image of the family thus imposed, it is not surprising that this extension of maternal duty was not met with a comparable
paternal accountability; in an era in which newly constructed "classes of
citizens" were being figured as "oppressed" (taxpayers, Christians, fetuses, white males), the focus was placed not on paternal *responsibilities* but
on father's *rights* (seen as endangered by feminist demands).[2] This has
created a double bind for feminists concerned with sexual freedom and
reproductive choice, a situation perhaps most apparent in the debates
revolving around reproductive technologies and the ambivalent responses
that these technologies yield from men and women alike. On the one hand
(and despite previous feminist goals of detaching "woman" from "nature"), many women fear that the disruption of "natural" processes of
reproduction will accelerate women's expendability under patriarchy,
producing new forms of medicalization and domination with which to
contain and control the female body.[3] On the other hand (and responding
to a contradictory fantasy), men may fear the ways in which these same
changes seem to enlarge the scope of the maternal generative sphere while
further removing husbands and/or fathers from the seat of reproductive
control.

Because of the controversies these issues engender, apart from news
shows and some made-for-TV movies, television has rarely entered into
debates surrounding sexual, reproductive, or family politics in a sustained
or explicit way. There have of course been some notable exceptions: *All My
Children*'s Erica Kane became infamous in the early 1970s for (among other
things) undergoing daytime television's first abortion, and there was a
national uproar when the situation comedy *Maude* (1972–1978) aired
episodes dealing with later-life pregnancy, abortion, and vasectomy in
1972 (an outcry which was exacerbated when CBS rescinded a promise to
the Catholic Church and chose to rerun these episodes the following
summer, provoking boycotts, affiliate cancellations, local rescheduling,
and advertiser withdrawals).[4] Indeed, no lead character of a prime-time
series has chosen an abortion since. More recently, segments of *The Silent
Scream*, produced in 1984 by the National Right-to-Life Committee, were
widely shown on network and cable television stations, sometimes together with Planned Parenthood's 1985 response. Portraying, its narrator
claims, a real-time abortion "from the victim's vantage point" (a 12-week-
old fetus referred to as "the living unborn child," a "human being indistin-
guishable from any of us"), *The Silent Scream* seemingly delivered, as one
critic remarks, "the live fetal image into everyone's living room."[5] Though
not explicitly marked as anti-abortion rhetoric, the award-winning documentary "The Miracle of Life" (which aired on PBS's science series *Nova*)
similarly penetrated the womb, providing what Valorie Hartouni describes as "vivid visual evidence of what [anti-abortion] activists regard as
the biological facts of fetal life" ("Fetal" 134).[6]

While somewhat atypical, these examples are hardly anomalous, fitting into many of television's usual formats (the language of discovery familiar from the science show, the fascination with health and its personal ramifications in television drama, the emphasis on "current events" found in several TV genres).[7] In fact, even though network television may attempt to avoid such "immoderate" subjects in the interests of its own "regeneration" (high ratings and renewals), it is necessarily enmeshed within the terms of reproductive debates. Truly a "family affair," U.S. television is a medium in which the familial is both the dominant theme and the typical mode of address, and thus, television's construction of family dynamics as well as its place within them is significant for any analysis of our society's "domestic policies." Within our culture, not only is television often figured as part of the family, but it is used to define notions of both domestic harmony and household authority: bringing its families into our living rooms and us into theirs, it asserts a national family unity even as its patterns of use in the home articulate relations of power, positioning family members hierarchically within a larger social field.[8] It should then come as no surprise that the operations of electronic reproduction, the relations that define TV's existence, intersect with those of sexual reproduction, relations that define the family's (and our own) existence, in a multitude of ways.

The discursive network by which the family and its modes of electronic and sexual reproduction are constructed necessarily establishes a relationship between television and sexual difference. Yet here again there is a complex dynamic between television's own cultural location and those constructions of gender by which television is articulated and which it, in turn, articulates. As I've elaborated throughout this study, television has been figured in gendered terms which both encode and direct our understandings of its texts and viewers. Said to foster a "feminine" look which accords with domestic conditions of reception, television works to keep the viewer caught up in an endless dispersal of consumer desire while "safely" tucked away within the confines of family life; like reproductive technologies that regulate female "labor," television regulates viewing in conformity with ideological notions of gendered work in the home.[9]

Yet despite apparent alignments between television and social constructions of domesticated femininity, television's gender inscriptions are more tangled than they first appear to be, and the positions that television maps for its viewers involve displacements and disjunctions that resist attempts to sum them up under any one label. Within several TV programs and genres, for example, the desire to reassert male control is readily revealed. As discussed in the previous chapter, the strategies used to achieve this end are themselves often riddled with contradictions and disruptions. As I elaborate there, in attempting to reverse its usual connotations by aligning itself with masculinity rather than femininity, television does not so much repudiate the feminine (although this, of course, also happens) as appropriate, and thereby reroute, these same clusters of meaning. Rather than preventing male viewers from assuming any kind of dominant position, TV thus assures them that the prerogatives of masculinity continue to exist even within the pacified family that television constructs (both within its fictions and among its "family" of viewers). In other words, while television may be figured as feminine or its viewers as feminized, it also attempts to restore a threatened masculinity, to reclaim any "feminization" in the name of a more encompassing vision of masculine self-sufficiency and plenitude.

In this context, it is interesting to investigate some trends in recent television history, particularly those pertaining to representations of the family—or as I will ultimately emphasize, representations of the search for an "acceptable" family. Employing a somewhat broad definition of the term, one can trace the ways in which women may be excluded from TV's "familial space."[10] For instance, some genres effect an erasure of the woman by defining the world as one big masculine home: in the cop/detective shows discussed in chapter 4, men within the police or investigative "family" usurp the traits of femininity, often dispensing with women altogether since the men themselves can play all of the roles. One might also consider various incarnations of the family situation comedy in which an appropriation of femininity/maternity allows men to move into the position of both mother and father (*Charles in Charge* [1984–1985, first-run syndication, 1987–1990], *First Impressions* [1988], *Mr. Belvedere* [1985–1990], *Raising Miranda* [1988], and *Who's the Boss?* [1984–1992] are just some examples).[11] Although the strategies of exclusion upon which these texts rely may seem to be opposed (in that the aggression of the cop show seems to stand in marked contrast to the warmth and humor of such situation comedies), in many ways, their results are quite similar indeed.

However, it is an episode of the 1985–1989 romantic comedy *Moonlighting*—a witty detective show pairing a polished ex-model with a cocky private eye—which will ultimately be my primary focus here. Going beyond the genres named above, this text brings violence and sentimentality together in a particularly striking way so as to forcibly expel women from the family—an expulsion that is only strengthened (rather than mediated) by the self-reflexivity associated with this series. By offering an in-depth analysis of the premiere episode of what, in fact, turned out to be *Moonlighting*'s last season—the show in which lead character Maddie Hayes loses the baby that is the visible result of the previous season's (and specifically Maddie's) "sexual excess"[12]—I hope both to expose the extent of television's engagement in sexual, reproductive, and domestic politics and to reveal how television may rely on specific textual devices to establish the prerogatives of masculinity within all of these domains. Reasserting the primacy of the patriarchal family by literally redefining this unit as a "family of man," *Moonlighting* performs a chilling excision of the maternal sphere. Yet in disrupting the "natural" course of both familial and narrative progression, the program disturbs the very ground of representation upon which television's construction of the family is based, unleashing a threat which it can only manage to recontain by turning in on itself in a particular way. In my discussion of *Moonlighting*'s "family practice," I thus plan to show not only how the text commits an assault upon the woman, but also how this series' noted strategies of self-referentiality, far from being radical distanciating gestures, contribute to a containment of femininity which allows the fathered-family to appear.

Paternal Precedents

Before elaborating *Moonlighting*'s (re)construction of familial space, though, let me briefly consider some of this detective comedy's (not so distant) televisual relatives by recalling some of the lines from which it evolved—the cop/detective show and television comedy. While, at first glance, it may seem odd to refer to such stereotypically "male" genres as the cop or detective show in an analysis of television's construction of the family, my prior "investigation" of these texts reveals that such a connection is not so far-fetched. Although the crime drama is usually linked with action and adventure, far removed from the genre of melodrama in which a focus on the family is the norm, the particular conditions of television discussed in chapter 3 have driven these forms closer and closer together. Because of the typical proportions and location of the TV set, as well as the budget and scheduling of TV productions, almost all television texts borrow melodrama's strategies for the intimate presentation of domestic life (an emphasis on interior shots, close-ups, background music to capture the attention of a distracted viewer, and so on). Furthermore, like the melodrama, television's cop/detective shows negotiate their social issues in primarily personal terms. Because of the institutional structures of U.S. television (which require the continuation of leading characters and, thus, the plot itself), TV's heroes are enclosed within a virtual echo chamber of repeated action and emotional pressure as the circumscribed parameters that define a privatized melodramatic sphere delimit the world of the cop show as well. Accordingly, the dramatic impulse of many cop and detective programs—the affective center that sustains viewer interest—tends to revolve around the struggles and dynamics that exist between members of the investigative unit or police "family" itself.[13]

Within this unit, the same "myth of complementarity" that supposedly holds the heterosexual couple and the nuclear family together binds the members of the hero pair or team into a functional whole; as noted in the last chapter, the members take up separate (but unequal) roles, becoming each other's own "better half."[14] These differences are often visually and ideologically expressed through racial or class distinctions, and by "marrying" cultural oppositions in this way, the crime show can insert a husband/wife or parent/child dynamic into the heart of its (usually) all-male detective pairs or teams while fully maintaining dominant norms. Yet as the familial and the "feminine" become subsumed within this masculine sphere, actual women often find themselves with no significant part to play. This can be seen in the distribution of positions along the axes of subject/object and pursuer/pursued as well as in the formation of a leader/helper dichotomy (the husband/wife or adult/child dynamic mentioned above). In the cop or detective show, women may appear in some scenes, but since they offer little in the way of textual enigmas, it is rarely their appearance which counts. Still trapped within the look but deprived of the power that this position might provide, they become just frivolous decorations, useful mainly as they contribute to the man's masquerade—his ability to perform a role and perfect a look which draws the criminal's (and of course the viewer/consumer's) attention.

The ways in which cop/detective shows like *Magnum, p.i.*, *Miami Vice*, and *Wiseguy* have aligned their male characters with spectacle and the pleasures of the look have been critically as well as popularly applauded. For instance, John Fiske suggests that the genre's appropriation of a "feminine" concern with masquerade, image, and appearance not only shifts conventional representations of masculinity but signals the demise of stable sexual identity itself (*Television* 221–22, 255–62). Yet as I recommend in chapter 4, rather than prematurely celebrating the death of gender in the postmodern age, it seems more important to analyze the ways in which statements of this death actually work to increase the scope of sanctioned male play. While both the effort to bring a "human" (read "family") focus into the precinct and the attempt to associate masculinity with the surface gloss of style may at first seem surprising or even subversive, the hegemony of male power is, in the last instance, still assured. By granting their heroes the best of both worlds, these texts extend the range of male dominance so that it is able to cover every narrative sphere. Furthermore, the alliance of masculinity with familial emotion or the image tends to result in the exclusion, rather than acceptance, of women. In appropriating the position traditionally reserved for femininity (as men take up both sides of the heterosexual coin, becoming, in turn, either husband and wife or subject and object of the investigatory gaze), masculinity gains a self-sufficiency that tends to leave no space for women in the narrative at all.

Indeed, in feminist discussions of reproductive politics, the appropriation of spectacle and the manipulation of appearance have hardly been lauded. For example, in her perceptive analysis of fetal imagery and optical/obstetrical technologies, Rosalind Petchesky critiques *The Silent Scream* precisely by suggesting that it "encapsulates the 'politics of style' dominating late capitalist culture, transforming 'surface impressions' into the 'whole message'" ("Fetal" 264). In this case, the "cult of appearances" that brings the fetus-as-baby-as-humanist-subject into view works to make the pregnant woman disappear; aside from occasional glimpses of a body on an operating table, she is "seen through" rather than truly seen. Not only does *The Silent Scream*'s self-described "dazzling" imagery limit our identifications (either to the narrating "paternal-medical authority figure" so familiar from TV dramas and ads or, of course, to the fetus "himself"), but its narrative "operations" do the same: in fact, according to Petchesky, its tale of "'victims' [of] . . . abortion clinics . . . 'run by the mobs' . . . [employs the] rhetoric, not of science, but of *Miami Vice*" (266–67). Making a similar argument in her analysis of the "fetal fascinations" found in medical literature and photography, Sarah Franklin also notes the use of interlocking adventure narratives in which the envisioned protagonists are all men: from the heroic scientists who have developed the technology by which we can objectively "see" the "facts of life" to "the fetus-commander, preparing his defense-mechanisms against the hostile maternal environment [which] speaks of a particularly militaristic genre of the masculine adventure narrative (*Rambo* fetus)" (201).[15]

This link between male action and paternal adventure exists within network television as well, albeit most often through more "sensitive" displays. Not only does masculinity regenerate its own image in the cop/detective show, erasing women from the screen by allowing men to usurp so-called "feminine" traits, but a vision of the world as one large masculine clan is enacted even more explicitly within other television forms. For example, many family situation comedies from the late 1980s promote male homosociality as their ultimate goal and reveal a disturbing desire on the part of men to appropriate women's reproductive and maternal roles. In fact, to take a glaring case, in television's 1987–1988 season line-up, not a single new "domestic family" (as opposed to "work family") sit-com featured an actual mother. Instead we were offered *My Two Dads* (in which a woman has died and left her "estate"—a twelve-year-old daughter—to two of her ex-lovers, either of whom may be the father, who raise her together); *Full House* (in which a woman has died and left her husband with three daughters to bring up with the help of his brother-in-law and best male buddy); and *I Married Dora* (in which a woman has symbolically died by abandoning her family, leaving her husband to raise his two children with the help of his "alien" housekeeper—a woman he must lovelessly marry so as to prevent her deportation). While, of the three programs, *I Married Dora* at least involved an adult female character, not only was this show the most blatant in its attack on "real" mothers (in its presentation of the mother as villain and father as savior, not to mention its racist portrayal of the woman who steps into the maternal role as somehow "alien"), but it was also the only one of the three to be cancelled at the end of the season, finding itself "terminated" when it wasn't picked up for renewal.[16]

Given the social and political realities of contemporary American culture in which women are the primary caretakers of children, men notoriously neglect both financial and emotional parental responsibility, and almost all single-parent households are headed by women,[17] TV's announcement through these texts of the strength of male "paternal instinct" appears quite curious indeed.[18] Commenting on this phenomena in an analysis of a similar text, the film *Three Men and a Baby* (a remake of the French film *Three Men and a Cradle*, and an inspiration for TV's own paternal themes), Tania Modleski discusses how anxieties revolving around paternal position and the threat of patriarchy's decline—fears provoked by abortion rights, new reproductive technologies, and changing social norms—are both manifested and allayed within such fantasies

of the fathered-only child ("Three").[19] Not only are women now synonymous, at least in the media's eyes, with the "sexual revolution," but, as
previously mentioned, the recent attention given to artificial insemination,
in vitro fertilization, embryo transfer, and other clinical procedures has
raised male concerns over the rights of the father—especially as these
technologies seem to increasingly minimize male participation in the
process of conception just as legalized abortion maximizes women's own
control. Giving voice to the contravening, almost contraceptive, fantasy of
a male "virgin birth" (71), the aforementioned programs thus attempt to
dispense with women altogether, conveniently ridding themselves of the
mother so that male homosocial bonding can occur, not, as is typically the
case, by exchanging women (although this is also implicit in the brother-
in-law relationship on *Full House* and in the competition for / sharing of the
woman that served as the premise for *My Two Dads*), but rather through the
intervention of the young child.

Providing the characters with both progeny and the pleasure of usurp-
ing feminine roles, these texts articulate a narcissistic fantasy in which men
can have it all (Modleski, "Three" 74–75). Assuming every family position
(and thus literally embodying the feminization and infantilization often
associated with television), these regressive "male moms" are not only the
perfect companions to their young, but by drawing the viewer into a world
of endless childish play, they also help "reproduce" the power of television
itself. In other words, they attract many viewers precisely because they
present their visions of the purely fathered family as simply the source of
innocent fun. The humor involved in these texts—a humor that depends
upon the absence of the woman—can then mobilize and authorize what
would otherwise stand out as a much more disturbing trend. Nonetheless,
as in television's crime dramas, the feminization that plagues such male
characters is not accepted without some form of defense. While on the
surface, this vision of nurturant and caring fathers may seem diametrically
opposed to the violent behavior engaged in by TV's detectives and cops,
we should be wary of valorizing it as a more humane, even feminist,
image. Not only does the role of "mother" and the accompanying fear of
being "unmanned" often give rise to the heroes' displays of masculine
prowess and strength (a phenomenon also found in reproductive science's
stories of conquering medical experts and the embryos/fetuses with
whom they identify), but, in allowing their heroes to play all the parts, the
programs implicitly suggest women's expendability and marginality in
the family (72, 76).[20]

As Modleski points out, though the desire to find alternatives to masculine aggression and to further involve men in the responsibilities of child
care may speak to justifiable and important female needs, we must be
careful not to unwittingly legitimize an aggressive male appropriation of
the maternal realm, thereby authorizing our own expulsion from familial
space (79–80). Similarly, the fact that these sitcoms employ the form of
comedy, constructing their role reversals as the source of "harmless"
humor and "mere" entertainment, should not exempt them from critical

scrutiny. If anything, the pleasure that they provide helps to mask the more sinister fantasies to which they give voice. While their humor may make these texts palatable and even appealing, it is precisely women's exclusion from the domestic sphere that engenders viewer laughter, allowing the negation of the feminine to become the cause for both enjoyment and applause.

Violation and the Law: Breaking and Entering the Female Body

While, given the obvious correlations between the television shows mentioned above and *Three Men and a Baby*, Modleski's analysis of paternal desire within this film is important to my own argument, I would like to expand the discussion to incorporate some other trends in U.S. television's representation of the family (or the desire for family) in the 1980s. It was during this decade that a whole range of women's behavior during pregnancy (from drinking alcohol or smoking to choosing an abortion) became construed as "child abuse."[21] Perhaps in response to (even avenging) such conduct, 1980s television did not simply promote male homosociality at the expense of women deemed expendable, but in some instances it actually enacted a certain violence on the body of the would-be-mother—a violence which, in *Moonlighting*'s case, extended to the very rhetoric of representation itself. Specifically, I want to discuss how the aggressive expulsion of women from familial space (redefined as a purely paternal domain) as evidenced in the 1987–1988 TV season was further exacerbated in the 1988–1989 season, which, instead of portraying an "unnatural" but desired male appropriation of feminine reproductive/ nurturant capacities, chose to penalize a threatening female procreative potency by stripping the woman of her seemingly "natural" role (demonstrating the double bind created for feminism by both articulations and disarticulations of women and nature).[22] Punishing the sexual woman who dares to claim her offspring as her own, or to put it another way, "castrating" the mother who wants both power and a child, three TV programs (*Hooperman, thirtysomething,* and *Moonlighting,* all on ABC) presented miscarriage stories in their 1988 season premieres—a surprising plot device under any circumstances, but absolutely extraordinary considering the goal of generating audience sympathy and loyalty that all premiere episodes share.

Because of the multiple and/or continuing plotlines that both texts involve, *Hooperman*'s and *thirtysomething*'s decision to use this device may not seem so far-fetched. The miscarriages in these shows intersect with plots regarding women's struggles over relationships versus personal autonomy, the decision for family or for career (a standard, if very limited, way in which options for middle-class white women are portrayed), and given the soap opera–influenced structure of both programs, a concern with romantic and family crisis is not totally out of place.[23] *Moonlighting,* on the other hand, had always revolved around the sexual tension, witty repartee, and unfulfilled passion between its two leads—Maddie Hayes (played by Cybill Shepherd) and David Addison (played by Bruce Willis). Maddie's pregnancy, carried over from the previous season and intro-duced when actress Cybill Shepherd was herself pregnant, raised the thorny issues of not only how to make a pregnant woman seem "sexy," but how to maintain the traditional focus of the show. In other words, due to its emphasis on a sole couple (until Shepherd's pregnancy frequently prevented her from appearing in the episodes) and a narrative premise that rested on the now obviously redundant question of "Will they or won't they?" both the pregnancy and *Moonlighting's* miscarriage plot stood out as much more disruptive textual breaks.

In an attempt to extricate themselves from this dilemma, the producers of *Moonlighting* ended Maddie's troublesome pregnancy in an astonishing way. While it incorporated shots of the actors preparing for work, clips from past seasons' programs, and brief scenes of Maddie and David at their detective agency and then at a baby shower, most of the action took place within Maddie's uterus—in fact, the show was entitled "A Womb with a View." Thus enabled to reveal all that (its producers presumed) we ever wanted to know, the episode served as an antidote to the paternal confusion informing texts like *My Two Dads*: while the previous season showed Maddie's sexual involvement with two suitors (hero David and rival Sam Crawford) and ultimate marriage to still a third man (Walter Bishop), this episode cleared up once and for all any doubts about the paternity of the child while still preventing Maddie from carrying to term. Recalling the fetal imagery familiar from medical science as well as from anti-abortion demonstrations where it is brandished as a weapon (after all, ultrasound technology derived from the military's use of sonar detection for submarine warfare), this show reveals the aggressive patriarchal underpinnings of such disciplinary techniques, participating in what Petchesky has termed our culture's "panoptics of the womb" ("Fetal Images" 277).

Yet perhaps even more peculiar than either the choices of subject matter or *mise-en-scène* was the vehicle selected to frame what one might expect would be a rather sad tale. Instead of portraying the loss of a child as a "weepie" and employing the more predictable melodramatic mode (or even borrowing strategies from the new discourse of fetology and con-structing it as a sci-fi adventure), "A Womb with a View" was actually presented as a classical Hollywood musical—a genre that is not only considered synonymous with Hollywood entertainment, but one that is associated with utopian fantasy as well. In utilizing this form, *Moonlight-ing* capitalized on a nostalgia not simply for a pre-television and pre–rock 'n' roll era (good-naturedly critiquing its own associations with youth and media culture), but also for both the mythical days of stable paternity (when women knew their place) and the program's own successful past. In fact, before the actual glimpse into the womb, the episode begins as the characters openly express their desire to regain their former popularity and the show's once-high ratings (prior to the previous season's fall from

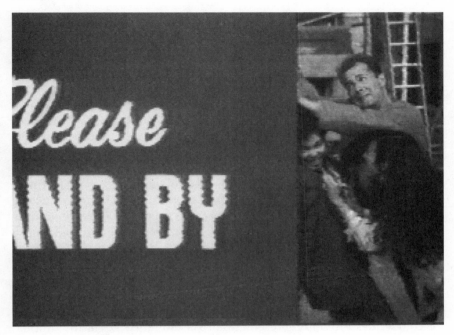

The performers clear the air.

grace, provoked, in part, by Maddie's/Cybill's pregnancy and the chaos that it brought both to the show's production schedule and to its founding premise of unfulfilled love). With this goal of revivifying their televisual existence, the performers directly address the audience in the attempt to create a sense of intimacy, familiarity, and community.

This strategy is a common one in the Hollywood musical as well as in *Moonlighting*'s own formula—through the abolition of proscenium space, techniques of viewer recognition, and the use of *I/you* pronouns that disguise the *histoire* of recorded media as the *discours* of interpersonal interaction, both the musical and many forms of television present themselves as live, spontaneous, and communal endeavors, the better to mask their mediations and interpellate the viewer into their ideological orders.[24] Keeping with both of these traditions, *Moonlighting*'s "A Womb with a View" paradoxically denies any technical intervention even as it draws attention to the medium of television. At the beginning of the episode, for example, the actors point toward the camera and call to individual and seemingly "familiar" viewers by name, creating an interesting reversal as the viewers are brought into the text while the characters themselves are allowed to move outside of it at will. Later, in another self-referential joke, they push a "Please Stand By" title that interrupts a song-and-dance number out of their way as if it is merely a part of the set that the cast is constructing rather than the evidence of electronic mediation. It is precisely through such ironic and self-reflexive strategies that *Moonlighting* had always been able to set itself apart from other programs and achieve its status as quality television.[25] Building on this reputation, the use of these techniques has a specific dual function here: not only does it under-score the innovative value of the show, but by drawing the production processes of the media into the fictional world of the program itself, *Moonlighting* manages to turn its extra-textual problems (including bad publicity and ratings) into the textual trouble that it sets out to resolve. Recognizing themselves as fictional constructs in search of our much-needed approval, the characters nonetheless seem to inhabit our own world, and the sense of intimate connection with the audience that is thereby established is exactly what is needed to get the program back on track.

Yet if *Moonlighting's* loss of ratings is the problem that these performers face, then, as in any good musical, the solution can be reached just by putting on a show. The episode thus goes into a typical backstage produc-tion number as the characters/actors express their wishes to reconstitute a new community of performers and viewers united within a utopian space. That this utopia is to be literally figured as prenatal existence is made clear by the fact that the narrative quickly shifts to the activity inside Maddie's uterus, minimizing her own relationship to the momentous event about to occur by concentrating almost solely on the state of life within the womb.[26] Of course, despite this representation of a universal Eden, the utopian sensibility of the musical responds to specific historical tensions in con-ventionalized ways. Playing almost a mythical or ritualistic role, the musical allows the spectator to heal oppositions and resolve current social problems—in this case, the tensions surrounding sexual and reproductive politics—by apparently offering timeless solutions that facilitate our re-dedication to traditional goals.[27] As a general rule, in its final "wedding" of cultural polarities, the musical asserts the triumph of communal harmony over personal, social, or sexual conflicts, and not surprisingly, this social integration (or the integration of the individual into a warm, loving community) most often occurs through marriage and the consolidation of the heterosexual couple (see, for example, Sutton).

In "A Womb with a View," however, rather than ultimately securing the Law through a contract of marriage, the desire for this Law (and the Name of the Father that stands as its sign) is directly expressed.[28] Though there are a few jokes concerning "Baby Hayes's" prenatal interest in the opposite sex (particularly in relation to his mother), he reserves most of his awe for the sight of his dad. For while Maddie's "promiscuous" behavior has precluded certain knowledge of paternity for those existing within the social world, there is no such confusion for those in the womb: not only is Baby Hayes played by Bruce Willis (the same actor who plays David Addison, but here, as an infant, dressed in diapers, blue pajamas, and a little blue bow), but the apparent angel who visits him in preparation for birth (Jerome, identified as the "emissary of the Creator") summons a giant, magical family album in which the new member is already in-scribed.

Fanciful as this might seem, it mirrors contemporary discourse on procreation and abortion in a number of ways—from the peculiar mixture

Moonlighting's familial inscription.

of religious and scientific rhetoric to the representation of the fetus as a "homunculus," a complete but miniature man.[29] The relevancy of this representation to reproductive debates should thus be obvious. By figuring the fetus in the womb as both a full subject (complete with language and already installed within the Symbolic Order) and as a familiar presence (played by Willis, the "fun" member of the *Moonlighting* pair), there is not only no question as to when life begins, but even as to whose life has priority here. In other words, the fact that Baby Hayes is truly Baby Addison—that he already carries the paternal legacy as a tiny yet autonomous human being, that he is properly assigned as male through his little blue outfit, and that he is indeed his father's rather than his mother's child—is visibly confirmed.

Nonetheless, Baby Hayes officially lacks his father's name—a gap that the narrative must eventually fill. When he is then confronted with the picture of his mother, Baby Hayes predictably lets out a low "hubba hubba," but he only attempts to attain recognition from the father he requires, calling out to him as "Dad!" Therefore if, as several critics have claimed, the musical number often functions as a means of "surrogate sex," there is here a crucial shift in both the surrogacy required and the value placed on sex. Instead of celebrating heterosexual love, this episode ultimately punishes Maddie for her interest in this "vice" and reveals a vengeful urge to make the woman merely the means of conception, to relegate her, in other words, to the position of "surrogate mother"—the term now used to discredit biological mothers so as to assert the overriding reality and rights of the father.[30]

Television Dystopia and the Maternal Scene

In the previous season, Maddie's maternal potential had already been somewhat disparaged and condemned. Indeed, her ability to maintain an acceptable feminine "propriety" was called into question not only by the text itself, but by many of the secondary discourses that circulated around it; tabloid reports on production battles and on-the-set power struggles, for instance, attacked Cybill Shepherd in much the same terms that the show used in attacking Maddie Hayes. Detailing the path of a former model who attempts to orchestrate a new career, *Moonlighting*'s premise both mirrored and relied upon the image of its star, and by blurring the distinction between fiction and "real life," Maddie's character elicited viewer fascination while at the same time provoking the hostility so often directed at women who attempt to take their lives into their own hands (whether this be through professional/productive or personal/reproductive choices). Always figured as a shrew and a castrating terror (a position made explicit not only in the popular press's depiction of the battle of the sexes on the sets, but also in another of *Moonlighting*'s tributes to the past, its re-presentation of *The Taming of the Shrew*), the pregnant Maddie was made to seem positively grotesque in some of 1987–1988's final episodes.[31]

This partially derives from the general shock and discomfort the gestational body seems to elicit within our historical and social formation. In an analysis of the changing parameters of reproductive debates in the 1970s and 1980s, Faye Ginsburg explains that pregnancy places women in a liminal position, temporarily located between two structural states and thus unassimilable to any one role (69–71). Furthermore, the legality of abortion allows for the uncertainty of the final outcome: the state into which the woman may move (motherhood or nonmotherhood) is no longer predetermined (or punitively enforced as such), and thus, the social and contingent (versus "natural" and necessary) order of reproduction is exposed. For this reason, while the pregnant woman is supposedly the revered object of "pro-life" discourse, she has largely disappeared from its visual imagery, posing more of a potential challenge to dominant conceptions of gender and familial status than this discourse can contain. The difficulty of visualizing and containing the pregnant body can be seen in more "mainstream" venues as well: witness the outcry surrounding the infamous August 1991 *Vanity Fair* magazine cover, which featured a nude and very pregnant Demi Moore (not to mention Moore's appearance on *Late Show with David Letterman* in 1994 when, again pregnant, "she" supposedly did handsprings across the stage in a skimpy outfit).[32] That Demi Moore, spouse of *Moonlighting* star Bruce Willis, carried the "real-life" Willis offspring is an amusing coincidence; nonetheless, the way in which Moore's "flaunting" of her pregnant body was denounced by comparing her behavior to more "dignified" (non)displays is telling, for this is precisely the way in which *Moonlighting* itself derided Maddie Hayes.[33]

For example, in the episode in which the pregnant Maddie marries

Walter Bishop (the only one of her three "suitors" who is not a biological candidate for fatherhood but who, temporarily, is the legally appointed choice), Maddie's position within the constellation of characters makes her monstrous status perfectly clear. Displacing viewer judgment away from one triangle (the men vying for Maddie's affection) and onto a competing triangular configuration, this episode sets Maddie up against another pregnant woman—a friend of David's whom he has been assisting in Lamaze classes—and stands as the logical precursor to the miscarriage story in "A Womb with a View." Within this first show, after chasing David out of the church and into the hospital where his friend is about to give birth, Maddie bursts into the delivery room and interrupts the course of its "natural" proceedings. Exaggerating the effect of this narrative disturbance through its construction of *mise-en-scène* (Shepherd, already a commanding presence, is here not only shown to be obviously pregnant while wearing a virginal, white wedding gown, but she is also inserted into a tiny, crowded room—a setting that makes her appear almost hideous because she is so out of place), *Moonlighting* produces Maddie as the monstrous shrew precisely by locating her in opposition to the good mother whose delivery she disrupts. Acting almost as a "prequel" to next season's miscarriage show, this incident establishes the parental prospects of the characters quite well; not only are David's capabilities proven, but Maddie's are denounced. Unlike the "good" woman who has taken care of herself and her baby throughout her pregnancy (even, or especially, to the point of finding a good man to assist her), Maddie has unleashed terror and disorder for all of those around her—for the guests at the wedding, for the people in the delivery room, and even for the *Moonlighting* viewers themselves.

Given our culture's codes of representation and gender, such figurations of terrifying maternity, existing both in relation and in opposition to the sentimentality also attached to notions of motherhood, are not at all rare. The (supposedly) dreadful nature of pregnancy is simply a variation on the alliance between the monstrous and the feminine commonly found within the genre of horror, and while presented as a musical-comedy, "A Womb with a View" has a horrific edge.[34] Blatantly dealing with issues that are typically idealized, repressed, or banished from the scene (sex, reproduction, birth and death, et cetera), the episode's vision of miscarriage is shocking at best. In fact, its very exposure of the deeply ambivalent fantasies at the heart of the nostalgia that it exhibits toward both motherhood and the musical form makes "A Womb with a View" a more dystopian than utopian dream. Referring to the Hollywood musical's self-fulfilling "utopian" promise in terms which are remarkably literalized in *Moonlighting*'s spectacle of prenatal life (and its termination), Dennis Giles writes, "[t]he show bears a resemblance to the state before birth, echoing its timelessness, its ultimate unity of lover and beloved. But it is also a preview of the death state, transforming all the terrors, all the flux of life into a state of permanent being" (87). Revealing the drive for death that's intimately intertwined with our regressive fantasies of utopian rebirth,

Moonlighting's musical–horror show raises the terrifying specter of the ultimate abject.

According to Julia Kristeva, the abject—that "pseudo-something" which is neither subject nor object, a "pre-object" which cannot yet be recognized as an "other" for a "me"—disrupts all borders and rules, disturbs any identity or location, and both terrifies and fascinates as it collapses the distinctions between inside and out, sacred and defiled, life and death (*Powers*; see esp. 2–17). Existing on the vacillating frontier of signification and subjectivity, the abject both engrosses and divides, attracts us but repels, seduces us with the desire for meaning but sickens us as it draws us to a place where meaning falls apart. While the horror of abjection is related to the fear of femininity (and its supposedly permeable boundaries), Kristeva particularly associates it with the maternal body and the threat that it poses to the very existence of subjectivity for the child: "that of being swamped by the dual relationship, thereby risking the loss not of a part (castration) but of the totality of his living being" (64; see also 70–72, 83–85). In order for the subject to be born onto himself (as subject), the not-yet-"it" of the abject must therefore be excluded even at the price of one's "own" death—an exclusion that not only revolves around separation from the maternal entity "even before ex-isting outside of her," but one that uncannily resembles the trajectory of *Moonlighting*'s own miscarriage plot. Dissolving the bounds of the subject through a glorious expansion of its anarchic drives, maternal abjection must somehow be hemmed in so that the Law can take its place. In other words, while the abject may offer a kind of sublime rapture as it carries us away, there must be some release from the stifling power that it holds. It is therefore the function of symbolic systems, rituals and myths—secular as well as religious—to "ward off the subject's fear of his very own identity sinking irretrievably into the mother" (Kristeva 3, 13, 64).

Frequently defined as a mythic or ritualistic form, the musical may seem to be a genre well equipped to enact just such a defense—dazzling us with its vista of boundless delights yet harnessing this in the name of the Law, the musical sweeps us off of our feet only to firmly plant us once again on Symbolic ground. Yet a musical that is, for the most part, located precisely within "the desirable and terrifying, nourishing and murderous, fascinating and abject inside of the maternal body" (Kristeva, *Powers* 54), as is "A Womb with a View," seems to raise more tensions than it is able to resolve.[35] While, traditionally, the musical's construction of the woman as image and object provokes viewer interest while still containing any threat that might be posed by the female form, in this episode, such allurement and mystique arise only in conjunction with the horror of the show (although the specularization that typically defines the female star in both the musical and in *Moonlighting* continues to operate even within this unusual text, albeit in a very literal way). Employing a notion taken directly out of the scientific debates on reproductive technologies—that of a "maternal environment"—in this episode, the mother no longer simply poses a possible threat of engulfment but is constructed as the realm that actually envelopes the text. The female body literally becomes a site for conflicts that cannot be directly represented in narrative terms.

Speaking of another text that crosses genre lines (in this case, those between science fiction and horror), Mary Ann Doane notes that within the 1979 film *Alien* (as well as in its 1986 sequel *Aliens*), the woman similarly "merges with the environment and the mother-machine becomes *mise-en-scène*, the space within which the story plays itself out. . . . The maternal is not only the subject of the representation here, but also its ground" ("Technophilia" 169).[36] In fact, the maternal body (and the abjection it involves) *cannot* be the subject of representation within these texts in any coherent or conventional way. Dissolving oppositions, the abject threatens to disrupt the possibility of signification itself (necessarily based on the paternal law of differentiation), thereby undoing the very systems upon which narrative, history, subjectivity, and knowledge are based. Relating *Alien*'s preoccupation with this threat of dissolution to the same crisis in the reproductive sphere that Modleski notes, Doane explains that the issue is "no longer one of transgression and conflict with the father but of the struggle with and against what seems to become an overwhelming extension of the category of the maternal, now assuming monstrous proportions" (169).

While, of course, *Alien* and its cinematic "progeny," the sequels, struggle with this horrifying expansion in terms which differ from those of "A Womb with a View" (the *Alien* films focus on the vacillating border between human, inhuman, and technological reproduction while *Moonlighting* is concerned with erecting a boundary between socially sanctioned and illegitimate procreation—in other words, between the sacred and profane, the pure and the impure), the threat of an ever-enlarging maternal domain, no longer as limited by biological or social constraints, hovers over all these texts. The anxiety provoked by this vision is strikingly figured in *Moonlighting*'s show as it transforms the pregnant body into a space of both dread and utopian song/dance. While the musical numbers, in part, serve as terror's mask, they actually increase the violence of the scenes, producing, through the lethal combination of horror and escape, a textual dissection of the glamorous female star. It is thus no wonder that the text insistently calls for paternal relief. Enacting Kristeva's observation that "fear of the archaic mother turns out to be essentially fear of her generative power . . . a dreaded [power] that patrilineal filiation has the burden of subduing," *Moonlighting*'s baby can only be "delivered" to the Father and the Law (77).

Courting precisely the kinds of fears that Kristeva here describes, a minor subplot within "A Womb with a View" (involving two characters who often function as less "desirable" versions of David and Maddie) actually details the terms of such a struggle for parental control, foregrounding both the anxieties and antagonisms that inform current reproductive politics as well. Arguing about Maddie's upcoming baby shower, Herbert Viola admits to Agnes di Pesto that pregnancy makes him uncomfortable—a confession that triggers all the aggression he can muster.

Finally revealing his feelings of inadequacy when it comes to fatherhood, he states that he wouldn't want to pass his genetic weaknesses on to a child. Defending the "rights" of a mother against male assumption of sole parentage, Agnes retorts, "It wouldn't be just your gene pool; who's to say that your oddball genes would be the ones to carry the day?" Going on to assure him that he'd be a wonderful dad, she exclaims, "I could really get into your genes," clearly punning on "jeans" as they go into a love scene on the couch (with Agnes as the dominant partner). Yet as she walks out of the door after having assuaged him of his fear, she makes a face and calls him a jerk, indicating to the viewers that all she really wants from Herbert (and, by implication, what all women really want) is simply a willing donor to supply her with a child (a projection indeed made possible by reproductive science). Both denying and "exposing" the way in which women today supposedly use men as impregnation machines—rather than the ways in which women have been used, sometimes through coercion, as incubators by men concerned with passing on their lines—this exchange reveals the threat posed by the devouring woman/mother to men's control over reproduction—a threat that the episode as a whole seeks to contain.

All in the TV Family of Man

In order to effect such a containment and closure, Maddie must lose her child so that he can be born instead into the midst of the paternal domain. Near the end of the episode and moments before the birth should take place, the angel who visits Baby Hayes within the womb receives a telephone call on his portable phone (a plot twist which suggests the same imaginative potential of intermixing spiritual and technological imagery exploited by religious broadcasting and anti-abortion campaigns). The call is presumably made by God himself to inform Jerome, his "emissary," of a major change of plans—a "last minute shuffle" which provokes a violent disruption within Maddie's life, but one that offers a solution to the problems in the text (not to mention a conclusion which upholds a patriarchal ideology at risk). Cutting between Jerome reassuring a frightened Baby Hayes with shots of Maddie collapsing as she's attacked from within, the text manages to reap vengeance on the body of the mother without having to damage the prospects of the child.

While thus adhering to some degree to the conventions of horror (which often gleefully exhibits the destruction of the family), "A Womb with a View" nonetheless offers a more "hopeful" view: it celebrates the destruction that it reaps merely to reconstitute the family in a more "appropriate" form—namely, by assigning Baby Hayes to a couple that can offer him a "proper" (father's) name. Furthermore, rather than making television or technology into an agent of horror and feminization (as occurs in several films, *Videodrome* providing the exemplary case), television is here what saves Baby Hayes. It offers one of its own favorite fathers to counter the

DELIVERED BY TELEVISION

Maddie loses the baby.

Dancing up the stairway
to heaven.

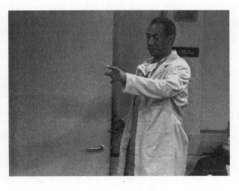

Dr. Cliff Huxtable,
Ob./Gyn. on *The
Cosby Show*.

(literally) maternal medium of "A Womb with a View" while still keeping
the birth "all in the [television] family."

After hearing of the change in plans for the child, Jerome informs Baby
Hayes that rather than having David and Maddie for parents, he will
become instead either Kirk Cameron's little brother (a plug for ABC's own
1985–1992 sitcom *Growing Pains* in which Cameron appeared) or Bill
Cosby's grandchild. Ultimately, of course, the choice comes down on the
side of TV's truly "big name"—Baby Hayes is magically zapped out of the
womb, and as the baby and "angel" dance up a stairway to heaven while
doing the episode's final musical number ("On the Sunny Side of the
Street"), birth into *The Cosby Show* is finally assured. It is indeed appropri-

ate that Baby Hayes's fetal transplant would be managed by TV star
Cosby—who not only presided over the top program of the mid-to-late
1980s (allowing rival network NBC to capture the ratings so desperately
craved by *Moonlighting*'s cast) but, as Cliff Huxtable of *The Cosby Show*,
portrayed TV's ideal dad and an obstetrician to boot. Critiqued by many
for its rosy portrait of upscale professional life (leading to controversies
over the notion of "realistic" images of African Americans), this 1984–1992
domestic comedy was nonetheless lauded for its "wholehearted endorse-
ment of family values" (Alex McNeil 166), even credited with "reju-
venat[ing] TV's interest in the traditional two-parent family" (Zoglin 33)
after a number of sitcoms of the late 1970s and early 1980s had revolved
around single-parent households.[37] For *Moonlighting*'s big (re)production
number, the significance of this nod to *The Cosby Show* is clear. Within the
televisual universe, this is truly utopia: a domestic heaven where all racial,
gender, and intergenerational conflicts are erased (at the price of natural-
izing the class biases of the program), where one can have it all in an
updated version of *Father Knows Best*.

The fact that this solution involves a reassignment of racial identity is
never posed as a problem in the text, for, if anything, such a prenatal
transfer helps to solidify the familial project of TV. Rather than acknowl-
edging the possibility of socio-cultural difference, *Moonlighting* implies
that, when it comes to the family, only one acceptable form exists. Indeed,
in a telling displacement, the reason why Maddie and David fail to meet
this requirement is that her independence prevents him from assuming
adult responsibility—a charge most often leveled by dominant culture at
"minority" couples (particularly at African Americans) and one which
thus assumes that any problem in the family, regardless of race, ethnicity,
or historical formation, is based on the failure of women to stay in their
place. Foreclosing any recognition of either cultural construction or so-
cial/familial diversity, the only choice that is offered by the logic of
the text—the choice between lawful (paternal) placement or the lure of the
(maternal) abyss—is portrayed as one that has already been made, as the
decision that has been ordained by the "Creator" himself. The Name of
the Father is the key to the gates of heaven approached by the child, and as
the musical number announces, the road to this fulfillment has but one
sunny side. Therefore, while this mention of *The Cosby Show* might seem at
first glance to promote another network at ABC's expense, it is only
through such a reference that *Moonlighting*'s own vision of the ideal family
can prevail. Not only does the power of this modern-day patriarch's name
allow him to claim his own show, but within the *Moonlighting* episode, no
mother (nor even an actual father) need even be mentioned—the grandfather's (or Symbolic Father's) name is all that really counts.[38]

Of course, there is a self-reflexive television joke at work here that, in
some ways, reveals the identity of the mother. Telling the baby to "keep the
Cosby thing under your hat; they're pretty self-conscious over there about
the whole pregnancy business," the angel makes reference to *The Cosby
Show* (and its spin-off, *A Different World*) actress Lisa Bonet's real-life

pregnancy, which NBC chose to mask by erasing Bonet from the screen (much as *Moonlighting* itself often did when Cybill Shepherd was expecting). As previously noted, *Moonlighting* is known for just these sorts of referential jokes; underscoring its own textuality and playing with the boundary between the fictional and the real, the program's knowing allusions had largely contributed to its popular and critical success. Addressing itself to an extremely media-conscious audience, *Moonlighting* commented on its production constraints, television conventions, and numerous aspects of American popular culture. Though not the first program to call attention to the structures of TV, in foregrounding the discursive and institutional practices of television, *Moonlighting* has achieved status as an innovative show and attained great critical acclaim—its wit and invention is based as much on exposing aspects of the media as it is on exposing criminals or even the characters' personal entanglements.

Yet there is a danger in valorizing the use of such techniques, of confusing textual practice with political commitment. The problem of lauding *Moonlighting* as a subversive or progressive program simply for its use of devices associated with radical media and/or the avant-garde (self-conscious commentary on the text and its context) becomes apparent when one considers the ways in which self-reflexive strategies generally function in television and especially how they operate in this particular case. As Mimi White has argued in a perceptive analysis of television's practices of self- and inter-program referentiality, rather than undercutting the illusions at the base of the media's appeal, television's imbrication of the fictional and real asserts a familial unity across temporal, spatial, and narrative diversity, a continuity that goes beyond the diegetic space of any individual show ("Crossing"). As the world on TV becomes increasingly equated with the world of TV, an imaginary coherency binds it together as a whole; securing the viewer across a variety of texts, television constitutes itself as a self-enclosed and self-perpetuating field. *Moonlighting*'s comical references to the world of broadcasting and to other programs then stand not as critiques of the medium, but simply as incitements for the consumption of more television—they both encourage further viewing in order to get all the jokes and make *Moonlighting* itself appear more "honest" and "live" through its exposure of television's usual artificiality. Portraying the world through media clichés (as Jerome describes life to Baby Hayes through recycled film/television images, introduces his parents and explains history through clips from past *Moonlighting* episodes, and reassures him of his birth through references to other TV families), "A Womb with a View" works to maintain television's dominance, remaining within this protective enclave so as to contain its own contradictions.

In addition to promoting television in this way, the intertextual joke of "A Womb with a View" provides the outlet that is needed to authorize the violence of this text. By assuring us that nothing bad is really going to happen to adorable Baby Hayes, *Moonlighting* can dispose of its "problem" in a most efficient way. The fact that "A Womb with a View" is presented as a musical pacifies the viewer all the more. Not only is our horror bought off by the relief of song and dance, but the text need only fall back upon itself in order to achieve its own alibi. In other words, by turning the womb into a theatrical arena, *Moonlighting* manages to stage TV itself as the answer to the loss that it presents: its characters simply assign themselves new roles in order to renew their hold on life. Arguing that within the genre of the musical—where self-referentiality is also the norm—such reflexive strategies function in a conservative and self-justifying way, Jane Feuer notes that

> [m]usicals are unparalleled in presenting a vision of human liberation which is profoundly aesthetic. . . . [T]hey give us a glimpse of what it would be like to be free. . . . But the musical presents its vision of the unfettered human spirit in a way that forecloses a desire to translate that vision into reality. The Hollywood version of utopia is entirely solipsistic. In its endless reflexivity the musical can offer only itself, only entertainment, as its picture of utopia. (*Hollywood* 84; see also Medhurst)

Like television, the musical exists within a self-enclosed world in which its own productions are the objects of its dreams—or in this case, where the celebratory numbers offer an escape from the nightmare it describes.

A "'Man' in Space": The Medium and Its Message

While some critics suggest that the musical's utopian moments cannot be fully recuperated by the closure of the plot, this strategy of removing the show in time and place and situating it within its own self-contained space limits the critical potential that the form might otherwise provide. By presenting its own protected sphere as already fully whole, the text is unable to comment on the confines of the status quo. As Richard Dyer has explained in regard to the class of Hollywood musicals that creates a self-enclosed world, the contradictions developed in these films "are over-ridingly bought off by the nostalgia or primitivism which provides them with the point of departure" ("Entertainment" 188). Pointing backward toward a golden age instead of forward to the future, they actually reverse a utopianism that might allow their viewers to envision a process of social change.

The fact that "A Womb with a View" engages in this type of regressive nostalgia seems plain enough. Yet the text reveals not only a sentimental nostalgia for life in the womb (or even for life in the tube); it also expresses a historical nostalgia for the (imaginary) days of unchallenged male rule—a fantasy that too requires *Moonlighting*'s construction of a self-enclosed space. In a perceptive analysis of the relationship between character and environment unique to the genre, Martin Sutton notes that "space in the musical is the most expressive of media" (192). Often located within areas that provide the excuse for both movement and play (theaters, parks, gymnasiums, carnivals, and, in *Moonlighting*, the womb figured as an inflatable bubble with a trampoline floor), the musical's space awaits activation by "an interpreter, an explorer" who claims it as his. Charged with meaning only by the dancer's performance, this site is encompassed by the figure who invades it, transforming it into a world of his own. Sutton argues that it is this imaginative use of space that makes the musical a utopian form, contrasting it to the horror film in which the situation is reversed (since in horror, the characters fear, rather than revel in, a space whose darkness and shadows menace instead of please).

Yet "A Womb with a View" combines music with dread—the abject space of the maternal always threatens to engulf the subject rather than the other way around. The conventions of the musical genre can thus offer a release. In allowing the little male hero to conquer the horror of feminine space, "A Womb with a View" makes the mother's body into a mere medium for man. In other words, within the most feminine sphere (in this case, triply feminized—located within the female body; within a genre that, like the melodrama, is often considered a "feminine" form; and within the "feminized" world of television), we discover a desire for the Law and the patriarchal Name.[39] Indeed, we are back to the patently patriarchal "fetal fascinations" critiqued earlier in this chapter: the popular and scientific representation of the fetus as autonomous, active, and athletic, a "'man' in space, floating free."[40] Even if recognized as attached to the mother, he is perceived as the dominant partner, considered, as one fetologist explains, "not as an inert passenger in pregnancy, but rather as in command of it," responsible for making the woman "a suitable host" and even "determin[ing] the duration of pregnancy" (Findlay 96; quoted in Franklin 193). If this tough and resourceful fellow is not exactly fetus-as-Rambo, then perhaps it is fetus-as-*Die Hard*'s-John McLane (Bruce Willis's wisecracking action hero from his 1988 film), the cocky fast-talker "tap-dancing" his way through the minefields, verbally if not also physically in each of these incarnations.[41]

This "genesis" into the action film is revealing: although *Moonlighting*'s spectacle that reformulates birth, like the preceding season's stories that had reconstituted the family as a purely fathered realm, may seem far removed from the blatant display of masculine power found within the crime genre previously discussed, all of these programs share a common desire to assert masculine dominance within the medium considered the most "feminine" of all. Revealing the concern for masculinity that underlies much of television's "feminine" world, television's exhibitions of male performance—whether through spectacles of strength or spectacles of song, camaraderie at work, or fun and games at home, the stylized "dance" of slow motion violence or an actual musical show—are efforts to achieve and flaunt a virility that is in danger of being aborted itself. Yet television's attempts to prove masculine potency are riddled with contradictions, and the tensions this involves are never finally repressed; both the exaggeration of maleness through a hypermasculine defense and the appropriation of femininity for the benefits of man produce ruptures that these texts can hardly contain. Able to succeed only by taking on the roles of the women they replace, finding their identities only through some form of masquerade (by way of virile poses or the staging of "paternal delights"), TV's male heroes are trapped within a circuit without end. More and more spectacle is always required, and this results in a curious situation in which television cannot help but disrupt the very divisions of gender that it strives to reinforce. Revealing the discord involved in attempts to manage the figurations of gender that TV itself helps to promote, these texts create their own horrific and violent excess.[42]

Resurrecting the Voice, or "Look Who's Talking" Now

Because *Moonlighting*'s family practice was prevented from ever reaching resolution within the confines of television, it may come as no surprise that Baby Hayes (or, more accurately, Baby Willis) would find his home within another media form. While the *Moonlighting* series suffered its own "miscarriage" when it was cancelled at the end of the 1988–1989 season, the narrative of "A Womb with a View" has almost had a rebirth that miraculously managed to resurrect its "blessed child." In the 1989 hit film *Look Who's Talking*, not only does actor Bruce Willis replay his role as a fetus in the womb (providing the running commentary for the pre- and post-natal infant Mikey), but he is able to project this role both forward and backward in time in order to ensure the security, legality, and ultimate dominance of the paternal function throughout every stage of reproductive and family life. From the film's first images of sperm attempting to penetrate an egg until its final moments when the family is complete, the male gamete cell / embryo / fetus / infant has a mind and a voice of his own (in fact, the only time that Mikey doesn't speak is when he is but a gleam in his father's leering eye). While not strictly a musical, in many ways *Look Who's Talking* mirrors "A Womb with a View" in its deployment of what might be called "re-production numbers" too. As in other films, the soundtrack plays an important role in supplementing the narrative; in this case, it is made up of songs that "twin" terms of romantic endearment with words that signify a parent / child relationship ("baby love," "my angel," "girl of my dreams," "daddy's home," et cetera). In fact, the film as a whole conflates romance and sex with parenting and procreation. While the love scenes are predictably tame (the movie had a PG rating), the text offers a remarkably blatant portrayal of reproduction; as in "A Womb with a View," the specularization commonly "operating" on female stars is here literalized as speculum in an extraordinary way.

Nonetheless, in continuing the project of "A Womb with a View," the idea that reproduction is nothing if not a father's own affair is once again made absolutely clear. Within *Look Who's Talking*'s world, not only does human subjectivity lie in the sperm alone (the egg just passively and silently awaits the orgasmic pleasure that "he" provides her),[43] but almost all that Mikey can "talk" about is his desire for a dad—a wish that's granted at the end of the film when Mikey (without Bruce Willis's voice-over) finally pronounces his first word for himself: "Dada" (of course). While the "dada" that he gets is not his biological dad, the film naturalizes this transfer by reproducing the conditions of his birth (just as *Moonlighting* naturalized its reassignment through the miraculous restagings of its self-reflexive joke): Mikey's mother (played by Kirstie Alley) goes into labor in the midst of a perilous cab ride, and later, our cab driver hero (John Travolta) repeats this same route in order to save Mikey's life, deliver him into the arms of his mom, and establish himself as the legitimate protector/possessor of his fated heir. Even the publicity for the film attempts to justify the hero's claim to the paternal position. Speaking of Mikey, the release poster states: "He's hip, he's slick, and he's only 3 months old. He's got John Travolta's smile, Kirstie Alley's eyes. And the voice of Bruce Willis. . . . Now all he has to do is find himself the perfect daddy." By noting the attribute of the would-be-dad that the child has supposedly inherited (and making it a priority by listing this before any mention of the mother), the advertisement implies that Mikey is truly his father's own child—even though it goes on to indicate the gap that lies between father and son.

As all of these details indicate, the similarity between this film and the *Moonlighting* episode is startling, and the characterizations of women in the two texts are basically the same. Although both Maddie and Molly (the heroine of *Look Who's Talking*) are tough, independent women, neither of them is able to maintain a family on her own, and they even lack the sense to (formally) bring in the proper man. It is up to the small male child to demand the family that he needs, which, in both cases, involves actualizing a paternal heritage that is already inscribed within the structure of the text (Baby Hayes's desire for Cosby, and Mikey's desire to be granted legal access to the nurturant man and grandfather with whom he is already spending time).[44]

However, the difficulties that both "A Womb with a View" and *Look Who's Talking* have in bringing to fruition a family structure that they pose as preordained is telling in the light of the upheavals that have plagued a traditional vision of the familial American dream. Though striving to establish an immediate connection between sexuality, reproduction, and the patriarchal family, the texts cannot help but expose the distance that lies between these terms. In figuring the fathered family as both natural and yet as a choice that must be made, *Moonlighting* and *Look Who's Talking* destabilize the very ground that they struggle to secure. Trying nonetheless to perfect the family practice conceived by these texts, *Look Who's Talking* itself spun off into the 1991 television series *Baby Talk*. In an ironic bit of casting, the voice of the wisecracking infant (now called Mickey to his mother's Maggie) was provided by Tony Danza, well known for his role as the ideal dad/mom-substitute in the gender reversal sitcom *Who's the Boss?* (1984–1992). While dealing with a single mother, *Baby Talk* thus also recalled television's construction of the fathered clan by attempting— unsuccessfully—to capitalize on the popularity of yet another paternal icon before this show too was quickly deemed "unviable."

The labor of technological reproduction thus intersects with the labor of sexual reproduction in a very complex way—although the media work to bind our multiple desires into one overruling Oedipal construction, they also reveal the contradictions within it, and it is precisely in the space that is thereby opened up that we must begin to formulate our interrogation of familial ideology. In fact, in the final moments of *Look Who's Talking*, the possibility of such a critical space is disclosed. After the hero and heroine have finally gotten together and solidified the family through the birth of a new child, the nuclear family seems to have reached its ideal form— mother, father, first-born son, and now a little girl. However, the sister's position within this family portrait threatens to unravel the narrative logic upon which the construction of the paternal order is based. Unable to be figured as a full-blown subject from the moment of attempted conception as was the little boy (for how can a little girl be figured as a talking sperm?), she nonetheless begins to "speak" (through Joan Rivers) once she emerges into the social sphere. Her first words, "Can we talk?" raise an important question for women in the text and in the audience alike—amid the discourses that structure both sexual and technological reproduction to- day, how can the female subject gain access to a voice?

The Final Word?

This question, in fact, has been posed explicitly by women working in reproductive politics. Responding to imagery which renders women both invisible and speechless, feminists have "labored" to produce other repre- sentations, filling in the picture in order to portray what might otherwise be eclipsed (through sonographic imaging or simply editing choices that erase women from the screen). Rather than "dismembering" the pregnant subject to see the seemingly autonomous embryo/fetus within, these discourses urge us, as Valorie Hartouni states, to "re-remember" women and their struggles ("Fetal" 145), or as Rosalind Petchesky suggests, to contextualize reproduction by clearly resituating the fetus within the woman's body and this body within its social space.

The demand that women be "restore[d] to a central place in the . . . scene" should, of course, also be leveled at television and its operations of media reproduction (Petchesky, "Fetal" 287). But perhaps this demand is, in some measure, already being met; after all, U.S. television has offered us some truly embodied, not to mention big-mouthed, moms. Roseanne— able, like Cosby, to "authorize" her own sitcom, *Roseanne* (introduced in 1988)—springs immediately to mind. As a working-class and avowedly feminist mom, Roseanne not only redefines notions of televisual mother- hood, but her wisecracking remarks and "shameless" bodily display— not to mention authorial control over her own textual and extratextual (re)productions—allow her to contest precisely those discourses of do- mesticity which are at the center of her biting wit.[45]

And who can forget Murphy Brown (played by Candice Bergen), lead character of the self-reflexive sitcom *Murphy Brown* (which also premiered in 1988)? This acerbic and strong-willed star reporter of the fictional newsmagazine series *F.Y.I.* (*Murphy Brown*'s TV show-within-a-show) became a single mom and so managed to lure Vice President Dan Quayle into a "dialogue" that one-upped any of *Moonlighting*'s attempts to inter-mix the "televisual" and "real." Quayle's 1992 speech lauding law, order, and family values—and then attacking the sitcom character for "mocking the importance of fathers by bearing a child alone" (quoted in Morrow 30)—not only exposed the hypocrisy at the heart of a political program that condemns unwed mothers (and anyone else who attempts to main-tain a household outside of the nuclear family model) yet tries to outlaw abortion; it also revealed (even in its absurdity) the extent of television's place within national, familial, and reproductive (trans)formations.

Of course, Murphy Brown's position of political prominence was par-tially achieved through a displacement—from an urban scene to suburban screens, from the young, poor, and unmarried black women that Quayle was apparently discussing to the older, successful, white career woman/female character that he actually attacked. Stating that "a welfare check is not a husband. The state is not a father. . . . Bearing babies irresponsibly is, simply, wrong" (30), Quayle reiterated claims about African American communities that have circulated in mass culture at least from the time of the "Moynihan Report," the 1965 governmental study on the "Negro Family" that traced the social and economic problems of African Ameri-cans to the "tangle of pathology" arising from a "matriarchal structure" in which women head households without sufficient "male authority" (quoted in Davis 13). As in *Moonlighting* (in which a family consisting of a powerful single mother and an adolescent—or worse, absent—father is shown to be no family at all), a reductive "diagnosis" used primarily against African Americans is both promoted and masked through a projec-tion onto a white professional woman (and a TV character at that). Given *Murphy Brown*'s relative unpopularity among the demographic group that spurred Quayle's critique (the sitcom was ranked as the third most popu-lar program for the overall U.S. audience, but fifty-sixth among American blacks [Morrow 30]), this displacement seemed particularly trivializing: young African American women were subjected to a discourse initiated on their behalf that failed to take into account the social issues—or even television programming—that most concerned them.

Yet whether her new central position within social, familial, and repro-ductive controversies was "illegitimately" gained or not, Murphy (who had earlier considered artificial insemination and whose TV child was played by twins conceived in vitro and carried to term by a surrogate mother) accepted the challenge and rose to the debate. Mixing various levels of mass-mediations, she responded to Quayle on her news show by suggesting that he expand his definition of family, emphasizing her point by introducing a racially, ethnically, and professionally varied group of single parents and their children both to the diegetic audience and to *Murphy Brown*'s own viewers. Such families, as well as many other alterna-tive models, might similarly be introduced on any number of daytime talk shows—programs that address a multiplicity of social subjects and which seem to respond even more directly to Joan Rivers's invitation "Can we talk?" (the tag line not only to *Look Who's Talking* but, more significantly, Rivers's own television act). These examples, of course, do not suggest that struggles over sexual, familial, or reproductive politics—not to mention television's place within them—have been resolved; *Moonlighting*'s Maddie Hayes was also a strong woman with a biting tongue. Yet in spite of a "family practice" that promotes a very limited set of "domestic policies," television also provides the glimmer of a different kind of familial space. Its outspoken women—Roseanne, Murphy, Joan Rivers, Oprah Winfrey, and others—and perhaps more importantly, the female producers who help "write" them—point toward a social arena in which women's voices will truly be heard.

"Alter-egotist": Max Headroom.

In-between identities: Pee-wee Herman.

VI

"INTO THE SYSTEM"
TELEVISION AND THE CYBORG SUBJECT(ED)

Technology/Reproduction/Simulation: Life and Death in the Cybernetic Realm

In discussing a male desire to usurp the cultural position of femininity in chapters 4 and 5, I alluded both to the presence of masculine fantasies of reproduction and to the tensions surrounding technological and social practices that threaten to disrupt traditional familial and gender arrangements—tensions which television attempts to manage through its fantasies of masculine self-sufficiency and prolific achievement. As I tried to demonstrate in those chapters, despite differences in their generic structures, both TV's cop/detective dramas and several portrayals of the family (those which "deliver" the child to a paternal sphere) construct an image of the post-industrial Western world as quite literally a "fatherland"—a space in which men might recuperate the feminine while managing to edge women out of the scene so as to maintain the primacy and usual prerogatives of masculinity.

However, the ideological (and legal) struggles concerning reproductive roles, rights, and technologies which are played out on television enact more than the battle of the sexes: they also involve the various conflicts surrounding the redefinition of life/death and reality/simulation that postmodern cybernesis necessarily provokes—conflicts and conceptual transformations which intersect with, and come to be figured by, relations of sexual difference.[1] In other words, while the questions of reproduction raised in the previous chapter may seem detached from the frightening visions of cybernetic experimentation evoked by references to militaristic, technocratic regimes (that is, "fatherland"), the possibilities of fetal engineering previously discussed indicate precisely such a connection, revealing the links between sexual and cybernetic struggles. Indeed, in his article "The Work of Culture in the Age of Cybernetic Systems," Bill Nichols treats even the simplest of new reproductive possibilities together with advanced biotechnologies, strategic "defense" deployments, and computer programming designs as comparable simulation systems. Considering the children produced through these reproductive procedures, he writes: "Such 'engineered foetuses' and babies become so much like real human beings that their origin as commodities, bought and sold, may be readily obscured. They become the perfect cyborg[s]," beings who radically throw conventional indicators of difference—here, between self/other, subject/object, organism/property, and consumer/commodity—into doubt (44).[2]

Cybernetic generation thus poses a multitude of questions for sexual politics as well as for the very conceptual systems we use to describe postindustrial life. As the medical, legal, and representational battles over reproductive engineering assert the overriding reality not only of the father, but also of the processes of postmodern fabrication, the maternal no longer seems able to maintain a discrete and discernible position. Its reproductive capacities, the ability to create and destroy life itself, are diffused into the very systems of simulation that recuperate it in the interests of a hetero-masculinist society. Yet as evidenced in the preceding chapter, the fantasies of a male usurpation of femininity/maternity also raise a number of tensions which are both the product of and the catalyst for these cybernetic convolutions. It is such anxieties that popular narratives often attempt to address, and television—itself a technology of reproduction that constitutes a type of "artificial life"—is a key site for the generation and administration of cyborgian fantasies and fears.[3]

For example, in the March 1987 premiere episode of the U.S. sci-fi series *Max Headroom*, one of television's most innovative explorations of our cybernetic world, Max is born through the miracle of computer technology and thrives through the wonders of corporate-controlled television; a literal "video subject," Max lives within the screens of a vast television system that monitors ratings by the second and can never be turned off.[4] In what appears to be a futuristic version of electronic organ donation, this cybernetic tele-offspring is created when a computer programmer downloads the mind of news reporter Edison Carter after he has crashed into a "max[imum] headroom" warning sign in a near-fatal motorcycle accident. Suggesting the confusing relationships between the self and the (m)other, consciousness and its dissolution that exist in cybernetic reproduction, the computer whiz-kid who "delivers" Max (mis)recognizes his first stutters, "Ma . . . Ma . . . Ma . . . Ma . . ."—Max's attempt to name himself by repeating the words that Edison has last seen—as an infant's cry for "mama."[5] Despite this moment of parental and/or proprietary satisfaction, Bryce, the young computer expert, later threatens to erase Max's memory and rupture what I am tempted to call, but cannot quite delimit as, his "identity," further demonstrating a convolution of pacification and aggression.

As in the *Moonlighting* episode discussed in chapter 5, the simulated maternal is here a space of both life and presaged death as well as a realm which must be re-presented as purely fathered (in this case by Edison and Bryce) and hence under male control. But the introduction of cybernetic (im)mortality additionally confuses the dualities at stake (life/death, male/female, self/other): Bryce gains the power to terminate his "baby" (both his child and his pet computer project) through the same program by which he was conceived—a program whose outcomes then cannot be singularly defined. Born into a computerized circuit of interfaced components, the cybernetic being also has some of his own powers of reassembly and control. Because he is what Andrew Ross terms an "electromorph" ("Techno-Ethics" 145) (not unlike the metamorphs discussed in chapter 1), when Max overhears the plan he is able to disappear from the screen and, as Bryce puts it, "escape into the system": he melts into the flow of television only to reemerge at will, playfully bringing the word of ratings, consumerism, and self-promotion to the postmodern wasteland of the program's *mise-en-scène*.

While ABC itself finally "aborted" Max and his series after the text's own cyborgian existence ("cloned" from a British program and then repeatedly switched on and off by network programmers),[6] *Max Headroom* nonetheless activates a number of tropes found not only in the media's depiction of the cyborg body but also in TV's idealized construction of its own "video subject," the television viewer. As the ultimate television creation—part of TV as well as TV's consummate consumer—Max draws us into a realm where the contrasting categories of absorption/escape, stasis/animation, dissolution/propagation, and technological reproduction/reproductive sexuality are confounded and transformed, and the representation of his "birth" is telling for a number of reasons. Not only does it illustrate our fears and fantasies of cybernetic doubling, narcissistic self-generation, and the control of death through a masculine assumption of female reproduction, but it also indicates postmodernism's curious conflation of diffraction and confinement. Just as Max merges into the television environment only through the deconstruction and reconstruction of his vacillating codes, so television viewers are drawn into what I've described as a "preoccupation"—a mediatized receptivity—precisely through their dislocation, their lack of a unified viewing position.[7]

As I've argued throughout this book, such a decentered multiplicity poses particular problems for the inscription of a masculine spectator and has contributed to the association of television and femininity. But the paradoxical mode of placement through displacement exhibited by the cyborgian video-automaton suggests the kinds of contradictions that face *all* postmodern subjects as well as the difficulties television critics have in defining the cultural effects of their object of study—an object which, like Max, is technologically produced to seem animated and "live," an entity which itself produces and reproduces viewing subjects who are at once consumers and commodities, statistical yet real. This curious construction exemplified by Max's condition—fusion through disruption, envelopment by difference, and a new holism of the part—is thus indicative both of many aspects of U.S. television in the 1980s and of the simultaneous fears of cultural critics beginning to outline a politics of the postmodern.

Like all discursive systems, however, postmodernism contains gaps and contradictions which open up a space for intervention and critique. The analyses that have been initiated by feminist cultural critics are especially important for my considerations here, for, as noted above, the fantasies of reproduction associated with the cyborg suggest that constructions of gender are very much at stake.[8] The struggles—political and conceptual—

that accompany cyborgian visions seem to involve both the recuperation and celebration of difference(s), and insofar as the cybernetic and sexed subject are connected in a number of ambivalent ways, postmodernity's implications for gender remain a vital area of concern. Rather than simply applauding the multiplicity and plurality associated with this age or bemoaning its rejection of (seemingly) universal standards and norms, the signification of these changes should be even further explored; the ways in which postmodern conceptions of disjunction and containment intersect with psychic investments that have already been formulated and analyzed in terms of sexual difference seem to me to be a crucial field of inquiry if we are to continue to engage critically with cultural and media formations instead of merely looking on in either resignation or dismay.

Since at least the time of Max Headroom's televisual existence, there has been a steady interest in postmodern culture and its relationship to television. Yet reading this relationship too through a politics of gender may open up a space that is otherwise closed off. Failing to frame the concept of difference in terms other than either absolute dispersal or the lure of the abyss, many media critics theorizing postmodernism are trapped within those same oppositions that maintain a hierarchized sex/gender system which they might claim to discard. By investigating the problem of a videocyborg "identity" against the question of a sexed subjectivity—by interfacing sexual, cyborgian, and televisual differences, so to speak—new possibilities may arise.

It is these possibilities that I would like to explore by analyzing the cultural and psychic determinants of two television texts that activate cyborgian fantasies and foreground the medium in which they are embedded: *Max Headroom* (1987 and then briefly in 1988) and *Pee-wee's Playhouse* (1986–1990). Not only are they "hypermediated"—ideal representatives of a postmodern televisual imagination—but both Max Headroom and Pee-wee Herman have also, even if surprisingly, been taken by critics as significant representatives of 1980s masculinity.[9] Max, the partial man, uses his powers of recombination to look forward to a time "20 minutes into the future"; Pee-wee, the "part-time boy," uses his to look back toward the past in a nostalgic regression.[10] In analyzing these figures and the sexual/textual differences they embody, I do not simply wish to advocate either route; that is, I am trying neither to celebrate nor to lament postmodern fragmentation. Instead I hope to reveal the ways in which the sexed and cyborg body have been linked in both the televised and the critical imagination, and to discuss the psychological appeal yet political risks of such discursive bonds.

This necessarily involves an attempt to articulate the relationship between psychoanalysis and postmodernism, a difficult and often confusing task. Because critics tend to see postmodern culture as a surface phenomenon—described, for example, as the appropriation of various styles divorced from a history or meaningful context with which to place these fragments—the use of a depth model of critical interpretation (such as the one that psychoanalysis offers) may seem antithetical to postmodernism's own concerns.[11] Similarly, in diffusing the intensity of the spectatorial gaze through its own textual and historical flow, television also poses problems for the kind of psychoanalytic criticism formulated in relationship to cinema studies.[12]

It is, however, precisely for these reasons that a combined approach—a hybrid discourse of psychoanalytic and postmodernist critique—might prove to be a valuable tool of intervention. Psychoanalysis may allow the critic to emphasize what is at stake in postmodern and televisual textuality; to see, in other words, how the contemporary re-articulation of cultural terms of difference is not simply a matter of style to be either merely enjoyed or dismissed but a political project that involves the very constitution of subjectivity and the (sexed) self. And just as psychoanalysis can remind us of the existence of these stakes within the cyborgian playground, postmodern theory can remind cultural critics of the existence of differences, pluralities, and networks besides those that are taken for granted by psychoanalytic theorists (and all too often by feminists) themselves. For this reason, it is important to encourage a dialogue between these two modes of analysis. It is through the interfacing of psychic and social cyborgian formations that the hypertelevisual *Max Headroom* and *Pee-wee's Playhouse* activate and administer TV's gender figurations; taking this into account might allow us to do a bit of our own "reprogramming" within both television culture and cultural critique.

Absorbed into the Screen: Reinventing the "Miracle of Television"

While television has often been devalued in comparison to film, there has been a paradoxical interest in shows such as *Max Headroom* and *Pee-wee's Playhouse*, which highlight precisely those conventions that have been most criticized.[13] Playing with TV's multiplicity of signs, time flow and mobile space, editing techniques derived from advertising, and fluctuating levels of reality/reproduction/fabrication, these texts carry television's form to its limits, almost transforming the critiques of TV into a celebration of its specificity. Suggesting, for example, how *Pee-wee's Playhouse* glories in the triumph of TV, one reviewer exclaimed, "Pee-wee has reinvented 'the miracle of television.' He's conjured up a different world . . . [where] everything is alive" (O'Brien 93). Extending the implicit promise of television's immediacy, this program's sense of all-pervasive "liveness" is not simply due to the animated vitality invested in all of the playhouse decor but is inscribed within the very structure of the show. Alluding to popular media trends from previous decades (old cartoons, talking puppets, beatnik musicians, retro design, and kitschy details), *Pee-wee's Playhouse* is, according to Ian Balfour, an "allegory" of television history, a "pervasively citational, recombinant" production that brings both television's past and its processes of construction to the forefront of the show.[14]

The recombinant, transformative quality of video is further illustrated through one of Pee-wee's toys. His Magic Screen, a kind of cross between a TV set and a drawing table (a device which mimics the operations of the media in both primitive and futuristic forms), allows Pee-wee to enter the screen and toss up a group of dots which are then linked together to construct an object or vehicle that takes Pee-wee away to another dimension. Involving, like the TV "mosaic" itself, a configuration of fragments and bits which transports us to imaginary realms (breaking down the barrier between "real" and simulated space), the Magic Screen mirrors the processes of television and, in fact, was initially designed as part of a game in which viewers at home would connect the dots on a plastic sheet attached to their own television screens.[15]

Employing strategies of self-referentiality so as to encourage our engagement with the set, *Pee-wee's Playhouse* explores the bounds of the televisual imagination. Similarly, *Max Headroom* can be seen as the quintessential TV series: using techniques of interruption, fragmentation, and self-reflexive mediation, it condensed the elements of video manipulation that also provided it with the material for its plots. Like *Pee-wee's Playhouse*, it made use of citations and allusions, detailing the workings of the media machine within its diegesis even as it relied upon video technology's most sophisticated effects in order to draw viewers into its own simulated realm. Located within the midst of TV itself—involving characters who either work in television or, like Max, *exist* in television—*Max Headroom* turns in upon its own mass-mediated form, encouraging a preoccupation with, indeed absorption into, a televisual realm. One reviewer remarked that "figuratively speaking, the series sucks viewers *inside* the tube" (Waters et al. 58). *People* magazine ranked Max as one of the twenty-five most intriguing "people" of 1986, yet in a comment much like the one praising Pee-wee's "miracle of television," they equate the character with the very video processes that compose him: "he is one of the most ingenious creations to be seen on TV since the invention of color" (101).[16] Thus calling attention to the specific patterns (technological, textual, and institutional) of television, these programs provoke a new fascination: rather than achieving a critical distance, we are bound to the flow, part of the same transformation that we view on the screen.

It is within this hyperreality of television that images of the cyborg, a postmodern hybrid of human, animal, and machine, are frequently narrativized.[17] Just as television provides us with a flow of bits and pieces to be combined and recombined into an endless screen of experience, the cyborg plays on the disassembly and reassembly of all parts, rupturing the boundaries of "natural unities" and interfacing components in innovative ways. For example, in addition to *Max Headroom*'s video-automaton who, as Barry King writes, "personifies the principle of networking per se" (134), in *Pee-wee's Playhouse* we enter a metamorphic and cybernetic space where people enter animation; adults merge into children; and toys, furniture, and technology become talking, living beings. Among the many characters in the playhouse are Globy, the living globe used to locate Pee-wee's pen pals around the world; talking flowers that let us actually converse with nature; Chairy, the chair that literally enfolds her guests; Conky, the robot constructed from film machinery and stereo components that are now truly able to call out to us, and so on. All of these personified parts plugged into Pee-wee's world keep us plugged in as well. As these examples demonstrate, Pee-wee and his toys are, like Max Headroom, fully "in the system," drawing viewers into a decentered, yet oddly complete environment in which conventional boundaries are joyfully transgressed.

A paradoxical relationship of holism and partiality is thus established. On the one hand, such transgressions subvert the authority of organic wholes, allowing new textual formations to emerge. As Donna Haraway notes, the language of the cyborg [as well as that of television] is not unified ("Manifesto" 94); it is a hybrid tongue, "spliced" like Max's computer scratch and the stutter of Pee-wee's robot Conky. This marked heterogeneity involves a play of codes and affords both Max and Pee-wee the opportunity to confuse and delight us in a spiral of signification. Reveling in the duplicity of words, they toy with double meanings and celebrate a pure pleasure in the signifier: sound for sound's own sake and the humor of a literal use of language. Pee-wee and his friends scream with joy when they hear the day's secret word (brought forth from the stuttering robot made of media equipment) and chant along to a genie's scat-like syllables that make wishes into realities (another allusion to media technology since this genie lives in a magic box that one critic describes as a "'50s futurist console TV" [O'Brien 91]). Similarly, Max remixes the "human" range of affect with the parlance of technology (what Ross calls "the assembly language of television itself" ["Techno-Ethics" 147]) and so creates a unique blend of literal and double meanings with which he both promotes and critiques the system he is in.

But as Max's condition demonstrates, the dissonance of a spliced voice does not prevent the possibility of operational networks engulfing us in a web of power and pacification. With "the translation of the world into a problem of coding," no small difference is immune to instrumental control. That is, the fissure of conventional unities, split into constituent parts to be recomposed at will, need not yield the more liberating potential noted above; new integrated systems also emerge, implying that disruption and enclosure are no longer polar terms. As Haraway explains, "no objects, spaces, or bodies are sacred in themselves; any component can be interfaced with any other if the proper standard . . . [is] constructed . . ." ("Manifesto" 83, 82). Consequently, as traditional boundaries break down, the possibility arises not just for unchecked play, but for fusion and containment: we may merge into the space of simulation through the very dissipation of constraints that we might otherwise commend.

The postmodern image of the cyborg thus suggests a new social and discursive order of U.S. culture, an order embodied in television which has confused critics precisely because it seems to be at once so open (fragmented in form and multiple in address) and yet so limited (seducing viewers into constrictive patterns of consumption and control—though, as audience theorists remind us, this is certainly not the case with all viewers, under all circumstances, or with any sort of univocal meaning or effect). Nevertheless, as fragmentation, multiplicity, and fluctuation (not to mention the self-reflexivity of the programs discussed here) define the strategies not only of radical artists, but of commercials, network promos, music videos, and other programming components—indeed, of U.S. television and multinational capitalism in general—it seems to many cultural critics as if there is no escape from the "consuming" logic of postmodern simulation. Exemplifying this attitude, Baudrillard writes (almost as if he is describing the narrative spaces of Pee-wee and Max): "This is a completely imaginary contact-world of sensorial mimetics and tactile mysticism; it is essentially an entire ecology that is grafted on this universe of operational simulation . . ." (*Simulations* 140). While theoretically and politically problematic, such pronouncements have a certain illustrative force, suggesting that the postmodern world is not simply a field of playful contradiction but that it encloses us as well; its very fluidity allows for new incorporations. Holding out both the promise of a liberating plurality and the threat of absolute control, the hyperreal is a field of both partial identities and total command.

This unique blend of disruption and integration (or integration through disruption) has prompted a disturbing return to totalizing holistic modes of thought—a process evident not only in these 1980s televisual productions but also in some of the popular trends and scientific, medical, and psychological paradigms of the time. Discussing the intersecting fantasies of postmodern narratives and contemporary science, for example, Gabriele Schwab finds "a new order of the whole and its parts emerging, inspired by a kind of holographic model or a holonomy of the subject" (71).[18] Implying that each part embodies the state of the whole, such social and scientific speculations correspond to cultural fantasies of the cyborg which similarly suggest the construction of an entire ensemble by way of partial difference. Demonstrating the prevalence of such models across disparate fields, cybernetic theory has influenced the development of cognitive psychology (which sees the human mind as a dynamic yet quantifiable apparatus which follows predictable laws), and "New Age" thought (which valorizes a commodified brand of holism and sees the entire universe as an integrated system of interfaced communication) is no longer considered a counter-cultural phenomenon but has moved into the computer-networked corporate world of big business, managerial training, and worldwide sales promotion.[19]

Encouraging what seems to be a dangerous conceptual/political trend, some media and cultural theorists have incorporated a similar rhetoric, locating a new holism in the irrational simultaneity of the TV mosaic. As detailed in prior chapters, for example, Marshall McLuhan claims that the tactile and primitive intimacy of electronic transformation draws us into a "global" (or in Pee-wee's case, "Globy") village—what Baudrillard less optimistically terms "the black hole" of simulation.[20] Short-circuiting the linear and categorical logic of print, both cybernetic interactivity and televisual flow rely upon configurations of integrated data which, according to these critics, create structural changes in our culture and our senses. These technologies are then seen as almost reproducing the sensation of preliterate and unmediated modes of interaction: with the erosion of distinctions between animal and human, organism and machine, comes the breakdown of the (always already fictional) line between "primitive" and "civilized," between oral and written forms. The video cyborg thus confuses patterns of communication that had previously been theorized in absolutely polar terms. Several examples of this can be found in *Max Headroom* and *Pee-wee's Playhouse*. As a children's program (if not one made for professional middle-class parents) which centers on a character who's neither an adult nor a child, all of *Pee-wee's Playhouse* seems to be based upon the joys of infantile investment and the play afforded by confusing suggestively sophisticated discourse with "illiterate" (concrete) forms. Similarly, Max's speech joins preverbal stutters to the high-tech language of computer science—a fitting combination for a subject who is both newly born and technologically "advanced."

While such conjunctions may seem particularly appropriate to beings who blend a naturally childish (or more accurately, as I'll elaborate, "boyish") innocence with cultural affectation, they also exemplify the curious constructions that define postmodern life. Examining, for instance, how electronic computation and digital communication may readjust our sense of reality, replicating the 'basic' modalities that Westerners are apt to associate with 'primitive man' as well as our own youths, Bill Nichols asks,

> Is it conceivable . . . that contemporary transformations in the economic structure of capitalism, attended by technological change, institute a less individuated, more communal form of perception similar to which was attendant upon face-to-face ritual and aura but which is now mediated by anonymous circuitry and the simulation of direct encounter? (26)

As he goes on to explain, the fascination of cybernetic systems—as well as, I would add, part of the appeal of television—is precisely that they seem both to offer and to demand an immediate response, mimicking the processes of direct interaction while frequently drawing the TV viewer/ video game player/computer operator into a self-absorbed state (a situation taken to extremes in the phenomenon of "computer sex," the epitome of user-friendly technological "intimacy"). Apparently allowed the instantaneous contact of a presymbolic bond, the cybernetic subject can regress to an almost undeveloped stage (though one still inflected by gender asymmetries), which is paradoxically supported through technological mastery and skill.

It is for this reason that the patterns of electronic permutation have been said to reflect and re-create the primary processes of infantile involvement. According to this model, we seem to have entered a "new orality," connected by circulating flows and boundary confusions, ingesting "formulas" of data in place of mother's milk.[21] Yet as the technological field takes on the role of "second nature," the organic holism, proximity, and intimacy previously associated with the natural (and its mythical exemplar, the mother) become curiously aligned with postmodern fragmentation—a situation posing new problems for feminist theory and practice even as it has been championed by popular movements from New Agers to enraptured computer buffs linking up with the global network.[22] Converting the fear of destruction to the promise of new birth, the hyperreal therefore exerts a strong appeal. The seduction that it offers—like the maternal matrix that it simulates—is that of both life and death, plenitude and chaos, confirmation and disintegration, fragmentation and fusion. Setting into play a series of somewhat contradictory fantasies and figurations, cybernetic simulation can provoke "the same form of intense ambivalence that the mothering parent once did: a guarantee of identity based on what can never be made part of oneself" (Nichols 28).

Set against this threat of ruptured boundaries are attempts to reassert hierarchies of distinction in order to maintain traditional certainties. Frequently articulated through conventional metaphors of sexuality and gender (and therefore often feeding back into a gender system that it has the potential to disrupt), cybernetic reproduction combines infantile desires with dreams of technological control. A struggle over relations of identity and difference thus seems to define the cybernetic world—the very struggle that is evident in those television programs which explore the limits of a cyborgian/video imagination. Both *Max Headroom* and *Pee-wee's Playhouse*, for example, move beyond linearity to a multiple dimension that paradoxically draws interest by dividing our attention. Yet even within this fluctuating field, there is an attempt to stabilize the viewer, a way in which unity is ultimately reassured. It is precisely this curious relation, a holism of the part (an illusion of wholeness even within fragmentation), that provokes our fascination; it is the psychic lure of a difference that returns as the same.[23]

Fear and Loathing in Hyperreality; or The Uncanny Creations of a Prosthetic God

As suggested in the comments that opened this chapter, psychoanalytic theory can help explain this fascination as well as illuminate what might be at stake in such cyborgian dreams; that is, it might underscore the implications (for both the construction of gender and the very relationship of the subject to the terms of life and death) that follow from simulation's perplexing logic. On the one hand, the nondifferentiation produced by hyperreality's conception of totalized difference recalls the lure of death— also a fantasy of union through disruption (the promise of final integration through absolute disintegration). Similarly, the repetition involved in the image of the cyborg—the creation of doubles that multiply our lives— suggests that even in the desire for immortality, a deadening stasis will paradoxically emerge.[24] As these correlations indicate, the cyborg plays

"Two minds but with one single memory"; character doubling
on *Max Headroom*.

out fantasies of mirroring and narcissism as well as those of death.
Discussing these contradictory urges underlying our images of cybernetic
simulation, Schwab refers to Freud's own remarks on the "cyborgian"
goals of humankind: "Man has, as it were, become a kind of prosthetic
God. When he puts on his auxiliary organs he is truly magnificent; but
those organs have not grown on to him and they still give him much
trouble at times" (*Civilization* 43).[25]

Going on to argue that such prosthetic attempts "'to increase man's
likeness to God' . . . always express, among other things, the relationship
of a specific culture to death," Schwab explains that the apparatuses we
employ to extend our mortality—the electronic media which act as ar-
chives of a frozen, buried past and the "technological ghosts [that] hover
over our dead bodies" in cybernetic efforts to prolong or create existence—
almost take the place of a missing death cult to restore what is lost in life
(73, 79).

This dream of resurrection does not come without a price. As Freud's
reference to "man's" need for "auxiliary organs" indicates, such narcissistic, "prosthetic" attempts signal a defense against men's "defects," raising,
in his account, the anxiety of lack (41–43). Techniques of compensation for
these limits thus necessarily involve feelings of inadequacy and hostility;
the self is both supported and revealed as incomplete, a particular problem
for the construction of the male subject (*the* subject in psychoanalysis).
Discussing, like Freud, humankind's estrangement from its own attempts
at self-extension and analyzing the very way in which the human subject

is first formed, Jacques Lacan discusses the connection between destructive instincts and the narcissistic libido in terms of "the alienating function" of the ego, the psychic structure that must be constituted for even any illusion of a stable sense of "I" ("The mirror" 1–7).[26] Caught up in "the lure of spatial identifications" (4), the child projects himself into a coherent bodily form that is always external, an ecological shelter that contrasts with the turbulent movement the infant may feel (2). This misrecognition constructs an identity and sets into play a series of fantasies which then reappear in the image of the cyborg: the "fragmented body" to the "fortified works" that buttress identity (4–5), the latter, according to Lacan, often represented by a statue or automaton "in which, in an ambiguous relation, the world of his own making tends to find completion" (2–3).

Yet while the cybernetic automaton may embody the completion of our world, it also has the power to destroy that world as well; as the ultimate "mirror of man," it is both the final mode of individual abstraction and an image portending catastrophic consequences. As Schwab points out, "the most terrifying counterpart of these fantasies of producing endless copies of 'oneself' . . . is, of course, the simultaneous self-aggrandizing fantasy that humankind is, for the first time in history, able to destroy all forms of life on this planet" (72). Similarly reminding us of the ways in which the cyborg intertwines visions of invulnerability with images of death, extending our capacity for both self-sufficiency and global extinction, Haraway notes that "the cyborg has no origin story in the Western sense; a 'final' irony since the cyborg is also the awful apocalyptic *telos* of the 'West's' escalating dominations of abstract individuation, an ultimate self untied at last from all dependency, a man in space" ("Manifesto" 67). This image of a being who exists on automatic pilot, unhinged from all life around it and surviving on its own, recalls the descriptions of the seemingly autonomous fetus, master of his realm (the mother-host) critiqued in chapter 5; more relevant to my purposes here, it also suggests the kind of terror that the cyborg (whether electronically reproduced or bio-engineered) may unleash.[27] Its threat must then be tamed if postmodernism's cybernetic subject is to provide pleasure rather than fear, a process evident both in the strategies discussed in the previous chapter and the operations of domestication that turn the cyborgs of *Max Headroom* and *Pee-wee's Playhouse* into humorous rather than frightening forms.

The monstrous aspect of the cyborg—its confusion of fantasies of invincibility with those of bodily destruction—is suggested in Freud's essay "The 'Uncanny',", in which he analyzes automatons, moving dolls, waxwork figures, mirror reflections dissociated from the self, and other "beings" which seem to hover undecidably between life and death, part and whole, animated agency and technical control (Freud, "The 'Uncanny'").

The cyborg, a living but "programmed" figure, is just such a manifestation, and not surprisingly, the cyborgian creations that populate television's universe fit right in with Freud's description.[28] Max Headroom is a case in point: truly one of television's "talking heads," Max is both a man without a body and a double who mirrors the TV reporter who "donates" his mind. *Pee-wee's Playhouse* is also teeming with sentient toys, furniture, and creatures that would be right "at home" on Freud's list of such uncanny beings as "dismembered limbs, a severed head, feet which dance by themselves" and other things that efface the distinction between imagination and reality (151).[29] Jambi, the genie who makes wishes come true, is, like Max, nothing but a head within a magic box; parts of the playhouse are equipped with humanoid limbs, mouths, or eyes; the food in Pee-wee's fridge has a life of its own (talking, singing, dancing, and tumbling when Pee-wee glimpses in); and as Constance Penley remarks, "Pee-wee himself seems like a bright-cheeked puppet that has come to life" (139).[30]

Although Max and Pee-wee do not elicit the same sense of dread that comparable cinematic figures might (the threat of the various replicants in sci-fi films, for example, or of *Videodrome*'s human/VCR body), a sense of uncanniness still permeates their shows as Max and Pee-wee rupture the naturalized form of the body and the conventional distinctions by which we understand it (such as age and gender, not to mention existential status). For this reason, while the terrifying aspect of the cyborg is tamed in *Max Headroom* and *Pee-wee's Playhouse*, these programs nonetheless seemed quite disorienting, even disturbing, when they first appeared. Writing on *Max Headroom* when the series premiered, a *Newsweek* article noted that the program is "not easy to access" and worried that audiences might not like its "chillingly surreal" quality, "eerie claustrophobia," and the "uncanny ability" of a "disembodied head" to poke his image into our lives (Waters et al. 64, 58, 60). Similarly discussing the kinds of hostile reactions that some viewers have to *Pee-wee's Playhouse*, Glenn O'Brien drily remarks, "It may have something to do with him [Paul Reubens as Pee-wee] making their skin crawl" (92). The feelings of disgust and confusion that these shows may evoke attest to the uncanny nature of their simulated realms, and even the humor of their "heroes" reveals an unnerving, aggressive edge that stands in for the outright hostility of their cinematic counterparts and indicates that the threat of the uncanny (its disruption of order) lurks beneath their surface charm.[31] It is precisely this combination of disruption and seduction, though, that leads to the possibility of viewer fascination, creating a state of excitement that lies between arousal and fear.

Investigating the dread and the lure of the uncanny, Freud notes both egoism and the death drive as components of this state; the confusion of living and lifeless objects, of the self and the other, and of the part and the whole repeats infantile narcissistic fantasies as well as embodying the return of the same. Commenting, for example, on both the menacing and self-aggrandizing elements in the uncanny effect of seeing one's own double (a fantasy which is literalized in *Max Headroom* and not unrelated to the substitutions and character "twinning" sometimes employed on *Pee-wee's Playhouse*),[32] he shows how what originally functioned as "a preservation against extinction" (the double as insurance against the destruction of the [presumed male] ego) ultimately becomes the "ghastly harbinger of death" (141). What marks the uncanny, in other words, is the

confounding of the self as it is multiplied, mirrored, divided, and inter-
changed. The boundaries of subjectivity are breached, and as oppositions
merge in this regression to an undifferentiated state, the stable identity
that the subject strives to achieve is threatened with destruction.

It is then no surprise that Freud associates the uncanny with castration
anxiety and crises of vision: as the knowing gaze is ruptured (unable to
distinguish between life and death, subject and object), all guarantees of
"proper" difference fail, and masculinity can no longer claim distinction
from the feminine. Hence, Freud notes the fear associated with the return
to an intra-uterine existence and the uncanny sensation produced (in men)
by the female genitals (151–53). This is illuminated by his well-known
etymological investigation of the word *heimlich* (familiar, intimate, belonging to the home) which comes to coincide with its opposite *unheimlich*
(strange, concealed, uncanny): the uncanny leads back to what is long
known, what is repressed yet reoccurs, and the maternal female body, once
home to us all, is the ultimate site of repression (123–31). In other words,
the difference usually contained within representation—that difference
which is unleashed, however, through the threat of the uncanny—is
precisely that of sexual difference(s), the very stake both concealed and
revealed in these uncanny figurations of cyborgian doubling and/or
disruption.

The cinema exhibits one well-known defense against the uncanny mystery of femininity and the fear of castration. Delimiting the visual and
narrative positions assigned to men and women, and enforcing, according
to the familiar Mulvian formula, a heterosexually opposed structure of
looking, classical cinema represses difference and reproduces dominant
relations of power (Mulvey, "Visual Pleasure"). Yet within the postmodern
world of television cyborgs, this strategy of defense may no longer hold.
According to the accounts previously discussed, television ruptures the
logic of hierarchized distinction, constructing instead the tactile connections of a "global embrace." For this reason, the medium itself has been
blamed for weakening the polarities that maintain the sexed gaze; establishing multiple positions of identification, enveloping viewers in an ever-
present flow, television, as I've elaborated, has been coded as feminine.

Given the popularity of cyborgian action toys for little boys, the cyborg
may not at first appear to be similarly aligned with representations of the
feminine. Yet its uncanny ability to confound the self and disrupt oppositions indicates a deeper correlation (and may explain children's, particularly boys', need to control its effects).[33] Bound to the TV mosaic (fully "in
the system," as Max claims to be), the television cyborg achieves a kind of
fluid animation, an egoless absorption of the patterns on the screen.[34] Thus
achieving a graceful harmony of being, the paradoxical holism born of
boundary confusion, the cyborg plays out phantasmatic images of femininity, which has also been described in terms of empathy and closeness,
excess and disruption; replacing the woman as cultural sign, the video
cyber-subject seems tied to the flow of a new nature (the technological and
TV matrix) as it is "hooked up" to the world. As video subjects ourselves,

equally a part of the system we survey, TV viewers have appeared to be likewise "plugged in."

There is a way in which this very situation defuses some of the terror associated with uncanny beings even as it positions the spectator in a way that some have found unsettling. The mechanical creatures that Freud examines are upsetting precisely because they disrupt the conventional dualities of part and whole, subject and object, masculine and feminine. The cinema, also a mechanical technology, attempts to maintain these oppositions within its specific textual and psychic economy (even if this necessitates a certain amount of disavowal), and so, as noted above, the presence of beings which threaten these norms results in great disruption and produces an uncanny sense of dread and fear. However, television (like the cyborg itself) utilizes an electronic information system which, according to the popular and critical discourses I've discussed, is *already* predicated upon multiplicity and contradiction, already subversive of stable "masculine" norms. Belonging to (at home with, *heimlich* among) a medium and discursive economy—the "irrational" and "implosive" order of postmodern culture—which itself has scrambled conventional oppositions, the television cyborg stands as less of a threat to the logic of its base.[35]

Nonetheless, despite familiar claims about the schizophrenic nature of postmodernity and the irrational confusion of television's "feminine," decentered mode, we have not simply moved into an amorphous black hole. In fact, as I've argued in the previous chapters, the very intimation of the danger that postmodernism poses to the order of rational expectation has produced renewed attempts to secure conventional guarantees—a process evident in many television texts that attempt to uphold traditional constructions of masculinity in the face of cultural transitions which threaten their demise. In addition to the programs already examined, such an operation can be seen in the TV shows investigated here: by foregrounding the representational strategies and discursive formations of television, and even further exaggerating them through a focus on the video cyborg, these texts would seem to be the most vulnerable to charges of feminization, most able to create their own kind of fear. In this way, *Max Headroom* and *Pee-wee's Playhouse* crystallize the struggle over gender that permeates television and television studies, revealing the dynamics of power that criss-cross postmodern culture and cultural critique.

"I Know You Are, But What Am I?": Amassing Identities, Playing House

Suggesting the permeability of once sacrosanct boundaries, these programs do, in many ways, raise the threat of feminization: as one might expect from texts that tie in with the uncanny, the specter of castration anxiety is never far from sight. Several critics have commented on the way in which *Pee-wee's Playhouse* revolves around this issue, even calling attention to it by Pee-wee's very name. It provides a space that is custom-

Pee-wee and Miss Yvonne "play house" as the "mail-lady" looks on.

built for childish curiosity—not surprisingly, much of which focuses on
sexual difference—but withholds the comfort of final guarantees.[36] In
other words, *Pee-wee's Playhouse* teases the viewer through its movement
between half-asked questions and only partial responses. As Penley observes, what goes on in the playhouse is largely "playing house" (133): the
investigation of sexuality and gender roles is central to the show, though
this is always handled as if it were a game.[37] There are several episodes of
Pee-wee's Playhouse that explore what girls and boys do or what girls and
boys have (the time Pee-wee and Miss Yvonne play daddy and mommy;
when Pee-wee looks up Miss Yvonne's dress; the day when the King of
Cartoons arrives with his wife, new baby, and "educational" film on
reproduction; the episode in which Cowboy Curtis is taught how to date
and Pee-wee stands in for the role of Miss Yvonne). Yet a satisfying answer
to the problem of sexual identity is never ultimately assured; as Pee-wee
responds to all teasing remarks, "I know you are, but what am I?"

What Pee-wee is or is not has been precisely the object of much critical
and popular attention, for as a cyborgian creature that lies between (or
coexists as) human and puppet, adult and child, masculine and feminine,
obsessive and hysteric, he breaks all the rules of the game—or, perhaps
more accurately, as the leader of the playhouse, he is able to create his own
rules at whim. Furthermore, given the uncanny nature of Pee-wee's furniture and toys, he is not the only one within this world who crosses the
traditional divide. Balfour, for example, bases his analysis of the program
on the metaphor of the playhouse's "mail lady," necessarily, given the
context of the show, suggesting "male lady"—a character who, in accor-

dance with Lacan's writings, delivers a message about the instability and ambiguity of sexual identity literally "through the letter" itself (the postal envelopes she delivers) (155–60).

As participating members of Pee-wee's universe, tied to him through both processes of viewing and the letters that they sent, *Pee-wee's Playhouse* viewers became similarly enveloped within a realm in which markers of gender were often (if only temporarily) obscured. Existing beyond any simple categorization, the audience of this program was unusually diverse, especially given the show's Saturday morning time slot in which it was surrounded by texts that were not only clearly aimed at children, but also geared for either boys or girls. Breaking the conventional wisdom of television programming (especially concerning programs targeted for youths), *Pee-wee's Playhouse* was neither cuddly cute nor militaristically aggressive, neither sexually innocent nor completely in the know, and the appeal that it held across age and gender demographics continues to be one of the most intriguing aspects of the show. On the one hand, as Penley remarks, this play to several audiences suggests that despite other differences, the investigation of sexual identity never ceases to fascinate or insist (136). Yet on the other, it is difficult to say anything definitive about the audience or its interpretations of and interest in the text.[38] For, as Balfour writes, working "to disturb what can only with difficulty be called the viewer's 'identification' with the characters on the screen," *Pee-wee's Playhouse* seems to demand double or multiple readings which cannot simply be divided between masculine and feminine, belonging to the grown-up or the child: "Neither the subject constructed on the screen nor the viewer-subject constructed in the television audience is a homogeneous one; indeed, there is no 'subject' to speak of" (157, 160).

There may be no *unified* diegetic nor spectating subject of the text, but it is nonetheless important to account for the ways in which *Pee-wee's Playhouse* does construct identity (or identities). In this regard, Balfour's claims indicate exactly what seems to trouble many deriders of this show. Breaking through the barriers that typically divide viewers into separate and standardized groups, *Pee-wee's Playhouse* seems to glory in the very thing that underlies much critical and popular apprehension: the way in which television invites its viewers into an inclusive but seemingly undifferentiated space, one that ruptures familiar oppositions and replicates an overpresence coded as feminine/maternal. It is for this reason that *Pee-wee's Playhouse*, emphasizing how television may undermine the stability of the hetero-masculine norm, embodies some critics' worst fears and other viewers'—particularly some feminist and/or queer theorists'—greatest hopes. Yet, as I will elaborate later in the chapter, even this text cannot be described in such partisan terms. Despite its flirtation with feminization (and thus with one cultural model of gay male identity), *Pee-wee's Playhouse* nonetheless enacts its own strategy of containment through the way in which it positions Pee-wee as the center of the show; it thus reverses what's been seen by detractors as the threat of emasculation, and in the process, I would argue, unfortunately also plays down the potential that devotees see for articulating a new (gyne- and homophilic) masculinity.

Max Headroom also seduces the viewer into a realm which diffuses all distinctions, both extending and defending itself against what it poses as the vacuum of simulation and the threat of a feminized world. To expand my earlier description of this series, the computer-generated Max is specifically created to answer a life-and-death enigma (a position that not only demonstrates the intimate connection between being and its cessation within a cybernetic universe but one that immediately ties Max to the riddle of existence, mimicking the place of the woman in much philosophical, mythological, and psychoanalytic thought).[39] The enigma at the root of this "birth" centers on a mysterious accident and cover-up—an event investigated by ace reporter Edison Carter, the man who provided the mind given to Max. In the scene that reveals the hidden information that Edison is seeking, a large and lazy man sits at home in his armchair, watching television as an ad comes on the air. The ad that he sees makes use of what we are to presume is a diegetically new representational form: instead of presenting a logical, linear argument, miniature narrative, or coherent series of associations, the commercial bombards him with impulses, involving a rapid flow of sounds and images which cannot be clearly identified or isolated.

While this ad, called a "blipvert," is simply an intensified microcosm of TV as we, the home viewers, know it, the effect of the commercial on the diegetic viewer is that of a literal inflation; the man swells up as consumer s(t)imulation builds up inside of him until he actually explodes (or perhaps in accordance with Baudrillard's theory, implodes). What we witness, then, can almost be described as a textual form of hysterical pregnancy: TV provokes a generation of confusing sensations and animating force until this energy bursts to the surface, in this case destroying the human body but providing the narrative origin of the cyborg, Max. Because Edison Carter has witnessed this event (though through a mediation—he has seen it on a video tape), he is chased and captured (at the crash site previously noted), and his brain is then scanned by a computer in order to disclose the full extent of his knowledge. In the process, Max Headroom is created. Eventually, of course, Edison recovers, solves the case, and reports the crime through another simulation; he broadcasts the contents of Max's memory, which contains the videotape of the viewer explosion.

In exploring the sexual and textual issues raised in this episode, it is first of all apparent that TV is caught up in a web of simulations; as we see in this program, any access to "the real" is mediated through a series of video images (the original video ad, the videotape of the ad and explosion, the computer scan of Edison's memory of the tape, and finally, Edison's retaping of Max's computerized memory of this tape—a broadcast which is at that point at least four times removed). Such simulations are even further exaggerated in the show's short second run (when, like Max within his own diegetic TV world, it disappeared and then reappeared after initial cancellation—in this case, to fill a gap in the schedule caused by the 1988 writers strike). Just as Max gained Edison's mind in the opening episode, in the series' next "start up," alter-egoist Max returns the favor, allowing Edison to be programmed with the contents of *his* memory in order to save Edison from, as they say in the show, "going out of his head" after being brainwashed by some junk-food and its accompanying prize.

The question of whose head/mind either Edison or Max can go out of or into points to precisely the threat of cybernetic culture: the effacement of distinction, the absolute reversibility of an all-encompassing order. As Ross drily states, "Max Headroom was Jean Baudrillard's best trip yet, and Todd Gitlin's worst nightmare" (145): the series presents a completely technologically mediated and televisually determined world, the ultimate hyperreality that, as the program's logo tells us, is only 20 minutes into our own future. Furthermore, in its form as well as content, the show draws on postmodern textual devices, refusing to subordinate its visual effects to a linear narrative progression and multiplying the look through a dense layering of video and/or computerized images. Thus foregrounding the specific configurations of a televised and cybernetic landscape, *Max Headroom* rejects the cinematic model and self-consciously announces TV's difference.

This difference, as noted throughout my argument, has been linked to that of gender: *Max Headroom*'s premiere figures both the receptive TV body and the threat of a simulated world in terms of denigrating images of femininity. The viewer-victim, while a man, is an emasculated one: flabby and passive, he sits in front of the TV set until his body blows up in the "pregnancy" that ultimately results in Max. As in Baudrillard's vision, hyperreality's perpetrators also share this feminized fate. Even the experts of simulation, the computer operators who help Edison solve his cases, lack the benefits of powerful masculinity. Max is created by an apparently pre-sexual whiz kid (the standard cliché of the "terminally" adolescent nerd) while Edison's computer guide is female. But it is Max, the cyborgian child of television, who seems most strikingly emasculated by the condition of his birth; literally a "talking head," he lacks the body of a man and the understanding of the sexual memories with which he is repeatedly plagued. While Max masquerades as male (like Pee-wee), his constantly shifting contours provide him with a fluctuation of being that refuses even the illusion of unity and stability. Unable to differentiate himself from the matrices that bear him, he does not master the order of hyperreality, but can only vacillate within it, losing the distinction between self and other that is (however fictionally) required to attain the status of a man.

As discussed in prior chapters, this same diffusion (the conflation of subject and object, part and whole) corresponds not only to descriptions of female subjectivity, but to the conditions that inspire consumer consciousness as well; an overpresence of the object/image which is almost taken to be a part of the self is the very incitement that lures consumers to the stores. It thus comes as no surprise that Max achieved fame with U.S. viewers not as the hero of a mainstream network program but as an adornment for a

Max the ad-"man."

product up for sale: it was his status as enticing weapon in the "cola wars"
that made Max a star (having only recently appeared on the cable channel
Cinemax after hosting a music video show on England's Channel 4).[40] As
the spokes-"man" for Coke, Max thus gained popularity through his
feminized position in the circuit of exchange; like the woman who both
purchases (commodities) and sells (herself as commodified object), Max, a
consumable product *par excellence,* akin to the televised objects he displayed, advertised the value of another item we could buy.

This relationship between, first, representations of femininity and consumerism (both of which have been figured in terms of an excessive
"closeness") and, second, a cyborgian breakdown of subject/object distinctions was particularly emphasized in the episode that reintroduced
Max Headroom to the television market in the ABC series' second birth onto
the airwaves (after the program was shut down and "recharged" in time to
help the network manage its own commercial problems in the face of
industry disputes).[41] Interweaving a plot concerning overspending in the
consumer arena with a running battle between Edison and Max, this show
demonstrates the threat posed to masculine self-sufficiency by the "feminine" logic of postmodern simulation. The episode opens with an argument between our heroes, these two sides of the same cyborgian coin,
which erupts when Max, who gets better ratings, steals Edison's airtime,
interrupting the investigative reporting with sarcastic remarks of his own.
Claiming that he is allowed more freedom on the air (as the medium's own
child, Max, unlike Edison, is able to say whatever he wants on TV), Max

asks, "As long as it's the truth, does it matter which of us tells it?" Edison's response reveals the deeper problem in their "relationship," which is signalled by Max Headroom's very name (implying that there is not room enough for two minds where only one head should be): "Yes, it does. You're in my way. . . . You exist, that's what matters."

The problem of Max's overpresence and excessive closeness to Edison is raised again later in the program when the episode's other storyline, noted previously, becomes the central focus: while investigating a plot by which people overconsume as a result of direct neuro-programming from prizes awarded at a fast-food chain (owned by Zic-Zac, the series' villainous multinational corporation), Edison becomes a purchasing zombie and must be saved from his lust for never-ending, senseless spending. To this end, Max (who shares his memories of Zic-Zac's evil deeds) is reprojected into Edison's mind in order to give him what is referred to as "a jump-start"—a phrase which implies that Edison, like Max, is simply an electronic being, another cyborgian creation. While inhabiting the same brain, Max and Edison continue the fight that they had begun earlier. Edison exclaims, "You're always in my way; you're too close to me," and Max responds, "I can't help being that close and being a threat to you." Edison then asks, "Have you any idea what it's like having a part of me competing against me?" to which Max replies, "And have you any idea what it's like just being a part?"

This exchange, coupled with the plot revolving around extravagant spending in a commodified world, is interesting for a number of reasons. For one, it relies on the same tropes of "nearness" and overpresence that have been raised throughout portrayals of the cyborg, the woman, and the "consuming" body, thereby suggesting the danger to a (presumed) autonomous and unified male subject that is posed by a "feminized" (consumerized and cyborgian) existence. The emphasis placed on the position of the "part" reveals this as well: not only does it express all too clearly a classic castration anxiety and its fetishistic denial (the possible separation of a part and a supplemental object overvalued in its place), but it questions the cyborg's status as being, mate, or possession precisely in the context of the "new holism" previously discussed that confuses the distinction between fragment and whole.

Pee-wee's Playhouse also revels in a part-and-whole conflation, activating forces that are central to consumption by embodying the kinds of projections that tie viewers to their things. As in *Max Headroom*, the overt "lessons" that are voiced throughout the program often seem to be opposed to commercialism, but the text itself actually encapsulates the dynamics of consumerism which are staged before our eyes.[42] Commenting on this problem, Balfour argues, "No network television show can resist the gravitational pull of the commodity, but the Pee-wee show does its unlevel best to resist or reroute that force": in what Balfour sees as a negation of capitalist reification, Pee-wee simply "personif[ies] everything in sight" (164). Personally engaged with all the items in the playhouse (which exist as cyborgian characters in their own right), Pee-wee counters objectification with social interaction: his possessions are "possessed" with a life of their own.

Yet the strategy to which Balfour refers is a risky one at best. As Karl Marx (and Balfour himself) points out, both the "conversion of things into persons, and persons into things" are part of the same dialectic that defines a commodified existence (209), and Balfour's claim that "Pee-wee counteracts a certain commodity fetishism precisely through an excessive, hyperbolic reveling in personification" (164) sounds suspiciously like Baudrillard's valorization of the masses' depoliticized hypersimulation (the "feminine" irony discussed in chapter 4)— a hyperconformity which simply leads to more consumption. Despite, then, the much-noted fact that every week on his show, Pee-wee slammed the playhouse door in the face of the Salesman (a giant puppet with news of an "incredible offer"), this apparent rejection of consumerism is, arguably, merely a ruse, a refusal that is primarily directed at the aesthetics, not the substance, of the sale.[43] Unlike the hard-line sales pitch that associates the Salesman with a dated model of commercial persuasion, Pee-wee is interested instead in a more seductive version of consumption: the glorification of postmodern style.

Evoking an entire sensibility based on "amassing," collection, and pastiche, Pee-wee's Playhouse celebrates consumption as a basic way of life. As Glenn O'Brien states, Pee-wee is "the shopper/collector as artist," one who consumes not just for mere pleasure, but for its [cyborgian] transformative effect (91). Making his entire world a showcase, Pee-wee closes the gap between object and eye/I: his possessions become part of his very identity, his belongings give assurance that he truly belongs. Thus effacing the distinctions that keeps us separate from our things, he draws the audience into a universe which is literally alive with objects that call out to us and entice our interest. Therefore, even though no particular product is advertised (and Pee-wee/Reubens himself shied away from this task), consumption in its most basic and general mode of operation is heartily endorsed. At one with his world, Pee-wee re-creates a pre-Oedipal moment in which everything is simply an extension of the self, a McLuhanesque nexus that defines consumerism's own appeal. As viewers sucked into a televised scene which is chock-full of seemingly innocent, childish delights, we are likewise invited to join in the flow, to participate in a consumption posed as equally harmless. In other words, not only are the heroes of television's cyborgian dramas figured as somehow feminine—intimately tied to a world that, in its consumer simulation of maternal plenitude, undoes the markers of identity and the stability offered by the masculine name—but the viewers of these texts, also enveloped by the cyborgian/ consumer matrix so temptingly portrayed, similarly entertain this "feminizing" fate.

His Majesty, the Ego: Ruling in Style

By thus immersing us in the curious constructions of the TV simulacrum, *Max Headroom* and *Pee-wee's Playhouse* both confound the security of masculinity that is protected in the cinema—the assurance of which allows Hollywood narrative film to present cyborgs who provoke a stronger sense of dread and the uncanny. Television, which lacks recourse to final resolutions and the same focused structure of the gaze, must then tame the cyborg by methods which may seem less extreme or less suspenseful, but are not without effects of domination and control. Indeed, the very fact that unease is transformed into a roller coaster ride of fun indicates that a process of containment can be found within these texts. While *Max Headroom* and *Pee-wee's Playhouse* then play with textual forms that have been linked not only to postmodern disruption but also to what is posed as the dangers of feminization, various strategies with which to delimit TV's "feminine" connotations are also employed, and though none of these strategies is fully successful, an effort of suppression is apparent in the shows.

Pee-wee's Playhouse, for example, hints at a fluctuating narrative space, yet checks its threat through Pee-wee's obsessive control of the look. Employing a strategy which is commonly used in music videos (another form initially heralded as the ultimate in postmodern TV), any disorientation provoked by an unusual or potentially disruptive mode of representation is countered by an insistent return to the star of the show.[44] By shifting all attention back to a single focus in such a way, Pee-wee regains command of his text: he fully dominates the visual field and governs his world with all the ruthlessness of "his Majesty, the Ego."[45] Thus acting as the fixed and centered point from which all power emanates—a "virtual playboy"—he actually suppresses the subversive potential of the playhouse itself; we are cut off from the energy of this "other scene" (the uncanny site that we strain to see clearly) and are led back instead to the master of the house.

Furthermore, while Pee-wee himself has been championed as a liberating model—a post-gender hero who offers a progressive alternative to mass culture's typical male—I would argue that as the Playhouse ruler, he nonetheless poses no real threat to conventional norms. We accept Pee-wee's escapades precisely because they enact a childish regression that can simply be dismissed: as pre-sexual antics, they refuse the burden of cultural solutions, sidestepping the problem of gender/sexual relations and the question of their possible reconstructions. Despite, then, the way in which its ambiguities seem to allow for the emergence of a different kind of affective regime, *Pee-wee's Playhouse* falls short of presenting *any* kind of social, familial, or sexual (either homo- or hetero-) arrangement as a serious cultural possibility, and it is precisely this evasion that allowed the program to achieve the level of acceptance that it had. Questioning, for example, how a network would allow a character to reign on the air who, in addition to being effeminate, also created a televised microcosm of gay male culture (populated with icons taken from campy comedy, homoerotic performance and pornography—Jambi, the genie in drag; the Cowboy; the Lifeguard), Penley inquires, "Could it be that the CBS executives have *scotomized* the show's sexuality, and specifically its homosexuality? That is, that like children who are not yet developmentally or psychically prepared to receive certain sexual information, they *see* it but do not *register* it?" (138). Given the program's own infantile nature, this possibility might seem quite plausible. However, Penley later states that such an epistemological block is still unlikely and revises her opinion to account for what I would argue is the show's *own* efforts at defense: "Surely CBS *knows*, but somehow feels that things are controllable, that the sexual meanings circulated by the show will somehow be contained" (145).

Later, of course, these sexual meanings burst out of their textual confines. When, after having ended his series, Paul Reubens was arrested in 1991 for "indecent exposure" within an "adult" movie theater (that is, masturbating to pornography), his image was shattered and his marketing potential destroyed: this display of full-grown sexual desire led CBS to pull *Pee-wee's Playhouse* reruns off the air, toy stores to remove Pee-wee items from the shelves, and Walt Disney's MGM Studios theme park to drop a two-minute clip that featured Pee-wee from its tours. The sense of panic created over this scandal of "Pee-wee's misadventure" (which brought Drs. Lee Salk and Joyce Brothers on the air to advise concerned parents about how to break the news to their kids) indicates how successfully Reubens/Pee-wee had previously been able to disavow the sexual connotations of his television act.[46] Undone by the very forces upon which his popularity was based (the curious exhibition yet containment of uncanny difference), Pee-wee was "cut down to size" when it became clear that there might be more to his escapades than a game of simply playing house.

Rather than applauding Pee-wee as a positive gay (or even male feminist) role-model as some viewers and critics have done, it therefore seems more important to analyze the ways in which within the text itself this potential is defused—or even worse, turned back against its own liberating possibilities in a move that demonstrates how male dominance and gay allusions can coexist.[47] As Bryan Bruce and Alexander Doty persuasively argue, the program's "homosexual subtext" might indeed have encouraged some viewers to claim Pee-wee as an embodiment of the image of the feminine gay man, providing empowering appropriations of network television for audiences who are not usually addressed. Bruce's and Doty's readings are invaluable in correcting the heterosexist assumptions of critics who fail to take the possibility of queer meanings into account. But these meanings, as Doty himself acknowledges, do not excuse what still might exist as sexist assumptions (even if they recontextualize and thus reframe them), and the way in which Pee-wee replays oppressive clichés about feminine narcissism and regression—and therefore also replicates stereotypes about homosexuality as merely gender inversion and "immature" object choice—suggests a much less enabling portrayal. In fact, the pre-adolescent humor that prevails in the playhouse not only works to restrain subversive impulses; it also provides an arena for misogynist jokes. While, as Penley notes, any homosexual references are "probably taken by children as no more than a perfectly adequate representation of their own dismissal of the opposite sex and all that 'icky stuff,'" even this "gross-out" fails to equalize the show; it is only the prospect of dealing with girls that arouses disgust (136).

In other words, rather than providing a competing model of male-male or male-female relationships, Pee-wee is represented as arrested at a single point along what is still presumed to be a traditional path: as a pre-Oedipal narcissist, Pee-wee simply adheres to the "girls are yucky" stage of hetero-masculine development. In the episode concerning dating, for example, Pee-wee initially refuses to help Cowboy Curtis practice talking to a woman by masquerading as Miss Yvonne, declaring, "No way I'm going to be a girl." Although he eventually gives in, the masquerade abruptly ends when the time comes for a good-night kiss. Dodging both a homosexual and a revised heterosexual position, Pee-wee offers no amendment to familiar sex/gender norms, making both his dismissal of women and his horror at being seen as somehow like a woman into a basic aspect of the show—one that is motivated only by his egoism, not by a different sexual choice. As an infantile version of the "new man" discussed in chapters 4 and 5, Pee-wee thus does not so much alter gender relations as claim all available positions for himself, refusing to settle on any one but relegating women to mere "housework" all the same.[48] Or as Tania Modleski incisively puts it in her own cautionary description, this "her-man" may seem different from the phallic heroes we are used to, but given the way in which he combines a desire to appropriate femininity with the privilege to denigrate it, we cannot conclude that he provides any real alternative to the more familiar "he-man type" (91, 103, 95).

Yet to shift the focus away from Pee-wee himself and consider what else the program has to offer, we might rather appreciate its humor as camp—a more complicated issue than the question of Pee-wee's suitability as a new, progressive hero. For instance, in a move that negates the show's own centering devices, Penley argues that too much has been made of Reuben's/Pee-wee's own persona, recommending instead that critics look at the entire sensibility of the text, at the way in which *Pee-wee's Playhouse* "*puts camp to work* as part of an overall strategy to playfully subvert the conventions of both sexuality and consumerism" (147). Whether or not such subversion succeeds, however, is not at all clear. While a camp aesthetic has been associated with gay subcultural resistance because of the way that it toys with style, roles, and the trappings of identity—its performative awareness of what Susan Sontag terms "the convertibility of 'man' and 'woman,' 'person' and 'thing'"—the cyborgian implications of such "conversions" indicate that camp all too easily correlates with, rather than contests, oppressive processes of simulation and consumption (101).[49]

Camp's combination of parody and admiration, its affection for mass culture's own throwaways, already points to the double-edged logic of this aesthetic, which is as likely to be celebratory as it is to be critical, stereotypically reifying as it is challenging (and certainly not necessarily queer).[50] The fact that camp may no longer be distinguished from postmodernism's own emphasis on artifice and style emphasizes the risks of this strategy even more, suggesting that in today's context (that is, in a culture often seen as contextless), it no longer stands out as an oppositional mode.[51] Indeed, in Sontag's influential essay, she defines camp as "the relation to style in a time in which the adoption of style— as such—has become altogether questionable" (118), a posture for a "culturally oversaturated" (116) sensibility in which the seriousness of traditional critical responses (irony, satire) is no longer adequate to the excesses of an over-aestheticized and overcoded landscape. As such, it recalls the practices of hypersimulation and pastiche theorized by Baudrillard and Jameson—the mimicry of style in a culture in which no stable norm against which to differentiate your own style exists.[52]

Like Baudrillard, Sontag sees this excessive hyperconformity and artifice as "seduct[ive]" in its "duplicity" (110)—it allows us both detachment and sympathy, cynicism and generosity, parody and love, providing a way to ward off the boredom of an affluent society. Making no distinctions between high culture and the objects of mass art, camp can increase our pleasure in the "course" offerings of a mass-mediated world while also pleading for an attitude of tolerance by embracing precisely those things (objects and people) that a society based on moral righteousness and rigid social placement has rejected (116–18). Yet despite a "democratic *esprit*" that recognizes the "equivalence of all objects" (what Walter Benjamin terms the "sense of the universal equality of things" that exists in a world governed by mass reproduction [Benjamin 223]), Sontag argues that camp is "apolitical" (117, 107), once again recalling the assessments of Jameson and Baudrillard.

This may particularly be the case in a text like *Pee-wee's Playhouse*, which, as Modleski suggests in her comments on the show, uses camp as part of an escapist fantasy, offering not so much a critique of dominant culture as amusement within it (101–103).[53] That is, just like the childishly "innocent" humor that I discussed earlier, the camp aesthetic of *Pee-wee's Playhouse* is in keeping with the regressive and narcissistic nature of its play. Simply enjoying (rather than re-writing) the world around him, Pee-wee offers little challenge to the less humorous aspects of the system he is in. In fact, as a symbol of eternal youth, Pee-wee upholds the American dream: he is the ultimate product of the television generation, embracing all that surrounds him by claiming it as an extension of the self and therefore existing forever as a child (at least until the post-series scandal that finally stretched this illusion of innocent boyhood to the breaking point and unleashed the sexual anxieties that lurked beneath his image all along).[54]

Old and New Myths: Splitting the Difference

Rather than lessening Pee-wee's ability to control the objects in his world, the ageless existence he enjoys within the confines of his show furthers Pee-wee's own command, giving him a curious power over sexuality and reproduction, gender and generation. Like the cybernetic being who, lacking mother and mortality, triumphs over both life and death, we can imagine him neither aging nor being born; in the words of Glenn O'Brien, Pee-wee "seems to have sprung into life (from Dad's forehead maybe) fully formed" (90).[55] As the center of textual creation and the apparent anchor of its meanings, Pee-wee is completely self-sufficient—the ultimate ego removed from his source, repudiating the feminine with glee in a clubhouse of his own.

The notion of Pee-wee's spontaneous generation from his father's forehead—an image which is in fact literalized in *Max Headroom* when, with the aid of technology, Max springs to life from the brain of Edison Carter, the symbolic father on the show—comes from the Greek myth of Athena, the goddess of knowledge and wisdom, who had no mother but was said to have emerged, fully grown, from Zeus' brow. According to the story, as a goddess "all for the father" (as the poet Aeschylus had her say), Athena was aligned with the patriarchal order against an earlier system of mother right, and her appointment as the patron of Athens depended on the women of the city accepting the requirement that they would no longer stand as citizens, vote, or pass their names on to their children (Monaghan 34–35). Reproducing this myth within their cybernetic worlds, both *Max Headroom* and *Pee-wee's Playhouse* reveal the paradoxical implications of the gender relations at stake within their texts; while Max and Pee-wee each take up the place of the woman (Athena) in this tale, this position has already been claimed for the paternal order as the feminine becomes subsumed under male control.[56]

Pee-wee's Playhouse also makes an interesting reference to another ancient myth—that of Oedipus and the Riddle of the Sphinx. Not only does Pee-wee wear a helmet with a single eye adorning the brim (a symbol of both Oedipus's excess and his loss), but the figure of the Sphinx—the emblem of sexual investigation—is in place on the playhouse roof.[57] According to Balfour and Penley, the presence of the Sphinx on this program is entirely fitting. Not only does *Pee-wee's Playhouse* offer its own brand of sexual exploration, but the Sphinx's recombinant, cyborgian form (part dog, serpent, bird, lion, and human) makes this character entirely at home in an uncanny world that is full of such reconstructed creatures.[58] Yet rather than menacing the viewers with revelations of the dangers of sexual identity, Pee-wee's Sphinx takes the playhouse, spatially and symbolically, "under her wing" (that is, Pee-wee plays beneath her but seems somehow "above" the questions she might ask). Safely tucked away within this haven, Pee-wee is then shielded from the riddle she proposed (the answer, which sent Oedipus toward his frightening fate, being "man"); having simply emerged into his timeless state, Pee-wee is able to circum-

Pee-wee's playhouse sphinx.

vent the enigma of life, death, and sexuality itself. In other words, rather than representing an alternative to conventional constructions of sexual identity, Pee-wee provides a means of disavowal, a way to be both male and female, young and old, without ever having to challenge the rules of the game.

In addition to sharing a camp aesthetic, *Max Headroom* might be compared to *Pee-wee's Playhouse* in such treatment of sexuality as well. Max is also allowed to have his cake (or Zic-Zac treat) and eat it too: he is, like Pee-wee, both post- and pre-pubescent, innocent yet wise, seductive but still chaste. His relationship to gender is equally contradictory: despite his "feminine" position in the logic of simulation and consumption, Max nonetheless reasserts the necessity of patriarchal rule. As a cyborgian Athena, his status as the patron of our hyperreal 20-minutes-from-now future merely masks the law of the father, the price that must be paid for Max's own ambiguous identity. Indeed, in its strategy of defense against a feminized existence, *Max Headroom* literally splits its hero in two, displacing postmodern consumer consciousness onto Max and leaving Edison free to play the role of traditional protector. While Max is there for comic effect (much of the show's humor is based on Max's lack of a stable identity as well as his lack of a body), it takes a "real man" to free us from the adverse effects of cyborgian chaos. Edison, a typical melodramatic hero, battles crime and exposes wrongdoing in order to keep his world in line. He thus reinjects salvation into a time that would dispel it (the regressive and synchronic ahistory of the TV simulacrum), returning the viewer instead to the linear project of masculine ascendence.[59]

As these examples demonstrate, both *Max Headroom* and *Pee-wee's Playhouse* enact a contest over power, rei(g)ning in the threat of simulation that they initially suggest. These shows, even now judged by many to be among TV's "most innovative," thus exist in the tension between modern and postmodern forms, projecting what are considered the "feminine" cyborgian elements onto a dominated other (Max and Pee-wee's feminized furniture and toys) while still allowing their male protagonists (Edison and Pee-wee himself) to control the diegetic space and the flow of the narrative. Rather than texts to be wholeheartedly commended for their radical visions or liberating play, *Max Headroom* and *Pee-wee's Playhouse* are battlegrounds of meaning—fields in which a struggle over difference (sexual and textual, as well as epistemological and existential) can be waged.

Such a struggle is suggested in Freud's own comments on the uncanny. Noting the existence of scientific programs that attempt to reduce mysterious events to formulaic laws "and so deprive them of their uncanny effect," he pointed toward the rise of modern communications and cybernetic research ("'Uncanny'" 144–45). Such fields may provide us with the knowledge required to develop the electronic media and the cyborg beings who populate their realms, but the "disciplines" of information and cybernetic theory also allow us to master their dissonance and keep them under strict command.[60] By formulating all "free play" in terms of quantifiable data and statistical constraint, the uncertainty of difference can be banished from our world (at least according to the myth of technoscientific progress). The more radical implications of cyborgian disruption are thereby dissolved, prompting many cultural observers (such as Jameson and Baudrillard) to describe postmodernity as a closed circuit of absolute control. Producing theories that are then as totalizing as the sciences they mimic, these critics are unable to see the dislocations of postmodern culture as anything other than disorder, as the death of a meaningful system of knowledge and expression—a view ultimately equal to its reverse formulation, the uncritical celebration of postmodernism's alterity.[61]

Rather than either championing TV and cyborg myths for transgressing the boundaries of hierarchical distinction or rejecting them in the nostalgic desire for a restoration of these bounds, we might thus be better able to find new modes of intervention if we learn to pose the problem of difference in a more productive way, neither reducing it to a mirror of the same nor projecting it onto a mystified other. By inserting the question of gender into the analysis, we can underscore what these shifts might entail, using the analysis of sexual differences to call attention to other differences as well. While *Pee-wee's Playhouse* and *Max Headroom* employ various strategies with which to rein in these possibilities, they nonetheless hint at such transformations and provide us with a pleasure that exceeds their efforts at defense. In this way, they truly are exemplary televisual texts, displaying both the unavoidable limitations of commercial television and an equally striking plurality, frustrating as well as fostering utopian hopes of

a less restricted playing field. By edging our way around the male protagonists who still dominate their worlds, we may enter this more imaginative
space that has otherwise been banished to the margins of the scene—a
space marked by mutable connections which can lead us not into the
system, but toward affinity groups that resist its circuit of control.

De-Regulations? Reprogramming the Cyborg

As the paradoxical constructions of *Max Headroom* and *Pee-wee's Playhouse* demonstrate, the politics of postmodern simulation must be analyzed in terms of a complex dialectic of freedom and constraint. Neither
fully replacing traditional representations with a different, more liberating
vision of gender nor totally disallowing such a vision to emerge, these
shows pose interesting problems for feminist cultural critics as they shift
sexual politics onto less charted terrain. It is precisely because these
programs provide atypical figurations, altering the ways in which difference is usually handled, that formulating an adequate response becomes a
challenging task. In giving us models of characters who lack stable gender / generational identifications (not to mention technological / existential
definition), these texts seem to bypass many of the ways in which sexual
difference has been managed in the past, particularly disrupting the
cinematic norm by which the uncanny and the feminine are tamed through
the power of the male gaze. In both *Pee-wee's Playhouse* and *Max Headroom*,
the uncanny is made lovably cute rather than menacing as the look is
scattered across a fragmented scene, and if any one image can be said to
hold our undivided interest, it is the male figure (not the female) who
claims this position. Like children, Pee-wee and Max vie for attention
without even the kind of "prophylactic" protection afforded by the excessive hypermasculinity analyzed in chapter 4 (although, as I've argued,
there is a modified version of this in some aspects of these shows, and even
the striving for "cuteness" indicates a certain force).

Yet at the same time as these texts' ambiguity yields some freedom from
the constraints of a hierarchy of gender, there are also efforts to circum-
scribe this outcome—attempts, that is, to reassert a masculine control.
Such a dynamic reveals the way in which U.S. society —both in the 1980s
and still today—attempts to manage the contradictory potential of postmodern simulation, forcing it to conform to existing modes of categorization and those established patterns of cultural organization which it has
the power to overturn. As Bill Nichols explains in his analysis of cybernetic
culture, while simulation may rupture the gender oppositions central to
the discursive and textual formations of modernity (including the Oedipal
narratives of classical cinema), a hierarchy of gender need not so much be
disrupted as dis- [and then re-] placed: rather than offering the woman as
a fetishized icon to be subsumed under male power, simulation instead
often focuses on the very operations of regulation that allow for such

mastery, emphasizing the *processes* of fetishistic control rather than the fetish *object* in and of itself (31–32).

To many observers, such an emphasis on techniques of domination seems to be the inevitable result of the changes that cybernesis yields. Given that the term "cybernetics" derives from the Greek "to steer, guide, or govern," and that the first cybernetic systems (intelligent apparatuses capable of predicting future states) were developed in order to track anti-aircraft weapons, a hetero-masculine fetishization of politico-militaristic command may seem intrinsic to the postmodern condition.[62] Yet this link between cyborgian transformation and technologies of control (the focus on order in the face of disruption, uncertainty, and ambiguity) need not be insurmountable; the cyborg also offers a competing vision of the world. To quote from Haraway's well-known, stirring manifesto, while,

> [f]rom one perspective, a cyborg world is about the final imposition of a grid of control on the planet, about the final abstraction embodied in a Star War apocalypse waged in the name of defense, about the final appropria-tion of women's bodies . . . , [f]rom another perspective, a cyborg world might be about lived social and bodily realities in which people are not afraid of their joint kinship with animals and machines, not afraid of permanently partial identities and contradictory standpoints. (72)

It is such prospects of non-unified identities and the joint kinships they allow—the possibilities deriving from the "transgressed boundaries" and "potent fusions" that the cyborg embodies—that define the best that *Max Headroom* and *Pee-wee's Playhouse* have to offer; those who have lauded these programs seem to be drawn precisely to the pluralities thereby engendered.

Despite, then, the way in which these shows defend themselves against the threat of the uncanny and the danger that is posed to the unified male subject when difference is unleashed, they nonetheless maintain at least an outward acceptance of the cultural and categorical diversity that accom-panies their heroes' own peculiar, nondesignated states. As hybrid beings who seem to fall in between the cracks of gender, generational, textual, and technological distinctions, Max and Pee-wee are necessarily linked to the worlds that they strive to command; they can never fully divorce them-selves from their amorphous realms in order to maintain the distance required for domination of an Other. The dream of collectivity is thus held out to viewers of these texts, and while in some ways this fantasy is simply part of a commodity lure, perhaps such utopian longings ought not be so easily dismissed.[63]

In fact, these programs (*Pee-wee's Playhouse* in particular) hinted at the potential of multicultural and queer coalition politics just as these political and socio-cultural strategies were being advanced. Though, as Doty notes, some of the playhouse characters may at times seem like "ethnic exotics" (85), the program does deal with racial/ethnic difference in a way that was (and remains) unusual for U.S. TV: as many commentators have stated, not

Buddies: Pee-wee and his friend Ricardo.

only does *Pee-wee's Playhouse* include several characters in nontraditional roles (for instance, the cowboy, king, and female 'mailman' are all African Americans), but race/ethnicity is simply seen as one factor among many others (sexual, cultural, "species") which need not define the position one is in nor even be explained in terms of some assumed dominant norm (for example, the Spanish spoken by the character Ricardo is often not translated for the sake of non-Spanish-speaking viewers) [Penley 149–50; Balfour 161–62].

As the presence of Reba the "mail [or male] lady" also indicates, *Pee-wee's Playhouse* equally points to some "queer" combinations; Pee-wee's friends include stereotypical macho men (Ricardo, Cowboy Curtis, Tito the lifeguard) and flamboyantly "faggy" figures (most notably Jambi, labelled by Doty as the "queeny genie"), femme "fag moll" types (Miss Yvonne, the Cowntess, Mrs. Steve, and Mrs. Rene) and tomboy/butch gals (Reba, Dixie the cabdriver) (Doty 93, 87, 89–90). Many of these characterizations are still quite problematic: Penley and Modleski have pointed to the misogynist and "fattist" biases undergirding the representations of the "ladies" on the show (Penley 149; Modleski 102–103), and Doty discusses the misunderstandings that seem to exist between Pee-wee and the characters who are coded as "dykes" (90).[64] Such an "interspliced" cast of characters is nevertheless remarkable for television; even in its failings (and these are not to be dismissed), it promotes a notion of affinity and alliance that we, as cultural critics, might want to keep in mind. *Max Headroom*, whose regulars ranged from career women to cyberpunks, network executives to computer hackers and video pirates, also suggested the power of cross-border alliances within its plots and, though perhaps in a less progressive way, in its own production history (moving across national, generic, and cable/network divides).

By constructing such a circuit of connections, cyborgs (and their group of playmates) have the potential to re-form our world. This possibility, though, does not arise on its own. Like everything else about cyborgs, there is no "natural" progression to their fate or their effects; there is only the opportunity—and the necessity—for struggle and redefinition. As Haraway reminds us, "[t]he main trouble with cyborgs, of course, is that they are the illegitimate offspring of militarism and patriarchal capitalism . . . ," a problem particularly relevant to Max's diegetic as well as extra-diegetic condition (part of a corporate cover-up in his world and a "weapon" of commodity warfare in our own). "But," she goes on, "illegitimate offspring are often exceedingly unfaithful to their origins. Their fathers, after all, are inessential" (68). The main trouble with *Max Headroom* and *Pee-wee's Playhouse*, however, may be that they reverse this assessment so that the opposite is true: while flirting with the threat of the uncanny, which has been linked to the maternal, if anything, these figures are shown as *purely* fathered, as postmodern-day Athenas who front a patriarchal rule.

Yet just as Max and Pee-wee dodge those thorny issues that would truly open up their texts, viewers might follow their example and likewise try to dodge even (or especially) the Fathers that they incorporate (Edison in Max's case and, in *Pee-wee's Playhouse,* the masculine, domineering side of Pee-wee's multiple persona). In other words, while *Max Headroom* and *Pee-wee's Playhouse* strive to contain the subversive force of cyborgian disruption by recentering attention on a controlling male personality, this containment is never total; in fact, many viewers find their heroes to be the least appealing aspects of the shows, taking pleasure instead in the fascinating worlds that form the backdrop of the scenes. On *Max Headroom,* for example, Edison Carter may be a typical hetero-masculine hero, the paternal leader in the text, but his characterization is so clichéd that his ability to master the diegesis is curtailed; he too became a humorous, excessive, and cyborgian creation who had to share the spotlight with his more amusing counterpart as viewer interest shifted to the contradictions which subverted his power of control. Similarly, Pee-wee may have dominated the creatures in his playhouse, but the disruption unleashed in this decentered realm extended even beyond the scope of his command. For instance, the secret word that he announced on each show (with instructions to home viewers to yell whenever they heard it) continued to provoke joy and screaming long after that episode had ended, producing a rebellion against parental authority that went beyond Pee-wee's own fixed domain.

Interestingly, it was *this* aspect of *Pee-wee's Playhouse* that, even more than its sexual/gender ambiguity, produced parental and network objections, thereby calling attention to the *real* threat of TV: the way in which television can spill over into daily "reality," putting it outside the regulation of any one authority, including the television industry itself.[65] A similar slippage occurred with *Max Headroom*: not only was Max's power to subvert media institutions narrated within the diegesis of the program, but in a case of reality reproducing television, Max's image and peculiar mode of talking took on a life of its own (often used in explicitly resistant or disruptive ways), extending his mischievous influence beyond the limits of his creators' and his sponsors' control.[66]

While *Pee-wee's Playhouse* and *Max Headroom* may then reveal only truncated versions of cyborgian simulation (a simulation that is still within the hands of the dominant powers within their, and our own, social fields), not all of their subversive force is necessarily defused. By pointing toward the issues at stake in cyborgian transformation—the ways in which those institutions that define both the media industry and the patriarchal family continue to preserve themselves in the face of cultural and technological change—they may help us formulate a politics appropriate to the postmodern age: a politics that can move as easily from television to other social/cultural formations as the cyborg can move between its own affinities and homes.

Jane Craig surrounded by images of Tom Grunick in
Broadcast News.

Murphy Brown surrounded by fellow *F.Y.I.* reporter Corky
Sherwood Forrest and "real-life" newswomen Katie Couric,
Faith Daniels, Joan Lunden, Mary Alice Williams, and Paula
Zahn at her baby shower on *Murphy Brown*.

VII

NETWORKING
INTERLACING FEMINISM, POSTMODERNISM, AND TELEVISION STUDIES

Transmissions: Textual Meanings, Sexual Receptions

Throughout this book, I have attempted to read the discourses of 1980s U.S. television against the simultaneous and intersecting discourses of television criticism, considering in particular the ways in which critics have aligned TV with a "feminine logic." At times, this charge is directly voiced in a derogatory manner, but it is even more likely to be indirectly suggested in attempts to define television's specific textuality and mode of spectator positioning (or, perhaps more accurately, its mode of unsettling any such singular position). As I've argued in the previous chapters, because television threatens both to rupture the (illusion of) stability and unity offered by the cinematic gaze—a gaze that has been largely theorized in relation to masculine subjectivity—and to envelop all of its viewers in an amorphous haze of consumer desire—one that plays on the same tropes of overpresence and "empathy" that have been associated with feminine subjectivity—TV seems to place all viewers in a position that has been culturally coded as "feminine."

Yet, as I've also attempted to demonstrate, the condemnations of television's "feminizing" force lead to a number of contradictions for cultural criticism. These contradictions in discriminating certain gendered meanings of media forms arise because it is precisely those aspects of television considered most "feminine" that have also been used to describe consumer culture in general (even in its reactions against these connotations). Postmodernity, in other words, has *itself* been seen as a discursive regime in which numerous textual fragments are appropriated and combined into a flow that lacks a stable history or context, in which cultural assumptions are reconfigured and replayed with no fixity nor confirmation, in which subjects are (dis)placed within a fluctuating field that both derives from and perpetuates hypersimulation and consumption.

The same fears of feminization that are frequently expressed within speculations about television's detrimental effects thus emerge from the very conditions of the postmodern era. If, as Andreas Huyssen has argued, a modernist aesthetic took shape only against a mass culture that was considered its feminized "other," then postmodernism, breaking down the divisions between mass and high art, has brought that feminine other

right into the heart of our culture as a whole (see Huyssen "Mass Culture"). Diffused onto a general audience (the hyperreal masses of which
Baudrillard speaks), the decentering (dis)order of mass-mediation does
not simply construct a "feminized" television viewer as much as it characterizes the way in which all postmodern subjects are figured. This juncture
of television, postmodernism, and femininity (the network of these psychic, social, and cultural formations) is therefore important to consider not
only for an understanding of televisual textuality but also, as I elaborate in
chapters 1 and 2, for an analysis of TV's impact, its critical and popular
reception. By exploring the ways in which these connections have been
taken up and played out, we can better comprehend the enormous role
that television plays in our lives and our culture and perhaps then "re-
tune" our interventions into feminist, postmodern, and media politics.

One effect of this discursive circuit, discussed in chapter 3, is the
significance of melodrama for U.S. television and for postmodernity.
Responding to a felt loss of meaning while providing its own grounds of
reference, melodrama is, in many ways, particularly appropriate to the
(often mis)perceived problems of both television and "the postmodern
condition." However, the use of a form historically associated with female
audiences does not mean that television promotes, accepts, or even explicitly recognizes either its "feminine" connotations or the value of actual
women in TV (be they producers, consumers, or objects of television's
representations). In fact, as elaborated in chapters 4 and 5, it was typical for
1980s television (as it is for much of today's programming) to recuperate
the feminine in the interests of a still male-dominated industry and
culture. In the portrayals of TV's "new man" and "new family" that I
examine, men are able to usurp the place of femininity, appropriating
whatever power might be derived from this position (the power of mimicry, excess and masquerade, reproductive abilities and familial rights, et
cetera) while managing to exclude women from even the small amount of
space to which they had been relegated in the past.

Also celebrating a male-controlled "reproduction"—in this case of both
a (quasi) sexual and technological order (the generation of subjects as well
as the dissemination of electronically simulated reproductions)—are the
programs examined in chapter 6: texts which emphasize television's
specific textuality through their celebrations of a hyperreal, hypermediated landscape populated by video cyborgs who are so connected to the
tube that they seem to merge into the space of TV itself. Calling attention
to the troubled (and troubling) gender figurations of mass-mediatized life,
these video cyborgs embody the threat of feminization associated with
both television and postmodernism even as they shield a masculine power
that continues to hold sway. Yet as I indicated at the end of that chapter,
such television creations do not merely pose a risk—they also hint at the
positive potential that is afforded by postmodern transformations. As
suggested throughout *Re-Viewing Reception,* by foregrounding questions
of gender in cultural analyses, we might better engage with the terms of
the televised and postmodern imagination so as to "broadcast" these more
hopeful possibilities.[1]

Broadcast Views

While the previous chapters have then focused on particular sites of investigation, I would like to conclude by offering a more general theoretical discussion of the possible intersections and alliances between feminism, postmodernism, and television studies. Given the self-perpetuating function of television's representations of itself, these intersections might come into sharper focus by considering less "interested"—that is, less self-enclosed—portrayals of TV: specifically, the films *Broadcast News* and *Network*.[2] Each of these films explores the personal, sexual, and professional politics behind the presentation of network news, a genre that I've only briefly discussed in my analysis of TV melodrama. This somewhat delimited emphasis on the existence of melodrama within the news, though, is fully in keeping with the concerns of these films, both of which attempt to "expose" the ways in which a "feminine" sensationalism, emotionality, and dramatic focus on the image threaten to take over the masculine domain of "hard" news reporting and programming.

Of course, one might object that filmic portrayals are hardly "disinterested"—indeed, that we should be somewhat suspicious of the cinema's endeavors to demystify TV. Part of the project of such movies about television is necessarily to chastise the media "newcomer" and assert the cinema's dominance by offering the "clarity" of film's visual and narrative form in place of what it poses as TV's own chaos and excesses. Yet it is for this reason that these films are useful for my argument, revealing the way in which sexual and textual dynamics become mutually embroiled. For film's (supposed) clarity is, to some degree, based on the cinema's reliance on a relatively strict system of gender oppositions—precisely the system that television seems to endanger. These films thus not only critique TV, but do so in explicitly gendered terms, attempting to tackle the menace that television hazards both to film's popularity and to the cinema's sexual hierarchy.

Nonetheless, in tracing out a presumed feminization of television (especially television news), *Broadcast News* and *Network* entangle themselves in conflicting ideological currents: in each case, a strange sexual reversal occurs whereby the news*man* assumes a "feminine" position (thereby gaining extreme popularity and a frightening amount of control) while the main female character, both estranged from her traditional sphere and somehow psychically "battered" by newsroom politics, strives to avoid getting pegged as "old news."[3] Consequently, these films indicate the complexity of mediatized gender politics, demonstrating (perhaps unwittingly) how a "postmodern" confounding of sexual roles, and even television's acceptance of its feminine connotations, can in fact work to challenge (rather than support) the power of women in this arena.

For example, in *Broadcast News*, the film's female protagonist, Jane Craig (played by Holly Hunter), seems to personify (at least publicly) the respected but outmoded, traditional "masculine" virtues of news production. As a woman depicted only as "fathered" (in scenes of her childhood as well as in the film's representation of her network mentors), she has mastered the precision of both language and technology, yet struggles with a personal/professional split. Tom Grunick (William Hurt), the man to whom she is reluctantly attracted, represents the encroachment of "feminine" values in the news (that is, everything that disturbs Jane about TV): an appeal to dramatized emotion, a focus on appearance, identification and empathy made visible, pleasure in the image, and, as the male character competing with him for both Jane's affection and job recognition complains, "flash over substance."[4] Yet in his childhood scenes, Tom too is portrayed as purely fathered, ultimately in control of the images that capture ratings and, particularly, the admiration of female viewers. Indeed, Jane herself becomes one such viewer, won over by Tom's 'sensitivity' and 'realness' as she watches his eyes tear up in a televised interview with a date rape survivor—a moment she is later devastated to learn Tom has artificially produced for emotional impact.

The problems that arise in mapping the constructions of gender at stake in U.S. television are most clearly revealed in two scenes in which these characters express their desires for one another and for personal and professional success. After collaborating on a special report in which Jane feeds Tom information through his earpiece that he then relates to the public, Tom exclaims, "What a feeling having you inside my head!" Jane replies, "Yeah, it was an unusual place to be." Later, on their first date, he pursues the thought and states, "More and more lately I've been watching you in action, seeing all your energy, wondering what it would be like to be inside all that energy." She nervously answers, "Me too." Not only are these scenes interesting for the ways in which they conflate and confuse sexual desire and the control of discourse, but the ambiguity of Jane's response is also telling, revealing, I would argue, some of the contradictions of women's relationships to television. Does her "me too" express her desire to be in *his* position, to be really allowed inside his head by letting his discourse—a masculine assumption and control of femininity—inhabit hers?[5] Or does it indicate that she too wishes that she could be in *her* position, that a woman's voice be inside her head as well? The questions thereby raised about the conjunctions and disjunctions between "Woman" in TV and women in TV—questions revolving around television's sexual figurations and their relationship to the social positions of actual men and women—are central to an understanding of gender in a mediated world.

Alluding to similar questions, the film *Network* also suggests the ways in which TV's confusion of gender figurations need not imply any real change in the distribution of power and, in fact, may even help to maintain the social and economic arrangements that consolidate this power structure. Centering on the paths of two characters—Diana Christensen (played by Faye Dunaway), a ruthless female executive who describes herself as "masculine," and Howard Beale (Peter Finch), an aging anchorman whose emotional ravings against consumer culture have attracted a large cult following—this film satirizes commercial television's obsessive concern with ratings only by enacting its own hysterical concern with gender and sexuality in its place. For while the heroine's rise to the top might be considered a "feminist" success story, she is also portrayed as the embodiment of TV's worst traits. In fact, at one point, Diana's disgusted lover, Max Schumacher (William Holden), a decent guy who resists the encroachment of TV into our lives, claims that she is "television incarnate." Fed up with the way in which, on the one hand, Diana takes a 'feminine' sensibility to excess in her demand for melodramatic fare even as, on the other, she exhibits an overly 'hard' and 'masculine' business sense, Max walks out on her at the end of the film, leaving Diana friendless and alone.

Furthermore, although the film represents consumer capitalism as an endlessly reversible (and therefore inescapable) order, it nonetheless implies the woman's special culpability for this as well. Diana enthusiastically promotes the anchorman when he rants against the system (garnering a huge audience for the retooled info-tainment "news" show she designs), but when this "prophet of the airwaves" is finally won over by the logic of multinational capital that he had initially attacked, the ensuing loss of ratings incites the "heroine" to arrange and then televise Howard's tremendously rated assassination, proving the invincibility of a consumer logic even against one who tries to intervene in its effects. Thus, though this anchor-spokesman and his followers may be so angered by the dismal state of such affairs that they unanimously vow that they're "not going to take it anymore," the viewers of the film may not be so sure about where to direct their own anger or dismay. Who is the culprit here? The heroine who, trading in on emotionalism, rises to the top only to forget her own "feminine" emotions? The TV network that exchanges sensationalism for ratings? The passive masses who allow these (femme) fatalities to occur? Or is it the complex intersection of all of these things?

Discursive Machines: Generating Dialogues between Feminism, Postmodernism, and Television Studies

Indicating the diversity of forces operative in this film, the title, *Network*, plays an important, yet ambiguous role, and within the fields of cultural and feminist theory, the term has a similarly ambiguous position. At a basic level, *network* refers to a powerful economic and technical alliance within the broadcasting industry, though the term has also emerged in descriptions of new media possibilities as well (that is, the internet and TV/computer interactivity).[6] Additionally, the word *networking* has attained a certain popular usage in feminist circles to describe a strategy for increasing women's power—one which has often come under attack for its practical emphasis on personal gain (on inserting women into, rather than challenging, the status quo). In other words, like the maneuvering of *Network*'s heroine, this strategy can be critiqued as a "postfeminist," rather than feminist, solution. Finally, as this prefix *post* also intimates, the term *network* has appeared in cultural studies in descriptions of postmodern culture, many of which claim that postmodernity's erasure of historical depth has resulted in the dispersal of positions across the intersecting lines of communication, consumption, simulation, and pacification.

This terminological "switch point" between the discourses of television, feminism, and postmodernism signals the existence of a complex interrelationship among these cultural formations—an interrelationship which has undergirded my project in this book. As I've tried to demonstrate, questions of consumer and gender dynamics, textual excesses and containments, media multiplicities and unifications—and the implications of all of these things for a possible space of female enunciation (or enunciation from any delimited space)—are crucial to pose in today's TV-saturated world, even if these issues are not explicitly named as "postmodern." In fact, there is something to be said for not reducing such questions to a form which would comfortably fit under the label "postmodern theory." As Dana Polan argues, the concept of "the postmodern" functions almost as a machine for generating discourse, and "one necessarily wonders if this machine doesn't . . . limit the range of possible outcomes through such mechanisms as negative feedback and the binding of output to input that . . . characterizes [sic] the very performativity of machines" (49). For example, our by-now-established familiarity with the stylistic markers associated with postmodernism (pastiche, repetition, the curious conflation of various modes of address) seems to predefine and so contain what might be said about any phenomenon labelled "postmodern": one merely demonstrates (as if armed with a checklist) how these elements appear in the text at hand.

In analyzing tele-textual and tele-sexual differences, it is particularly important to avoid simply feeding terms through the postmodern machine. Rather than treating mediatized genders or genres merely as further instances of the postmodern condition, we need to understand how they provide an important ground of this condition as well as much of the language through which postmodern debates are articulated. In other words (to shift from the metaphor of industrialization to the related one of militarism, or to return to my comments in Chapter 1, from one mode of "occupation" to another), it is essential to see how television and gender are battlefields of postmodernism rather than simply isolated casualties of a war whose meaning and determinants critics tend to locate elsewhere.[7] Contested territories, crucial sites of struggle, these formations are "hot spots" of postmodernity. Indeed, television, one of our culture's major modes of communication (*the* major mode according to both its own and numerous critics' proclamations), is not so much one case of postmodern simulation as it is a prime representative of total consumer and technological infiltration. While Fredric Jameson points to architecture as the form most revealing of the postmodern condition ("Postmodernism" 54, 56)— not unrelated to his claim that it is the art most closely tied to the economic—U.S. commercial television is at least as closely bound to consumer capitalism as architecture is, and its multiple, segmented, and disrupted form has been seen by many critics as implicitly postmodern.[8] Involving a heterogeneous yet constant offering of several narrative and discursive forms, it deters the construction of a unified diegesis or position of spectatorship. Moreso, rather than being a window on the world, the reality that TV reflects seems more and more to be that of the world of TV itself, apparently portending the kind of fully enclosed hyperreality that many postmodern critics seem to fear most.[9]

It is for this reason that Baudrillard has called TV "the ultimate and perfect object for this new era"—an object which seems to make "our own body and the whole surrounding universe become a control screen" ("Ecstasy" 127). Not surprisingly, as television becomes the new postmodern body—an object of seduction requiring its own set of defenses—it also seems to become the primary "feminine" form of our time, assuming the woman's stereotypical position of alluring but perilous threat. Yet if the modernist figuration of mass culture as feminine threat continues to hold sway in some modified form (that is, in discussions of television's "inferiority" to film or to literature), it now does so in a world which is thoroughly imbued with the signs, codes, and images of the mass media, involving all of us in the "otherness" of this denigrated realm. In other words, as the "great divide" between mass and high art collapses, the threat of a feminized world hovers over all subjects, prompting the dismay of those who see this culture's fluctuating yet enveloping closeness as precluding the possibility of any fixed subjectivity—as denying the stability (or even the fiction thereof) of the masculine position. As a result, many critics feel the need to *divorce* themselves from the engulfing ooze of the postmodern masses—either, as Jameson does, by calling for the return to older modes of aesthetic production, or, as in Baudrillard's elitist tactic, by refusing to recognize themselves within the "black hole" that they otherwise so vividly describe (*In the Shadow* 4).

Such formulations involve situating postmodernism itself in the place traditionally aligned with femininity; just as the woman is figured as chaotic maternal body or menacing sexual other, postmodernism is the formless matrix from which the adventuring analyst must separate (employing, as Polan suggests, the figure of the cultural theorist as hero [50–51], a mirror of TV's own conquering heroes), or it is the seductive but dangerous object which must be investigated in order to put it finally to rest.[10] The differences that *do* exist within the media are then ignored as the specific textualities of television and of mediatized postmodernism as a whole become spaces to differentiate *from* rather than spheres to be engaged *with* in their own heterogeneity. Given this construction of the debates, it is clear that the shifting terms of gender are not simply additional cases of postmodern fragmentation; rather, the discourse of sexual difference is intrinsic to the very ways in which this debate has been posed as well as offering a significant stake.[11] Yet these connections have largely been ignored within a critical framework that tends to pose the problem of the postmodern in binary terms—as a question of either pro or con or before and after. Insisting on a polarized logic, this framework necessarily limits the analyses that may be offered and neglects the insights of feminist critique.

Postmodern Positions

Following these binarisms, two opposing positions have developed involving either the separation noted above or a contrasting immersion within the "feminine" realm, neither of which really questions such figurations. On the one hand, there are those who condemn the post-modern for leveling all distinctions and so effecting a totalized commoditization. According to this dystopian model, by imploding the oppositions of high and mass art, past and present, outside and inside, and, one might add, masculine and feminine, postmodern culture disallows the possibilities of analytical distance, historical consciousness, and political resistance.[12] As a medium which combines multiple narratives within an omnipresent flow, television might consequently be seen as a form which neutralizes any position which might be established: before the viewer has time to consider the meaning of any one segment, before in fact, he or she has time to even assume a meaningful position, another position is offered in turn, disrupting the possibility of critical reflection. The role of consumer may then be the only reliable option: among the open-ended and decentered texts of TV, the commercials alone provide stability and resolution; among the multitude of messages, consumption is the single certain value.[13]

The contrasting utopian model, on the other hand, claims postmodernism's self-reflexive strategies as radical transgressions which allow for a liberating play of differences. According to this theory, television's multiplicity may construct an open or, in John Fiske's words, a "producerly" text—the viewer is allowed to wander freely through the collage, producing whatever meanings best accord with the cultural competencies brought to bear upon them.[14] Taking a related position but focusing more on TV's fluid deployment of affect than on its effects of meaning, Lawrence Grossberg writes of an "emerging contradiction between affect and ideology" evidenced in postmodern culture, and particularly, in television's strategies of excess—a contradiction which leaves a gap between our norms and our feelings so that "it is as if one were to experience and in certain ways live values without actually investing in them" (44). Rather than bemoaning what other critics might see as television's "waning of affect," Grossberg affirms what he sees as its freedom, producing an account which, while different from the usual condemnations of TV, nonetheless offers problems for a feminist analysis of representation, subjectivity, and media culture.[15]

According to Grossberg's analysis (indebted to the work of Gilles Deleuze and Félix Guattari[16]), television offers a strategic response to the rupture he finds between values and emotion "by placing the nomadic subject [the viewer who roams through the assemblage of texts and the shifting positions that they offer] within an affective democracy which is . . . constitutive of almost all of the televisual apparatuses" (44). Free to construct a series of identifications and to 'spend' their emotions however they choose, viewers are less disempowered by television's multiplicity than enabled to do just what they please; having no particular grounding, affect also has no limitation and therefore allows for a kind of liberation despite its mediated base. Or to put it again in Grossberg's words, since "every image is equally open to affective investment because everything is a media event, a style, a pose," ultimately, in his view, the very power of affect and ideology are negated: "TV re-establishes a site of and source for affective living within its democratic economy . . . an empowering one for many of its viewers precisely because *it is not ideological*" (44–45, emphasis added). Here, Grossberg takes many of the familiar pessimistic assessments of postmodernism and stands them on their head.

As evidenced by such contrasting appraisals—that is, the dystopian view of a world that offers consumption and little else versus the utopian view of a culture that affords unlimited investments (precisely because none is required)—evaluations of television have polarized around the question of postmodernism and ideology, claiming that we are either in a realm of complete pacification due to an endless dispersal of meanings or in an affective and semiotic "democracy" in which this very dispersal negates the power of ideology itself. Both arguments, however, tend to suffer from a reductive totalization which precludes recognition of the differences *within* mass-mediated culture and the ways in which they have repercussions for, and are mapped onto, the terms of sexual difference. While text and audience critics alike have noted the ways in which the pessimistic dismissal can collapse all forms of textual and economic production onto a single homogeneous essence, even the optimistic celebration of absolute difference may become a discourse of "indifference"—one which fails to recognize distinctions between various cultural forms, all of which operate within distinct contexts and, thus, hardly offer equivalent possibilities.

As mentioned above, such totalizing tendencies result in part from the perception of a historical duality: critics tend to speak of the disjuncture between a previously ordered world in which subjects were centered within coherent structures, and a postmodern, mass-mediated culture in which representation lacks reference, history is dispersed in a constellation of mere allusions, and subjectivity is split across a number of conflicting constructions. Not only does this deny the fact that representation was never unmediated nor subjectivity ever so unified, but it also tends to map this distinction onto a temporal model that suspiciously resembles the before and after pictures so common in television advertising.[17] While there certainly have been cultural disruptions, the continuities against which these "breaks" take place must also be explored so as to avoid both an apocalyptic tone which offers no possibility of resistance or a triumphant one which fails to see how not all disruptions are equally beneficial—or as a feminist analysis might show, how they do not equally benefit all members of society.

Rather than maintaining an opposition between the utopian and dystopian models, the empowering potential of postmodernism should be considered together with its consumer implications; focusing on the multiple components of particular textual and contextual "networks"—on the interwoven relations that exist within specific instances—allows us to avoid the kind of totalizations that simply reproduce (sexually coded) binaristic thought. In "re-viewing" television, this means attending to the ways in which TV's displacement of previously dominant forms (such as the institutionalized classical realism of the cinema which stood as modernism's other) still maintains a complex relationship to social demands. Though postmodern culture, with television as one of its most influential formations, may disrupt the grand narratives that worked to center us as subjects within ideology (disrupting the coherent emotional investment associated with classical realism as well), the dispersal of the narrative function does not necessarily mean that we are no longer so positioned or that the affective economy offered by television is a purely liberatory or "democratic" one.[18] Rather, this dispersal may itself be seen as ideological, cut to the demands of the hierarchies that define a "post-industrial" society. While, as Polan and Bill Nichols also point out, a centered subjectivity may have been crucial to the interpellation of productive workers, our consumer and reproductive economy seems instead to demand decentered subjects—masses situated within a broad, diffuse network that disallows discursive mastery as it disenfranchises its viewer-consumers.[19]

Analyzing, for instance, how television soap opera constructs a multiple and distracted form of identification, Tania Modleski persuasively argues that this creates pleasure in a state crucial to women's work within the home; in the terminology of my opening chapter, it offers a "pre-occupation" that is fine-tuned for particular "[non]occupations" (that is, occupations not quite granted "career" status). Yet the conditions of such home labor are no longer confined to the housewife. They have become a central facet of the postmodern economy, not only for the many workers who actually do piecework at home, but for the un- or multiply employed as well. Commenting on the decentering experience of watching TV, Modleski refers to Walter Benjamin's notion of "the art of being off center" which "flourished . . . with unemployment."[20] Within today's society, the art of being off center and the pleasure of a fragmented life that had been especially crucial for women and the unemployed have become equally crucial for more and more people as power divisions sharpen rather than dissipate and as we are all caught up in the endless consumption of multiple images (a condition which requires the dispersal of affect in order to function).

The way in which the particular "postmodern" textuality of television thus arises in conjunction with specific social practices must then be analyzed so as not to lose sight of the very differences that the utopian theorists strive to free; particularly important to consider here are practices of home viewing and consumerism, as well as the discourses of gender and generation which structure these within a domestic and familial realm. Furthermore, the trajectories of identification and desire that position us within this realm must also be addressed, despite the fact that some critics declare the end of the unconscious along with the end of reference and the centered subject. While Baudrillard, for example, may reject the applicability of psychoanalytic theory to our historical situation because, in his view, the unconscious too is hyperreal (a realm of simulated, rather than actual, desires),[21] to argue that unconscious figurations need be taken into account only when they are based upon 'reality' or when they haven't been 'contaminated' by historical formations seems to rely upon an odd notion of the unconscious: one which treats it as an insulated zone comprising particular, set contents rather than a site for constituting difference.[22] Like the dismissal of Marxist analysis, this rejection of psychoanalysis allows critics to further ignore processes of differentiation—in this case, those associated with sexuality and gender.[23] Denying the sexual dynamics of unconscious fantasy, we will simply produce another phantasmatic scene—a fantasy of nondifferentiation that is able to appear only because relations of difference, even if masked, are nonetheless maintained.

Forming New Networks

A number of critics have argued that the indifference of postmodernism operates on the basis of necessary divisions and exclusions, particularly those of class; Fred Pfeil, for example, has analyzed the way in which what is often considered a general 'postmodern sensibility' is actually determined by the cultural emergence of a specific socio-economic formation, the professional-managerial class.[24] But the way in which it is also based on divisions of gender (on one's "occupation" within a sexual economy as well as within the economy "proper") has yet to be fully explored. In the discourse of postmodernism, the position of the feminine is either rejected or it becomes available to all theorists as an effect of absolute heterogeneity, a position "in-difference" which allows us to evade the disparities that do in fact exist for men and women.[25] Whether a condemnation or a celebration, postmodern theory may then ignore the particular differences that feminism is committed to interrogate as it focuses on the ways in which, despite "postfeminist" claims to the contrary, gender continues to be structured according to repressive binarisms while, in turn, structuring postmodern formulations.

Perhaps it is for this reason that, as Meaghan Morris notes, feminist theory is treated as a separate and limited field, a women's sphere, within contemporary criticism (*Pirate's* 14–15). Commenting on how postmodern theorists tend to neglect feminist work or regret its absence (and so presume that it is, indeed, absent), Morris insists that we recognize the many ways in which women *have* been engaged in this critical arena. Making a similar point, Barbara Creed objects to the fact that even critics sympathetic to its goals "attempt to 'introduce' feminism into the postmodern debate . . . on terms which situate [it] as if it were a 'guest,' the other brought in from the cold to join the 'host'" (Creed 66). In such a scenario, gender almost takes the place of a visitor invited to a reception (a postmodern media party); the way in which "reception" itself has been coded through gendered tropes is thus blocked from sight. That is, by situating feminism *for* postmodernism (or vice versa) rather than seeing the two as already intertwined, their complex connections cannot be analyzed; instead, postmodernism is either given as the answer to the question "What do women want?" (in accounts that consider its disjunctions as the solution to feminist demands[26]) or else it is posed as an issue outside our concerns. In either case, women involved in cultural theory are rendered silent.

Yet if women's voices are to be heard, the difficulties of postmodern theory for feminism also need to be addressed. Though dismantling oppositions may accord with certain feminist goals, the strategic need to speak in the name of women is rendered problematic by a discourse which claims that all such categories have disappeared, producing precisely the slide from "postmodernism" to "postfeminism." Our attempts to critique the media from the standpoint of gender thus become easily dismissed. As an example, in a discussion of music videos that disrupt conventional Oedipal patterns while still enacting a frightening gendered violence, E. Ann Kaplan observes that these self-conscious disruptions may disarm potentially critical female viewers, making them feel as if they are taking the sexual sadism they see too seriously, as if textual experimentation somehow overrules sexual stereotypes ("Feminism" 37). In such cases, faced with both the ruptures of "postmodern" televisual texts and the continuity of the oppressive contexts in which these ruptures take place, the feminist critic is put into the by-now-clichéd positions associated with female complaints: we are either feminists without humor—women who take these things too seriously—or we are hysterical nags—women who fail to curb our complaints even in the face of cultural change.

Of course, there is a certain symmetry to placing feminist television critics within these positions: we become reflecting screens of what we critique, not only mirroring the complaining women so common on TV sitcoms, let alone on Oprah and Phil, but producing, just as television does, a limitless stream of discourse with no guarantees of reception at all.[27] This, in fact, is much like the image that *Broadcast News* offers of women in television. Earlier, I described Jane Craig's behavior as a performance of "masculine" news ethics, but this performance functions largely as a mask: the almost hysterical heroine talks so fast that no one can keep up with her, and she spends several minutes every day in timed crying jags— outlets for those emotions that she must otherwise bury in order to make it in the world of TV. A "feminine" discourse may be impossible in this representation—men appropriate the terms of emotionality in order to further their own power, while women's thoughts and feelings are simply not received—yet such cinematic portrayals are necessarily enmeshed in the hierarchies of evaluation that I interrogate throughout this study.

Television, commenting on its own figurations in moments of "self-receptivity," may offer a more useful depiction for feminist critics. I refer to the example with which I began this book: that of *Star Trek: The Next Generation*'s professional empath, Deanna Troi. I certainly wouldn't want to valorize *ST-TNG* or Troi herself by proclaiming this show and character as the solutions to the problems I've discussed; *ST-TNG*'s expansionist mission into outer—as well as televisual—space, along with Troi's often postfeminist position within this model of heroism, make any such uncritical celebration suspect. Yet used strategically, this representation might unsettle the utopian/dystopian opposition previously critiqued. Specifically, the way in which Troi not only receives impressions from the vast networks around her (complaints and all), but also manages to turn this into a worthy occupation may offer an interesting image for women in the occupation of television studies.

Unlike Jane Craig, Deanna Troi need not enforce a personal and a professional split; her world of emotions is part of her field of command. But even more important for my purposes here, she transforms the work of reception, articulating particular possibilities out of the flow of sensations around her. These "enterprises" often insert a dose of (not necessarily intentional) women's humor into *Star Trek: The Next Generation* plots; but they also suggest that receptivity itself can "lift off" and become mobile, that its constellation of feminine connotations can be played with rather than dismissed. Perhaps in our television "preoccupations," we too can reach out to systems not yet fully explored—even, or especially, systems that are right here at "home." In this way, women in television (producers, consumers, critics, other types of "re-viewers") might construct our own discursive interconnections, networks with which to receive impressions, ideas, and further thoughts on the politics and pleasures of postmodern life.

NOTES

1. Universal Reception

1. Many of the papers presented at this conference were later published in Mellencamp, *Logics of Television*.

2. For analyses of *Star Trek*'s and *Star Trek: The Next Generation*'s female fan community, see Jenkins, "*Star Trek*" and *Textual Poachers*; Lamb and Veith; and Penley, "Brownian Motion" and "Feminism."

3. *ST-TNG*'s other original female officers are, of course, also of interest, even though they are less central to my immediate concern with the figuration of feminine receptivity. Perhaps not unrelated to the way in which the figure of Deanna Troi uniquely mediates the tensions between feminism and postfeminism, gender and television (as I argue in the text), these characters also proved to have less consistent staying power than Troi. Dr. Beverly Crusher was introduced as a potential love interest for Captain Jean-Luc Picard but was dropped after the first season to be replaced by the irritable Dr. Kate Pulaski before returning again in the third season. Even more instructive was the fate of Lieutenant Tasha Yar: as head of security, she seemed to promise a powerful place for women on the show, but she was killed by an alien in the spring of 1988. Reduced to only a holographic statuette kept in a drawer, her duties as chief security officer were taken over by Lieutenant Worf, the rampantly masculine Klingon warrior. For a more detailed discussion of these aspects of gender in *ST-TNG*, see Wilcox.

4. Indeed, it has: see Hastie. The actress who plays Deanna Troi, Marina Sirtis, also speaks quite insightfully in public appearances about Troi's wardrobe changes and their significance.

5. This promotion of continuous consumerism (in which clothes, like other commodities, have a kind of built-in obsolescence which prevents one from ever being done building up one's wardrobe) is particularly true of women's fashion: not only are women identified with the body, but the female body is identified as never quite good enough, always in need of further adjustment and improvement. The constant adjustment of Troi's wardrobe plays into this construction of femininity as both consumerism and commodity. Furthermore, in addition to this relationship to fashion, Deanna Troi is marked as a stereotypical female consumer in other ways as well, most notably by her love of chocolate and desserts—another sign of frivolous consumption associated not only with women but with the genre toward which (as I argue later in the paper) *ST-TNG* is itself evolving (the clichéd image of the woman watching soap operas while eating bonbons).

6. This description of Troi as "the ultimate helping professional" comes from Kottak.

7. Indeed, the series was on the air for some time before viewers ever actually saw Troi in her office. However, since Troi is physically and/or psychologically "occupied" by receptivity (it is an essential, in this case "racial," trait), she continually enacts her empathetic role. The fact that Troi does embody a form of work (whether confined to an office or not) might seem to suggest, however, that she isn't the model of idealized femininity that I describe her as being. For example, one of the running issues in the series is the conflict between Troi and her mother over Troi's single status: her prioritization of career over marriage, Starfleet duties over wifely and parental responsibilities. Yet I would argue that this confirms, rather than undercuts, my argument: representing precisely the professionalization of femininity (the way in which it may become work), Troi conflates

womanhood and a career, thus providing an image that seems perfectly cut to the demands of our "postfeminist" society.

8. For specific analyses of the media in relation to the "postfeminist" phenomenon, see (among others) Modleski, *Feminism*; Press; and Probyn.

9. As I note later in this chapter, this might be seen as not simply TV "self-reflexivity" (the textual inscription of the medium) but TV "self-receptivity" (the textual inscription of notions of the audience). Whether they are contemplative or distracted, one might then argue that viewers are in fact "pre-occupied," invited to occupy a position marked by gender that is already acknowledged by the apparatus itself. I am grateful to Jim Castonguay for these thoughts.

10. This mention of the "logics of television" obviously refers to the evocatively titled collection in which Heath's essay appears. Because I attempt to read this cultural logic in relation to that of cultural criticism, my project might be seen as a metacritical one, an analysis of a historically constituted domain of "knowledge" (one that draws from both the "popular" and "academic" spheres). As such, it clearly owes much to Foucauldian analysis and to larger trends within "poststructural historical" methods (trends which themselves owe much to Foucault). For discussions of this type of approach, see the very interesting interviews and essays in, for example, Foucault, *Foucault Live; Language*; and *Power/Knowledge*. For comments on the way in which a poststructural historicism has influenced feminist thought, see Melosh, especially 3–5.

11. Analyzing the gender norms inscribed in 1960s "fantastic" sitcoms (programs which, like *Star Trek*, were influenced by science fiction), Lynn Spigel discusses a similar process of both solidification and "making strange" in "From Domestic Space."

12. The "maternal" and/or feminine presence that I locate in *ST-TNG* then in no way marks the show as somehow matriarchal. Indeed, as I note in the text, a remarkably high number of the episodes deal in one way or another with paternal issues, exploring not only actual father/son relationships, but the paternal potential of every male officer on the ship (including the android, Data). I discuss both television's fascination with fatherhood and the defensive strategy of "hyper-masculine masquerade" by which television may deny its "maternal" and/or "feminine" connotations in more detail in upcoming chapters.

13. Bennett and Woollacott discuss "occupational ideologies"—the professional decisions, institutional norms, and conscious and unconscious views held by media executives and workers that contribute to the shape and visibility of the ideology of a text—in their study of James Bond (which in fact appeared the same year as Heath made his remarks on the "occupation" of viewing and *ST-TNG* offered its own image of the occupation of reception). Suggesting the "occupational ideology" behind *Star Trek*, Stephen Whitfield and Gene Roddenberry explain that the network's and test audience's lack of acceptance of a woman in a command role contained a "valuable principle." They state, "Although *Star Trek* was a show about the 23rd century, it was being viewed by a 20th century audience—who resented the idea of a tough, strong-willed woman ('too domineering') as second-in-command" (128). It is interesting to consider the legacy of this "valuable principle" in *Star Trek: The Next Generation*, particularly in the cases of the characters Tasha Yar, the security chief (played by Denise Crosby) who was killed off after her character deteriorated in narrative importance, and Deanna Troi, actress Majel Barrett's diegetic daughter in *ST-TNG*. While I discuss the characterization of Deanna Troi in more detail, see Wilcox for further discussion of both Denise Crosby's and Majel Barrett's roles.

14. Barrett's role as the voice of the *Enterprise* computer also suggests the way in which technology might itself carry gendered connotations. For a variety of perspectives on this subject (some specifically related to television, others addressing other media/technological forms), see Karen E. Altman; de Lauretis, *Technologies of Gender*; Ann Gray; and the essays in Penley and Ross.

15. The "familiarity" of Guinan's service position refers, of course, to racial stereotypes and to the material conditions under which African Americans have worked in this country. In relation to gender, however, this specific service job is a bit less familiar: one might argue that as a female bartender, Guinan appropriates masculine space (the barroom and, particularly, the space behind the bar). Like Troi, her "occupation"—in both senses of the word—thus involves (and must mediate) a number of contradictions concerning sexual, racial, and class differences.

16. I discuss this in much more detail throughout the book, but for key analyses of the historical association between women and mass culture, see Huyssen; and Modleski, "Femininity."

17. I am indebted to Jim Castonguay for this formulation.

18. In fact, according to the series, television "died out" by the year 2040. Interestingly, this information was provided in an episode hurriedly put together during the Writers Guild strike ("The Neutral Zone," which aired during the week of May 16, 1988), and thus its prediction of the death of TV may be something of a revenge fantasy!

19. Wilcox makes a similar point in her discussion of *ST-TNG*'s creation of "synthetic women."

20. This episode first aired on April 30, 1990, and it starred Dwight Schultze as Reginald Barclay.

21. While Barclay suffers from a kind of media addiction, he does not exhibit any such dependencies around drugs or alcohol. Indeed, Barclay's favorite drink to order in the Ten-Forward bar is warm milk—another "feminizing" detail that links him to representations of *Star Trek* fans themselves (who are similarly figured as emasculated).

22. Confirming this analysis of "Hollow Pursuits" as a self-reflexive text, Sarah Higley, who (under the name "Sally Caves") wrote the episode, describes its main character thus: "Barclay is a *Star Trek* fan, making these wonderful *Star Trek* characters in the Holodeck say and do whatever he wants them to do" (quoted in Robert Rowe 20–21). *ST-TNG* producers, however, deny that "Hollow Pursuits" was making a comment on *Star Trek*'s own "obsessive" fans (Nemecek 125).

23. For discussions of the (changing) organization of television institutions and technologies, see, among others, Ang, *Desperately*; Barnouw; Hughes; Mattelart et al.; Morley, *Television*; Schiller, *Culture Inc* and *Who Knows?*; Schwock; and Whetmore.

24. By using the term "pre-occupied," I'm not trying to imply that television viewers are necessarily distracted rather than contemplative viewers—as I note in the text, it is impossible to generalize about television viewing, precisely the reason why critics describe TV as they do (as an amorphous black hole, an emblem of postmodernism, et cetera). Furthermore, as Meaghan Morris points out, the contemplation/distraction dualism is itself implicated in the gendered figurations of television and television viewing. Rather, through this pun I am attempting to move away from this dualism and toward an analysis of how TV's occupation is already in place, managing and assuring us of the appropriateness of our viewing regardless of how we actually watch. This is, indeed, the point of my discussion of *Star Trek: The Next Generation*'s representation of its "universal receiver." See Morris, "Banality," for her critique of the "distraction" model of cultural studies, 23–24.

25. Discussions of the approaches developed at the Centre for Contemporary Cultural Studies can be found in, among others, Hall, "Encoding/Decoding"; Hebdige, *Subculture*; and Morley, *Television*. Michel de Certeau provides the basis for many analyses of popular appropriation and "the everyday." Ethnographic studies of fan communities include those by Jenkins, *Textual Poachers*; Radway; and Seiter, Borchers, Kreutzner, and Warth. Communications and social science research which draws on and/or has been useful for the development of cultural

studies models includes Lull, "Family" and "A Rules"; and Press. Very useful summaries of the contributions and the limitations of such models can be found in Mayne, *Cinema*; and Morley, "Changing."

26. Scholarship produced within the field of cultural studies is too voluminous for me fully to list or characterize here. For a good overview of this work, however, see Fiske, "British." For a sample of the type of cultural studies argument that I describe here, see Fiske, "Moments."

27. The encoding/decoding model of cultural studies might also be refined in light of the fact that television now already "encodes" its own sense of viewer "decodings" within "the text itself" (a phrase that does not at all do justice to the permeable and expansive boundaries of the television text). In other words, because television is self-conscious about addressing viewers, discussions of television textuality are as crucial as discussions of television viewing (and vice versa). The formative work on the encoding/decoding model is Hall, "Encoding/Decoding." For an analysis of a specific television program that makes use of this method, see Brunsdon and Morley, and Morley, *"Nationwide."* Providing useful commentary on this model is Wren-Lewis, "Encoding-Decoding," and Morley's essays in *Television,* some of which look back on his earlier research on the *Nationwide* audience.

28. For an extremely useful review of the issues facing audience studies and, in particular, an illuminating discussion of this dispute over what constitutes the text, see Morley, "Changing Paradigms," especially the section in which he cites Jane Feuer's lucid critique of reception studies (23–24).

29. Similar critiques of cultural studies have been suggested by a number of critics. For one particularly interesting discussion of these issues, see Morris, "Banality." For a number of interesting comments that relate the debates between viewer and text-centered approaches to the particular concerns of feminist film and television studies, see the essays in *Camera Obscura*'s special issue on "The Spectatrix," particularly the introduction by Janet Bergstrom and Mary Ann Doane (5–27) and the selection by Patricia Mellencamp (235).

30. For discussions of this attention, see, for example, Allen, *Speaking,* and Hobson, "*Crossroads.*"

31. See McRobbie, *Feminism* and "Settling"; and Long.

32. For a discussion of the way in which the streamlined American commodities have been seen as leading to a "'feminization' of the authentic muscle and masculinity of the British industrial working class," see Morley, "Changing" 33.

33. For a provocative discussion of some of the problems plaguing studies of female audiences from a different perspective than the one offered here, see Ang and Hermes. Their critique of the assumptions behind (unwittingly) objectifying and essentializing accounts of female viewers is very interesting, yet I would argue that their proposed solution—discontinuing the research emphasis on women's experience, culture, and media consumption for a perspective more attuned to the dynamic, unstable, and even potentially neutral ways in which gender is articulated in concrete practices—partakes of the very logic that I am trying to critique: it figures television reception according to the same tropes of multiplicity and fluidity that have been coded as feminine even as it denies the power structures operative in such gendered imagery. In other words, it seems to me to be symptomatic of the stresses and contradictions facing recent television and television studies (the tension between the modern and postmodern, feminism and postfeminism). Rather than simply explaining the political binds of feminist (or perhaps more accurately, postfeminist) criticism, it thus may also unwittingly participate in the creation of these binds.

34. Mellencamp makes a similar point in her introduction to *Logics of Television,* a collection of essays written by a group of critics with quite different relationships to a number of television traditions (6–7). For an article that places the discussion

of the intellectual's relationship to the "ordinary" television viewer in the context of postmodernism, see Collins, "Watching."

35. The question of "experience" is a very complicated one in both feminist and media studies. While the debates are too numerous and complex to summarize here, for some very interesting theoretical discussions of the concept of experience, see de Lauretis, *Alice Doesn't,* and Scott for comments on the way in which the notion (and indeed experience of) the term *experience* intersects with debates about female spectators in film and TV; see also *Camera Obscura*'s special issue on "The Spectatrix" (as it is addressed, for example, by Bergstrom and Doane [10, 19] and Sandy Flitterman-Lewis [155]). This journal issue marks feminist film and television studies' attempt to reconsider and/or reinvigorate discussions of the spectator (particularly, but not merely, "the female spectator"). In exploring the ways in which the TV viewer is figured as feminine or feminized spectator and considering what this might mean not only for television and television studies but also for (all sorts of) men and women viewers, I see this book as extending that project.

36. Discussions of the soap opera include those by Robert Allen, *Speaking;* Brunsdon, "*Crossroads*"; Butler, "Notes"; Flitterman-Lewis, "All's Well"; Kuhn; Modleski, *Loving;* Nochimson; and Seiter et al., "'Don't Treat Us.'" On the prime-time serial, see, for example, Ang, *Watching Dallas;* Feuer, "Melodrama" and "Reading"; and Geraghty. On other specific programs, texts, and/or genres particularly related to women, see Bathrick; D'Acci, "The Case" and "Defining Women"; Kaplan, "Feminist"; Mayne, "*L.A. Law*"; Rabinovitz; Rapping, *The Movie;* and Taylor. See also the following collections: Baehr and Dyer; Brown, *Television;* and Spigel and Mann.

2. Good Reception?

1. It is true that some progressive scholars assume an attitude of liberal tolerance toward television (and television studies)—TV is, after all, what (some) people want. Yet this attitude is often expressed in patronizing ways, as an uncritical embracement of television based on populist sentiment rather than an informed engagement with TV texts themselves.

2. However, the division between "high" and "low" forms is reinscribed within TV itself in the divisions between daytime and prime-time programming and between shows marketed as "quality" programming versus television's regular fare.

3. There are many examples of the tendency to associate mass culture with the threat of femininity, and many of them will be examined throughout this book. For other analyses of gendered imagery in mass culture criticism, see Huyssen 44–62; Modleski, "Femininity"; and on TV specifically, Petro.

4. Other scholars have traced a history of mass culture criticism in more depth than I am able to do here. One very cogent and interesting example is Patrick Brantlinger, who discusses many of the critics and positions that I address in this chapter. However, gender as an organizing, if unspoken, principle in cultural critique (my immediate concern) is not the focus of his study; indeed, often gender remains somewhat unspoken in histories of cultural criticism.

5. That MacDonald clearly employs such a humanist discourse is evidenced by his claims that "unity is essential in art" and that art axiomatically refers to expressions of human quality, individuality, and identity (65). Interestingly, these comments are made in the context of a specific attack on radio soap opera—the "feminine" form *par excellence.*

6. As MacDonald's reference to "ooze" suggests, such complaints arise most strongly in regard to television, a medium defined by an endless "flow" that, like the flow of maternal care (according to some critics), invokes fusion, passive

surrender, and infantile longings in its viewers. The term *flow* to define the specificity of American television was first coined by Raymond Williams in *Television: Technology and Cultural Form*. Earlier media critics, however, had often noted this facet of television. Rolf B. Meyersohn states that the appeal of TV lies in "the glow and the flow" (347) and Gunther Anders writes that TV delivers events to us "like water ready to flow from the faucet" (363). Through such images of maternal presence and warm fluidity, TV is often gendered as feminine.

7. See, for example, Horkheimer and Adorno; Adorno, "Culture Industry"; Bloch et al.; Marcuse; and the essays by Lowenthal, "Historical"; and Adorno, "Television."

8. On the "reaction" of American social scientists against the cultural critique of the Frankfurt School, see Kaplan, "Introduction" and Boddy, "Loving." Social science approaches have been summarized and/or discussed in many places; some that may be useful include Robert Allen, *Speaking*; Fiske and Hartley; Morley, *"Nationwide"* and *Television*; and Real. For commentaries on the changing discipline of media studies, see the essays in Avery and Eason; Curran and Gurevitch; and the special issue of *Journal of Communication* on "Ferment in the Field."

9. Robert Allen makes a similar point in his Introduction to the first edition of *Channels of Discourse* (10–11). For good discussions of these research trends and some of their oversights, see also Lewis; and Morley, "Changing."

10. An overview of the founding scholarship on women and the media can be found in Tuchman, "Women's." Many feminist theorists have offered critiques of the method of content analysis on which this type of scholarship rests. For some of the early statements that have influenced the development of feminist cultural studies, see Cowie; Gledhill, "Developments" 18–22; Johnston; and Pollock, "What's Wrong." For more recent approaches to these questions (some of which critique the very conceptualization involved in researching "women and the media") see, for instance, Ang and Hermes; the essays in Bonner et al.; Kaplan, "Feminist"; and van Zoonen. For a summary of current media trends that suggests the continued importance of social science attention to questions of gender, see the *Media Report to Women* 4.

11. For a discussion of the way in which female audiences might also be pathologized, see Robert Allen, *Speaking*.

12. My discussion of this work is indebted to Horace Newcomb's critique of Glynn's sweeping generalizations and the way he makes television "both cause and effect, stimulus and response" (see Newcomb, *TV* 10–12).

13. For a more recent, yet remarkably similar, psychoanalytic analysis of television, see Houston.

14. A good example of the use of such models in the area of humanities and public policy is Herbert Gans's *Popular Culture and High Culture*, which Boddy critiques in "Loving."

15. There is much too much important work within cultural studies to offer any sort of a representative list here. Some of the more influential studies include Ang, *Watching Dallas*; During; Hobson, *"Crossroads"*; Morley, *Family* and *"Nationwide"*; Grossberg, Nelson, and Treichler; Radway; the essays in Baehr and Dyer; and Seiter et al. For an overview of this approach and a good bibliography, see Fiske, "British." See also Fiske's *Television Culture*.

16. See Barnouw; Boddy, *Fifties*; Gitlin, *Inside* and *The Whole World*; Spigel, *Make Room*; and Raymond Williams. See also Castleman and Podrazik; Sterling and Kittross; and the essays in O'Connor.

17. The quote from the *New York Times*—"Indispensable reading for modern feminists and, indeed, anybody else of serious attention"—appears on the book jacket along with several other applauding reviews. Not all reports, however, have been so glowing: critiquing Douglas for her thesis on "feminization" is Tania Modleski in "Femininity as Mas(s)querade."

18. Furthermore, as Modleski points out, Douglas considers all nineteenth-century women, even the writers, to be first and foremost readers, thereby effacing female production in the shadow of consumption ("Femininity" 40–41).

19. Obviously, I cannot provide an exhaustive list of recent work within television studies here. But some of the primary anthologies of theoretical work on television are Bennett, Boyd-Bowman, Mercer, and Woollacott; Drummond and Paterson; Kaplan, *Regarding Television*; MacCabe, *High Theory/Low Culture*; Mellencamp, *Logics*; Modleski, *Studies*; Newcomb, *Television* (fourth and fifth editions); Seiter et al.; and Spigel and Mann. Robert Allen offers an overview of a number of theoretical approaches to television studies, providing textual examples and bibliographies for each mode of analysis (*Channels*). Other very useful overviews include those provided by Jeremy Butler, *Television*; and Fiske, *Television Culture*.

20. I note the construction of Roddenberry as auteur within *Star Trek* fan culture in chapter 1. For a scholarly discussion of a television auteur, see David Marc on Paul Henning in *Demographic Vistas*; see also Marc's "TV Auteurism." Other auteur studies include Merritt's consideration of the question of authorship in relation to Bill Cosby and Thompson's "Stephen J. Cannell." With the greater recognition and/or opportunity for women writers and producers, some women have recently been considered as television auteurs: Linda Bloodworth-Thomason (*Designing Women, Evening Shade, Hearts Afire*), Diane English (*Murphy Brown, Love and War*), Roseanne Barr Arnold (*Roseanne*). Given the traditional association between authorship and the paternal function, it is no surprise that attempts to elevate women to the position of TV auteur have met with some resistance in many of these cases: the battles over who deserves the credit for creating *Roseanne* (one-time producer Matt Williams or the star, Roseanne, herself), the containment (in representations if not in actual practice) of Linda Bloodworth-Thomason within a heterosexual couple, et cetera. For interesting comments on these female TV auteurs, see Mellencamp, *High Anxiety* 71–72, 340–41, 345, 353, and 389–90. For a useful analysis of women and auteurism in general, see Mayne, *The Woman*.

21. Just to give a starting point for some of the many discussions on these matters, see, for example, Betterton; Butler and Scott; Gates, *Reading Black*; Miller, *Poetics*; Parker and Pollock; and Showalter.

22. Some of the influential earlier work on "images of women" in the media include Tuchman et al.; Weibel; Rosen; and Haskell. Betty Friedan's *The Feminine Mystique* was one of the first books to analyze the relationship between images of women in popular culture and women's social roles. Critiques and/or reappraisals of these methods are cited in note 10 above. Yet, as suggested in the text, while recent feminist criticism has taken up other issues than the call for "realistic images" put forth in much of this previous work, the demand for "reality" by the viewing public—signaled by the growth of "reality programming" throughout the 1980s and early 1990s—seems as strong as (if not, indeed, stronger than) ever. Arguing that feminists should reconsider the paradigm of this early work is Carroll.

23. This term (and my description of it) comes from Jean Baudrillard, *Simulations*. See also the essays in Foster; Huyssen; and Wallis. Much work on postmodernism and television has focused on music videos. See, for example, Kaplan, *Rocking*; Wollen; and the essays in *Journal of Communication Inquiry* 10.1, a special issue on music video. A sampling of other analyses of television that rely on Baudrillard's theory include Grossberg, "In-difference"; Mellencamp, "Situation"; Poster 43–68; and Sorkin. Several of the essays in Mellencamp, *Logics,* also address Baudrillard's influence on television studies. For a good discussion of postmodern theory and television studies (and suggestions for further reading), see Collins, "Television."

24. See Eco, *Travels*. For contextualizations of notions of "hyperreality" in relationship to cultural practices, see, for instance, Collins, *Uncommon*; Connor; and Kaplan, *Postmodernism*.

25. My references in this section are to Baudrillard's *Simulations*.

26. In other words, while Baudrillard's accounts of "hyperreality" have a certain descriptive force (particularly when it comes to television), I would certainly want to take issue with many of his conclusions concerning both the geneology and the implications of such phenomena. Rather than examining the validity of Baudrillard's theories, however, I am more interested in exploring the stakes and imagery within his (gendered) discourse. Many scholars have, though, offered insightful critiques of Baudrillard's position, stressing (as I would) the problems that he poses for any politically engaged criticism and pedagogy. On the potential and the limits of a Baudrillardian television criticism, see, for instance, Heath; and Morris, "Banality." For a more general discussion, see Kellner, *Jean Baudrillard*; and the essays in Rojek and Turner. For some of Baudrillard's own responses and comments, see *Baudrillard Live*.

27. For discussions and / or complications of this binary logic, see, among many others, Judith Butler, *Gender Trouble*; de Lauretis, *Technologies*; Felman; Irigaray, *This Sex* and *Speculum*; Kristeva, *Powers* and the essays in *The Kristeva Reader*; Moi; Rose; and Silverman, *Acoustic*.

28. This claim derives from "apparatus" and / or "screen theory." For an introduction to many of the founding works in this approach to cinema studies, see the essays in the collections edited by de Lauretis and Heath, and by Philip Rosen.

29. Important and interesting works in feminist film theory are too numerous to encapsulate here. For an introduction to the field, however, see the essays in the following anthologies: Diane Carson, Dittmar, and Welsch; Cook and Dodd; Doane, Williams, and Mellencamp; and *Camera Obscura*, particularly the special issue on "The Spectatrix," in which many feminist film theorists reflect on the field and which contains an excellent bibliography.

30. While I take the title of the anthology *Re-vision* for these comments on feminist film theory, reconsiderations of Mulvey's analysis go well beyond the essays in this volume alone (and well beyond what I could simply list here). For a discussion of the question of the spectator for feminist film studies, commentaries by a number of critics, and an excellent bibliography, see *Camera Obscura*'s special issue on "The Spectatrix."

31. For an excellent discussion of the way in which the televisual "apparatus" differs from that of film, addressing not cinema's "isolated, immobilised pre-Oedipal" individual reader / spectator but rather a "post-Oedipal, fully socialized family member" (102–103), see Feuer, "Narrative."

32. See, for example, Chodorow; Gilligan; Irigaray, *This Sex*; and Montrelay. Theories which associated the subversion of binary logic with "the feminine" include (among many others) Derrida, *Spurs/Eperons*; and Baudrillard, *In the Shadow*. See Jardine for an analysis of this tendency.

33. For a discussion of the way in which female viewers are figured, see Doane, *Desire*, especially 1–37. My reference to Doane's theory of masquerade comes from "Film and the Masquerade" 81–82; her reference in turn comes from Riviere, "Womanliness." See also Doane, "Masquerade."

34. While not referring solely to her very provocative theory of the gendered social subject, I take the term *space-off* from de Lauretis, *Technologies* 25–26.

35. While I attempt to demonstrate the widespread occurrence of the tendency to associate television and femininity, few people make this association explicit. One exception to that is Beverle Houston, who uses a Lacanian analysis to expressly argue that the specificity of the television text positions the TV spectator as feminine.

36. This point will be further elaborated in the next chapter on television melodrama; for discussions of the relationship between viewing and consuming in regard to literature and film, see Jeanne Allen 481–99; Bowlby, *Just Looking*; Doane, *Desire*; Friedberg; and Moore.

37. See Sandy Flitterman's analysis of the narrative structure of daytime TV's programs and ads in "The Real"; and Modleski's comment on commercials and

soaps (*Loving* 101). More generally, Raymond Williams explores the relationship between TV programs and commercials in the chapter "Programming: Distribution and Flow" in *Television*.

38. For an interesting discussion of the interpenetration of program and commercial, as well as a consideration of the intersection of dominant and subcultural readings (specifically, those supporting consumer capital and those produced by gay male audiences), see Feuer, "Reading *Dynasty*."

39. See the references to discussions of music video cited in note 23 above.

40. See Mimi White, *Tele-Advising*, for some brief but insightful comments on the generic hybridity of the infomercial (a combination of home shopping, the talk show, entertainment news, and educational programming) and the way in which it is structured like a "typical" program with advertising interruptions (for price and ordering information) despite its overall commercial function (181).

3. All That Television Allows

1. For a detailed examination of television's introduction into the American family home and the way in which this relates to such material, ideological, and spatial oppositions, see Spigel, *Make Room*.

2. For a discussion of postmodernism, nostalgia, and tradition, see Huyssen. Huyssen mentions the relationship of postmodernism to the "emergence of various forms of 'otherness'," including feminism, which are perceived as a threat to cultural tradition and so provoke nostalgic reactions on 199 and 219–220. Studies which concentrate on nostalgia in relation (and reaction) to feminism include Doane and Hodges; and Modleski, *Feminism*.

3. In referring to the image of "powerless spectatorship" in my discussion of television and the melodrama, I am not trying to suggest that spectators *are* necessarily powerless, fully at the mercy of the text. I am, indeed, attempting to discuss a particular *image* of spectatorship—one which I argue has important effects on both the representation of television and television's own representations. As I've explained in previous chapters, recent television studies have devoted considerable attention to the meaning-making processes by which viewers actively appropriate and interpret texts, but this attention to decoding should not come at the expense of a rigorous examination of generic conventions, encodings, and address. Thus, in what follows, I will concentrate on melodramatic form and its mode of address in order to explore the position of the melodrama within U.S. television and postmodern culture. Of course, audiences "work on" these texts as much as texts work on viewers, but before we can evaluate the possibilities and the limitations of their various readings, we must first understand what it is that is read (the melodramatic moments not just in the soaps but also in less expected places like the news or "reality" programs). Only then can we understand the implications of viewer subversion (which, in and of itself, need not be good or bad, at least in any politically progressive sense). What exactly is it that viewers negotiate with (or don't), and how is this negotiation itself represented and understood? It is in an attempt to answer such questions that I offer the analysis that I do here.

4. As Peter Brooks's study, *The Melodramatic Imagination*, indicates, melodrama need not always be associated with a female audience and certainly women are not the only ones to recognize its appeal. Yet, particularly in the cases of film and television melodrama, such associations are nonetheless very strong, having particular effects on viewers' and/or critics' readings and on the construction of viewing communities. The following anthologies (among others) contain essays which discuss film melodrama in relation to gender: Aspinall and Murphy; Gledhill; and Landy. For a discussion of how gender informs such viewing communities in the case of TV, see, for example, Brown, *Soap Opera*; Hobson, "Soap Operas"; and Seiter, Borchers, Kreutzner, and Warth, "'Don't Treat'."

5. Even soap operas, though, may be traced to traditions other than melodrama,

and different soap operas exhibit varying degrees of "melodramatization." For a discussion of the distinction between soap opera and melodrama and an analysis of the evolution of soaps toward melodramatic form, see Gledhill, "Speculations."

6. There are very many discussions of the narrative structure, generic specificity, and gendered, familial, and ideological bases of the soap opera. Just a sampling includes Robert Allen, *Speaking*; Jeremy G. Butler, "Notes"; Derry; Hobson, *"Cross-roads"*; the essays by Robert Allen, Brunsdon, Flitterman, and Modleski in Kaplan's *Regarding Television*; Kuhn; Lopate; Mumford, "Plotting"; Nochimson; Seiter, "The Role"; and Timberg.

7. Also noting this trend is Ellen Seiter, who looks at the rise of male protagonists in recent melodramas and argues that the genre is no longer the exclusive domain of women's popular culture. See "Men, Sex and Money." For discussions of "the male melodrama" and/or the relationship of masculinity to melodramatic conventions, see, for example, Curti; and Torres.

8. Indeed, space has been figured on television as "the final frontier," linking TV science fiction to the western and so suggesting that it might be resistant to the encroachment of the melodrama. Yet as the example of *Star Trek: The Next Generation* demonstrates, this is not the case. *Star Trek* fans themselves have noted (often with the scorn typically directed at soap opera) the shift from classic *Trek*'s construction as a space western to *ST-TNG*'s "evolution" toward a space soap: while the original series provided fairly linear plots that moved from problem to resolution, *ST-TNG*'s narrative progression is frequently upset by circularity, multiple identifications, and failed closures. The importance of family is marked not just by the inclusion of "real" families on the new *Enterprise* but by the familial connection that defines the crew itself; the exploration of character relations has become just as important as the exploration of space; and there has been a gradual progression toward continuing narrative that extends beyond the increasingly common two-parters to the general development of characters, memory, and textual history—all of which indicate that this program too has taken on more and more of the formal and thematic concerns of serialized melodrama.

9. For various discussions of comedy and its relationship to melodrama and/or gender, see, for instance, the essays in Brunovska ; and Mellencamp, *High Anxiety*. For discussions of the dramady, see Vande Berg; and White, "What's the Difference?" Also providing an important analysis of *Frank's Place* is Herman Gray.

10. Analyses of the made-for-TV movie which discuss these "trauma dramas" in terms of melodrama include Rapping, *The Looking Glass* and *The Movie of the Week*; Schulze, *"Getting Physical"* and "The Made-for-TV Movie."

11. This, of course, has implications for melodrama's construction of sexuality as well as gender. For an interesting discussion of the melodramatic TV movie and representations of homosexuality, see Leo.

12. For discussions of masculinity and the TV action or cop/detective show, see, for example, Jeremy Butler, *"Miami Vice"*; Deming; Gitlin, "'We Build Excitement'"; Fiske, "Gendered"; Flitterman, "Thighs and Whiskers"; Scott King; and Ross, "Masculinity."

13. For analyses of the news, see, among others, Brunsdon and Morley; Mitchell; Morse, "The Television"; Stam, "Television News"; and Feuer, "The Concept." These articles elaborate the melodramatic conventions used in the news, often indicating the ways in which news shows promote a sense of familial unity—a news "family," which extends to the viewer, linked together by the anchor's glances and a sense of shared space and time. On the organizational patterns that "frame" TV news, see also Gitlin, *The Whole World*; and Kervin.

14. The television coverage of each of these "events" demands much more detailed analyses than I am able to give here. Comments on the *Challenger* explosion are provided by Mary Ann Doane, "Information"; and Mellencamp, "TV Time." For critiques of the Thomas-Hill hearings, see Fiske, *Media Matters*; Smith; and Morrison's excellent collection. For discussions of television and the

Gulf War, see Jeffords and Rabinovitz; Kellner, *The Persian Gulf TV War*; Marks; and Stam, "Mobilizing." Suggesting the importance of these events for considerations of what has been referred to as "male melodrama," Penley and Willis note "the urgency of examining male subjectivity" in the light of the Thomas-Hill hearings, the Gulf War, and other such dramatized news stories as the William Kennedy Smith and Mike Tyson rape trials in the introduction to *Male Trouble* (viii).

15. As my comments indicate, it becomes exceedingly clear that any analysis of the media must investigate the shifting and ambivalent relationship between the public and the private. Of course, the concern with the complicated status of public and private within mass culture is not a new one: film has been seen as a public occasion for private fantasy while the reception of television, however private, is often considered crucial to the participation in a collective national culture. However, recent events within both media history and the history of film / television criticism itself have made the contradictions in mapping these relations even more apparent, making, in turn, an analysis of such questions even more pressing. With, on the one hand, the rise of programming strategies that extend our access to ongoing public forums (cable stations like C-Span, the continuous coverage of certain "newsworthy" events) and, on the other, the increased segmentation of television's time flow (the minute codification of the newsbreak yielding ever more momentary interruptions of the public into the private sphere), television announces its ability to cover public / private life by domesticating reality even as it calls attention to those instances that threaten to disrupt the smooth operation of the private sphere. This same ambivalence about the public and the private exists within television's fictional programming as well. For instance, TV dramas' attempts to re-present "private matters" (sexuality, disease, aging, et cetera) for the viewing public are riddled with gaps provoked by the very weight of what can't be publicly aired even within the context or expectation of private consumption. Not surprisingly, these fragile divisions of public and private are often supported by power divisions, particularly in relation to sexual difference. As television scholars, we must remember that the tension surrounding the mapping of public and private (and the way in which this is inflected by gender divisions) is not simply an issue for television itself; this tension also raises questions that must be directed toward television criticism, particularly given the recent shift away from an interest in psychoanalysis—now criticized as being too vested in the purely personal—toward a cultural studies approach considered more rooted in the social. While this move has been rightly praised for allowing television studies to recognize the political dimension to what were previously seen as purely private differences in viewing habits and interpretations, such an evaluation of critical methods may also rest on unexamined notions of the public and the private, reproducing within television criticism the same contradictions found within television texts.

16. It is also interesting to consider the ways in which television itself has commented on these events. For example, in November 1991, an episode of *Designing Women* was shot in response to the national debate surrounding the Hill-Thomas hearings. Here, a television "story" was brought right into the midst of the *Designing Women* "family" just as it was brought into our own homes; fascinatingly, the characters alternated between discussing this issue, playing out television's various interpretations, and literally "playing out" (in a dramatic production) the film melodrama *What Ever Happened to Baby Jane*? James Castonguay has discussed similar issues of television's self-representation in relationship to the Gulf War in the conference papers "Domesticating the Gulf War" and "The Masquerade of Massacre."

17. On the relationship between melodrama and periods of ideological crisis, see Elsaesser, particularly 3. This issue is also discussed in many of the essays in Gledhill; Landy; and in the useful summary that Gledhill provides in her section

on melodrama in Cook 73–84. For some discussions of postmodernism and the notion of "cultural crisis" from a number of different perspectives, see Baudrillard, *Simulations* and *In the Shadow*; Foster; Hutcheon; Huyssen; Jameson, "Postmodernism"; Lyotard; Norris; and Wallis.

18. Compare this statement on the dispersal of narrative and subjectivity in postmodernity to theories of the dispersal of identifications in television serials, as explained, for instance, by Flitterman-Lewis in her chapter "Psychoanalysis, Film, and Television" in Allen, *Channels of Discourse* 203–46.

19. For an elaboration of this argument, see 630–31 and 638–41.

20. For a similar observation on the contradictions between the optimism of the ads and the misery of prime-time soap opera diegeses, see Ang, *Watching Dallas* 78. For an analysis of the ways in which commercial narratives work together with soap opera narratives (here, in daytime TV), see Flitterman, "The *Real* Soap."

21. For similar arguments concerning the ontological confusion/conflation of media "records" and original or "real" events, see Boorstin; and Sorkin.

22. Other theorists who share Baudrillard's pessimistic assessment include Fredric Jameson, who discusses the waning of affect, evacuation of expression, death of history, and schizophrenia of subject positioning in "Postmodernism"; and Arthur Kroker and David Cook, who discuss the "ruins" of the body, science, history, and philosophy in the "excremental culture" of postmodernity in *The Postmodern Scene*.

23. See *Simulations* 23–26 for his analysis of Disneyland, and 71 for Baudrillard's claim that "all media and the official news service only exist to maintain the illusion of actuality—of the reality of the stakes, of the objectivity of the facts."

24. For an analysis of Ronald Reagan's position within political and media history (and the way in which he marks the convergence of the two), see Rogin's *Ronald Reagan, the Movie*. Pointing toward the process of melodramatic simulation discussed above, Rogin writes, "During Reagan's lifetime the locus of sacred value shifted from the church not to the state but to Hollywood. Reagan was born again to embody America through his sacrifice and rebirth on the screen. It was D. W. Griffith who made Reagan possible as a presence who feels real to himself and his audience because he is seen" (5). Interestingly, while Rogin uses film as his reference for Reagan, he still relies on television terminology ("episodes") and imagery (TV's pseudo-reality), collapsing film into television in the very title of his book.

25. On the distinction between the cinema star and the TV personality, see Ellis. See also the discussions of television character and acting in Jeremy Butler, *Television*; and Fiske, *Television Culture*.

26. The rise of consumption-oriented therapeutic discourses can also be seen in the popular growth of today's New Age movement—a movement which embraces both consumerism and the discourses of femininity that are often applied to contemporary culture.

27. White offers an alternative interpretation of the pervasive evidence of these strategies on 17.

28. Mimi White has provided a compelling account of TV's invocation of history in "Television."

29. For an excellent discussion of television narrative form that investigates (among other things) the movement of American series in the 1980s toward serialized form, see Feuer, "Narrative Form."

30. Also discussing this issue is Ang, *Watching Dallas* 75; and Modleski, *Loving* 85–109.

31. Also discussing the soap opera's curious construction of time are Jeremy Butler, who notes the contradictions between the temporal relationships internal to soap opera scenes and those that link the scenes and programs together in "Notes" 60–64; and Charles Derry, who distinguishes between the two (potentially conflicting) temporal structures of Extended Time and Landmark Time employed by the soap operas (6–7).

32. For example, on a computer newsgroup that I read, the bizarre time manipulations of daytime serials are regularly discussed (to predict revelations of maternity or paternity, for example) and/or mocked (in amusing postings on the glandular growth disorders and accelerated educational programs found in these fictional communities). For scholarly discussions of how viewing communities (not only "virtual" but "real") decode texts, see, for example, Brown, *Soap Opera*; Katz and Liebes, "Decoding Dallas" and "On the Critical"; Press; Hobson, "Soap Operas"; and Seiter, Borchers, Kreutzner, and Warth, "'Don't Treat Us'."

33. For an interesting analysis of television's self-promotion through strategies of self-referentiality (including the regulation of TV actors and personae across various programs), see White, "Crossing Wavelengths."

34. For another discussion of this example, see White, "Television."

35. An extensive list of articles and books which explore the question of melodrama and female subjectivity/spectatorship would be too numerous to provide here. However, for an introduction to these debates and a useful bibliography, see the collections edited by Aspinall and Murphy; Gledhill; and Landy.

36. Also on the disempowerment of the female spectator due to this lack of a single controlling protagonist, see Modleski, "The Search for Tomorrow," particularly 91–92.

37. For a discussion of such tropes of feminine "nearness," see Doane, *The Desire*, "Film," and "Masquerade." The way in which these tropes may irritate viewers is suggested by the quotation that provides the very title of the article by Seiter et al. on audience responses, "Don't Treat Us Like We're So Stupid and Naïve."

38. Doane's clarification of her argument can be found in her "Masquerade Reconsidered." In addition to this particular example, there are a great number of attempts to reconsider the question of female spectatorship which suggest the vast complexity of identifications, investments, and readings available for viewers who are variously situated within the social field. In my comments here, I state that many such discussions try to "realize" more powerful and pleasurable textual engagements for women. I use this term in order to suggest a double process: how feminist criticism has begun to recognize a wider range of viewers and interpretations, and how this very shift in critical focus helps to bring new readings into existence ("real-izing" them in quite a literal way). Yet I would argue that theories of "the masculine gaze" and the difficulty of feminine spectatorial pleasure (interrogations of dominant formations) do not contradict this extremely productive work on the multiplicity of possible positions for female viewers (explorations of fantasy and/or viewer negotiations, psychic and/or social relations)—instead, these theories complement one another in outlining both the limits and the possibilities offered by the cinema (and other cultural forms). For an extremely useful discussion of theories of spectatorship, see Mayne, *Cinema*. For statements from a variety of feminist theorists on these questions and an excellent bibliography, see *Camera Obscura*, no. 20–21.

39. Accounts that figure femininity in terms of a lack of a firm subject/object division and a "closeness" to the maternal body—qualities which are often positively assessed—can also be found in American feminist and psychoanalytic thought. See, for example, Chodorow; Dinnerstein; and Gilligan.

40. Peter Brooks discusses the importance of gestural and visual codes for the melodrama in terms of a crisis of meaning in which language is considered inadequate and a more "immediate" form of expression is sought (66–67). While TV melodrama similarly employs facial expression, gesture, and tableaux to crystalize meaning, there is nonetheless a complexity of dialogue, particularly in the soap opera, which is polyvalent. There is thus a certain ambivalence about language in the soap opera: it exhibits both the urge to present an essence of experience through direct expression (the summarizing close-ups held at the end of every scene) and the recognition that meaning is often veiled or ambiguous (when characters refuse to say all, say more than they intend, or mask their "true" feelings as they play with the network of meaning and its failures).

41. Thus, in her study of *Dallas,* Ang writes that "it is mainly women who are susceptible to the melodramatic imagination, a type of imagination which appears to express mainly a rather passive, fatalistic, and individualistic reaction to a vague feeling of powerlessness and unease" (82). Writing on the same program but with a more generalized sense of audience (his inclusive "we") that suggests melodrama's broad appeal in this era, Horace Newcomb states, "What we get is a sense of place, of tradition, and of true character. And we like what we hear because such qualities are in very short supply these days" ("Texas" 223).

42. For a discussion of the difference between television and film in terms of the status of "the ending," a cogent summary of the debate regarding melodrama's subversive force, and an analysis of the political significance of television melodrama, see Feuer, "Melodrama."

4. Threats from within the Gates

1. The concept of the cyborg body is derived from Haraway, "Manifesto." See also Modleski's discussion of *Videodrome* in "The Terror" 159, 163. For another reading of the film, see Shaviro 137–43.

2. I take the term "machine-subject" from Margaret Morse, who discusses the ways in which TV seems to address its viewers from a position of subjectivity ("Talk" 6).

3. The image of "invagination" comes from Jacques Derrida, who writes of the "invaginated text" in "Living On/Borderlines"; he also discusses this term in his interview with Christie V. MacDonald. I further comment on such uses of figures of femininity in literary and critical theory in the text above.

4. There are a great number of feminist scholars investigating constructions of masculinity, many of whom specifically address film and/or television representations. See, among others, Cohan and Hark; Jeffords, *Hard Bodies* and *Remasculinization;* Kirkham and Thumin; Lehman; Penley and Willis; Silverman, *Male Subjectivity;* and Studlar. While writing on literature, Eve Kosofsky Sedgwick has produced some of the most important work on masculinity, which is certainly relevant to my discussion of film and television. See her *Between Men* and *Epistemology.*

5. Huyssen's discussion of modernism as a "reaction formation" is on 53–55.

6. See for example, 15, 85–87, 112, and in particular, the section entitled "Oral and Literate Traditions in Television Discourse," 116–126.

7. The chart of oppositions between television and literate media that Fiske and Hartley offer in *Reading Television* (124–125) may be productively compared to the one that Fiske employs to differentiate feminine and masculine forms in Fiske's *Television* (203).

8. This is the process which Alice Jardine has termed *gynesis*. See also Spivak; and the debates that run through Jardine and Smith.

9. Ellis takes the notion of the "photo effect" from Roland Barthes, *Camera Lucida.*

10. This intimacy and complicity is what Robert Stam refers to as television's "regime of the 'fictive we'" in "Television" 39.

11. Perhaps the most obvious case of this tendency to associate television with the feminine is the Lacanian reading by Beverle Houston. I don't discuss her analysis in detail here precisely because the thesis that TV is feminine is explicitly offered in her work. The more interesting cases, in my opinion, are those in which gendered metaphors appear in discussions of television by critics not expressly making this claim.

12. Huyssen also notes the emergence of nostalgia in response to postmodernism's "various forms of 'otherness'" (including feminism) on 199 and 219–220.

13. This notion of television as a genetic "program" is not only indebted to McLuhan's theory of media as extensions of the human brain; it also recalls *Videodrome*'s image of a world in which television signals alter both consciousness and the very shape and substance of the body itself.

14. See, in particular, Laura Mulvey, "Visual." As noted in the previous chapter, this description of the male spectatorial ideal seems to leave little room for theorizing alternative viewing pleasures, and hence many feminist film/television theorists have reconsidered spectatorship so as to account for more powerful positions for female viewers, shifting identifications, and progressive readings of classical texts. Yet while male and female social subjects do not neatly line up on the sides of these binary oppositions, the categories *subject/object* and *seeing/being seen* are nonetheless crucial for feminist film analysis, and the notion of the masculine gaze continues to influence film and television studies.

15. The masses are thus like simulated savages, lunatics, children, *women*—all metaphors Baudrillard uses to describe the masses, though their femininity is explicitly named only once.

16. Irigaray, *This Sex* 76, 150–51; Doane, "Film" and "Masquerade"; Russo; and Case. As I remark in the text, these theorists employ and expand the concept of masquerade developed by Joan Riviere in "Womanliness as a Masquerade."

17. I take this point from Rey Chow, who, in a discussion of discourses of mass culture and their implications for gender (and specifically for Third World feminism), writes: "Baudrillard's theory does not reverse Adorno and Horkheimer's view of the [feminized] masses; rather, it exaggerates it and pushes it to the extreme by substituting the notion of an all-controlling 'industry' with that of an all-consuming mass, a mass that, in its abandon, no longer allows for the demarcation of clear boundaries" (109).

18. Also addressing this issue is Schor; and, in regard to TV specifically, Mellencamp, who examines sitcom simulations that are inflected differently by the female voice in "Situation," esp. 87.

19. These, of course, are not the only genres in which such a strategy is found: a hypermasculine reaction against women and "the feminine," often through an appropriation of this very field, can also be seen in many situation and romantic comedies, as I elaborate in my reading of single-father sitcoms and particularly *Moonlighting* in the next chapter.

20. Among many other studies, see, for example, Ang, *Desperately*; Morley, *Family* and *Television*; Press; and the essays in the anthologies by Baehr and Dyer; Brown; Seiter et al.; and Mann.

21. For examples of theorists that use such tropes, see Chodorow; Gilligan; Irigaray, *This Sex*; and Montrelay. For an illuminating discussion of the notion of feminine proximity, see Doane, *Desire.*

22. On advertising and self-image, see Lears, "From Salvation." Relating this to the specific position of women are Coward, *Female Desires*; and Doane, *Desire*, esp. 13 and 22–33.

23. Making a similar point, Modleski remarks that "[c]ommercials, of course, present the housewife with mini-problems and their resolutions, so after witnessing all the agonizingly hopeless dilemmas presented on soap operas, the spectator has the satisfaction of seeing *something* cleaned up, if only a stained shirt or a dirty floor" ("Rhythms" 71).

24. On MTV and postmodernism, see, for example, Kaplan, *Rocking*; Wollen; and the essays within *Journal of Communication Inquiry*'s issue on music television.

25. The analysis of crime/action shows as "hysterical" texts that yield contradictions emerging as textual fissures suggests a reading of these programs as "male melodramas" which inherit some of the historical and ideological tensions of melodrama as well as the tensions provoked by generic hybrids. For specific discussions of "male melodrama," see Deming; and Torres.

26. Within this chapter, Fiske (basing his theory on the work of Nancy Chodorow) makes a sharp differentiation between "feminine" texts (which are multiple, polysemic, contradictory, and open) and "masculine" narratives (which are unified, linear, and closed). The problem with the distinction as he makes it is not only (as he admits) that it is overly simplistic and that, given TV's specific visual and narrative form, all television texts lean a bit to the "feminine" side of this

,divide. Confusions also arise from the fact that Fiske tends to directly equate "feminine" texts with female viewers and then oppose this equation to the alignment of "masculine" texts and male viewers. Not only does this blur the important theoretical distinctions that can be made between narrative form and textual address and between the inscription of spectatorship and the empirical viewer (positioned by a number of other discourses and power relations in addition to the text), but it also denies the ways in which, in their attempts to construct a masculine viewing subject, many shows of male spectacle are just as contradictory (if not more so) than "feminine" texts. For his list of distinctions between these two gendered forms, see 215–20.

27. Sandy Flitterman discusses the way in which components of manliness are distributed among the characters of *Magnum, p.i.* so that Magnum himself emerges as "*magnum opus* of masculinity" (42) in "Thighs and Whiskers," esp. 42 and 48. Fiske discusses *The A-Team's* various attempts to narrativize or manage the contradictions between opposing aspects of masculinity in *Television Culture* 198–210.

28. Dyer discusses the "strain" in images of men in his article "Don't Look Now." Discussing the "excessive, even hysterical quality of so much male imagery" and the instability involved in constructing the man as an object of the gaze, he writes:

> The clenched fists, the bulging muscles, the hardened jaws, the proliferation of phallic symbols—they are all straining after what can hardly ever be achieved, the embodiment of the phallic mystique. . . . Like so much else about masculinity, images of men, founded on such multiple instabilities, are such a strain. . . . And the real trap at the heart of these instabilities is that it is precisely *straining* that is held to be the great good, what makes a man a man. . . . [M]en and women alike are asked to value the very things that make masculinity such an unsatisfactory definition of being human. (71–72)

Dyer's analysis of male excess and hysteria complements and broadens my own argument. While I agree that such strain can generally be found in images of men (none of which can adequately embody phallic power), I think that this stress is heightened by the specificity of television's form and look (multiple and interrupted without closure), which prevents even the illusion of mastery that is central to the masculine gaze of the cinema.

29. Dyer traces this panic even in images of men created for female audiences (male pin-ups, star portraits): "On the one hand, this is a visual medium, these men are there to be looked at by women. On the other hand, this does violence to the codes of who looks and who is looked at (and how), and some attempt is instinctively made to counteract this violation" ("Don't" 63). One common way in which the model's presumed passivity may be disavowed is by having the man portrayed return the spectator's gaze with a vengeance, displaying a look that is often called "castrating" or "penetrating." Yet Dyer concludes that since women have little to fear from castration and that the taboo on penetration applies to anal sex, such terminology reveals the real stakes of this system of vision—its threat to hetero-normative men: "In looking at and dealing with these castrating/penetrating looks, women are caught up in a system that does not so much address them as work out aspects of the construction of male sexuality in men's heads" (66). In other words, just like male imagery found in texts directed at men, images supposedly created for women viewers may be less concerned with female desires than with soothing male anxieties about the spectacle of masculinity.

30. A number of critics have expanded Neale's analysis, also providing interesting discussions of male spectacle. Particularly of interest for my discussion of television's male masquerades are a number of essays in the collection *Screening the Male,* edited by Cohan and Hark, which investigates similar issues in regard to film. See, for example, Fuchs, "Buddy"; Holmlund; Tasker; and Jeffords, "Can Masculinity."

31. For a discussion of the splitting of the hero in the western, see Mulvey, "Afterthoughts" 12–15. The theory of the continuum of male homosocial desire comes from Sedgwick, *Between Men*; see particularly her introduction, 1–20.

32. On the complicated "ins and outs," appearances and disappearances, exclusions and assimilations of the heterosexual/homosexual polarity, see also Diana Fuss's introduction to her edited volume *Inside/Out*.

33. Also suggesting the importance of narrative resolution in these moments of threatening loss is Herman Rapaport, who writes, "The annihilation of the subject . . . can be warded off only if the subject can convince himself that annihilation (castration, death) can be defeated by means of mastering events through overcoming time" (64). Cinema's narrative closure and its immortalization of the image can be seen as just the kinds of techniques for mastering time that would be required (techniques which are lacking in TV's evanescent flow).

34. This, of course, is a reference to Judith Butler's *Gender Trouble* and the theory of performativity contained therein.

35. For an illuminating discussion of another example of male spectacle that also suggests how these shows are positioned in relation to "the feminine" (even in the absence of female characters), see Flitterman, "Thighs."

36. The way in which the crisis in masculinity provoked by Vietnam informs these television shows has also been noted by Ross, "Masculinity" 150. Similarly, comparing *Miami Vice* to *film noir*, Jeremy Butler reminds us of the historical connection between the cinematic genre and post-war disillusionment in *"Miami Vice"* 129; just as *film noir*'s popularity can be attributed to this "dark" ideology, the popularity of *Miami Vice* may be related to post-Vietnam despair.

37. On this core dilemma, see Jeremy Butler, 131–32. On the double meaning of "vice" as it relates to masquerade and the "right stuff" of masculinity, see Ross, 152. Ross refers to *Miami Vice*'s premiere episode, in which Crockett's wife, about to divorce him, exclaims, "You and your vice cop buddies are just the flip side of the same coin from those dealers you're always masquerading around with." It is precisely the dissolution of difference that men "masquerading around" with other men provokes that *Miami Vice* must commit itself to solving.

38. "Duty and Honor," produced by Michael Mann, aired on NBC, February 6, 1987. The cast includes Dr. Haing S. Ngor as Nguyen Van Trang, Michael Wright as the Savage, Edward James Olmos as Martin Castillo, Don Johnson as Sonny Crockett, and Philip Michael Thomas as Ricardo Tubbs.

39. For further discussions of racial stereotypes in mass cultural representation (and the problems that these pose for film, television, and cultural studies), see, for example, Bogle; Gaines; and the essays in Diawara. For a historical analysis of the myth of the black rapist and its political effectivity in promoting violence against African American men and women alike, see Davis 172–201.

40. Fiske also briefly discusses the history and use of mixed hero-pairs in *Television* 214.

41. Theorists who associate femininity with the duplicity of style, the pose, and masquerade range from Friedrich Nietzsche ("Reflect on the whole history of women: do they not *have* to be first of all and above all else actresses? . . . The female is so artistic" [317]) and Jacques Derrida ("That which will not be pinned down by truth is, in truth—*feminine*. . . . Because woman is (her own) writing, style must be returned to her" [*Spurs* 55–57]) to the psychoanalysts Joan Riviere ("The reader may now ask how I define womanliness or where I draw the line between genuine womanliness and the 'masquerade.' My suggestion is not, however, that there is any such difference; . . . they are the same thing" [213]) and Jacques Lacan ("Paradoxical as this formulation might seem, I would say that it is in order to be the phallus, that is to say, the signifier of the desire of the Other, that the woman will reject an essential part of her femininity, notably all its attributes through masquerade" [*Feminine* 84]).

42. Craig Owens makes a similar observation about the effects of posing as an object in "Posing" 17.

43. In a chapter called "Carnival and Style," Fiske argues that television is frequently condemned for the same "vices" as that of the Rabelaisian carnival analyzed by Bakhtin: both exhibit the excess and degradation provoked by the collision of the official language of writing and high culture with the vernacular tongues of oral culture and the people themselves (241–43). Given these similarities, he argues, television can then operate (like carnival) to liberate the disempowered from established "truths" and order, suspend hierarchical ranks and norms, and open up a space of creative play through exaggerations, parody, and inversions—elements that Fiske locates in television's blooper, joke, and outtake shows; *Rock 'n' Wrestling*; and such figures as Mr. T, Hulk Hogan, and even Madonna. For this theory of carnival, see Bakhtin.

44. See, for example, Ed Cohen's comments on Judith Butler's theory of performativity; and Butler's own clarification of her position in *Bodies That Matter*.

45. Mary Russo, for instance, reminds us of the way in which the carnival might actually reinforce the existing social structure and of the "especial dangers for women and other excluded or marginalized groups" within its complicitous play (214–15).

46. Fiske acknowledges that TV's "postmodern" spectacles are intrinsically tied to consumerism and most often found within those television forms with explicit market purposes that are meant to be viewed more than once: music video, program title sequences, and commercials. Yet he claims that the pure visual pleasure that they offer (through special effects, rapid cutting, extreme angles, glossy images, and so on) allows the signifiers to overcome the signifieds:

> Style is a recycling of images that wrenches them out of the original context that enabled them to make sense and reduces them to free-floating signifiers whose only signification is that they are free, outside the control of normal sense and sense-making, and thus able to enter the world of pleasure where their materiality can work *directly* on the sensual eye, running the boundary between culture and nature, *between ideology and its absence. (Television* 250–51, emphasis added)

47. For example, *The Dukes of Hazzard* and *Magnum, p.i.* placed in TV's twenty top-rated programs (as measured by the A. C. Nielsen Company) in 1980–1981 and 1981–1982; *The A-Team, The Fall Guy, Magnum, p.i.,* and *Simon and Simon* made the list in 1982–1983, joined by *Knight Rider* and *Riptide* in 1983–1984; *The A-Team, The Fall Guy, Magnum, p.i.,* and *Simon and Simon* were again in the top twenty in 1984–1985; *Miami Vice* appeared on the list in 1985–86; and *In the Heat of the Night* was in the top twenty in 1987–1988, joined by *Hunter* in 1988–1989 and 1989–1990. Throughout this period, *Monday Night Football* was also in the twenty top-rated programs. The expansion of television sports is most evident in the growth of cable channels, "superstations," and pay-per-view services strongly emphasizing (or even fully devoted to) sporting events; the debut of ESPN2 (a second Entertainment and Sports Programming Network) in 1993 is particularly noteworthy in this regard. These Nielsen figures come from Brooks and Marsh 1104–1107.

5. Tube Tied

1. For discussions of these trends, see Eisenstein; Luker; McKeegan; Petchesky, *Abortion*; and the articles in the collections edited by Franklin, Lury, and Stacey; Ginsburg and Tsing.

2. I am indebted to Maureen McNeil for these points. See especially 151–52.

3. For a feminist critique of reproductive technologies, see, for example, Arditti, Klein, and Minden; Corea; Corea et al.; Oakley; and Stanworth. The primary feminist text which had earlier advocated the separation of sexuality and the family through the technological development of "artificial reproduction" is Shulamith Firestone's *The Dialectic of Sex: The Case for Feminist Revolution*. For an

interesting analysis of the general shifts in feminist sexual politics and, specifically, of the way in which some branches of feminism seem to have moved from a critique of biological and "natural" explanations of gender, sexuality, and reproduction to an embracement of the "natural," see Echols. For an analysis of reproductive discourses that reasserts the need to refuse discourses of "the natural," see Hartouni, "Containing."

4. The original episodes dealing with abortion, vasectomy, and birth control (alluded to in a conversation about why "the gismo" didn't work) aired on November 16 and 23, 1972, perhaps in response to a contest sponsored by the Population Institute for television programs supporting population control. Supposedly, CBS itself suggested the "postponement" of the two-part story and initially refused to pay for it, but they backed down when Norman Lear, *Maude*'s producer, threatened to pull the show entirely if this story didn't run. It was also Lear who insisted that Maude herself, rather than a friend, as first proposed, have the abortion. The November 16 show received a 46–48 percent share of the New York/Los Angeles audience and the program jumped from eleventh to sixth in the national Nielsen ratings; the second episode got a 44 percent share of the New York/Los Angeles audience (before this, the highest share was 38 percent). However, two CBS affiliates (in Champaign and Peoria) refused to put the two-part show on the air—the first time any CBS station had refused to run an episode of a continuing series. After the programs aired, CBS president R. D. Wood met with angry Catholic officials and told them that the episodes would not be rebroadcast. When they were nonetheless shown in reruns on August 14 and 21, 1973, the church called for a boycott. In response, thirty-eight local affiliates declined to carry the episodes, five more moved them out of early-evening viewing hours, one provided time for the presentation of an anti-abortion viewpoint, and most national advertisers withdrew from the time period—in fact, CBS could fill only one of twelve half-minute commercial slots. The National Organization of Women then called for its own boycott of seven companies that pulled their advertisements, and they picketed outside of various corporate headquarters (events that were also covered on television). Ultimately, it was estimated that sixty-five million people saw the episodes and CBS received twenty-four thousand critical letters in the campaign launched against the show by anti-abortion activists. The *New York Times* ran several stories on the controversy in the winter of 1972 and again in August 1973. See, in particular, Harmetz 3. For further details, see also the issues from August 10 (61), August 18 (53), and August 30 (67). For the debate between the United States Catholic Conference (USCC) and the Population Institute, see Beusse and Shaw; and then the response by Mrs. Theodore O. Wedel of the Population Institute and the final word from Beusse and Shaw of the USCC.

5. These quotes from *The Silent Scream* are spoken by the narrator, Dr. Bernard Nathanson, and cited by Rosalind Petchesky, who is also the critic that I refer to here. See "Fetal Images"; her reading of *The Silent Scream* is given on 264–68, the quote I use is from 265, and her quotes from Nathanson are on 266. For other interesting analyses of fetal imagery, see also Hartouni, "Containing" and "Fetal"; Rapp; and Stabile.

6. The images in "The Miracle of Life" (Swedish Television Corporation , 1982; WGBH, 1986) are provided by Swedish photojournalist Lennart Nilsson, whose fetal portraits have been made famous not only by *Life* magazine but also by "pro-life" activists who widely circulate his work. See also Stabile, 183–90, for a discussion of Nilsson's work, including that found in "The Miracle of Life."

7. Both Petchesky ("Fetal" 276) and Hartouni ("Containing" 38) cite the physician Dr. Michael Harrison on the value and implications of ultrasound:

> The fetus could not be taken seriously as long as he remained a medical recluse in an opaque womb, and it was not until the last half of this century that the prying eye of the ultrasonogram . . . rendered the once opaque

> womb transparent, stripping the veil of mystery from the dark inner sanc-
> tum and letting the light of scientific observation fall on the shy and
> secretive fetus. . . . The sonographic voyeur, spying on the unwary fetus,
> finds him or her a surprisingly active little creature, and not at all the passive
> parasite we had imagined. (Harrison et al. 774)

There are a number of things one can say about this amazing passage: the
presumption in the first sentence that the fetus is a "he" (only to be revised later in
the passage with the introduction of voyeurism and the realization that the object
of the look might be a "she"); the assumption that the fetus "could not be taken
seriously" until medical science could witness it (thereby discounting women's
experience and knowledge through other sensations such as those marked by the
now-outdated term "quickening"); the articulation of voyeurism and scientific
observation; the combination, indeed supplanting, of religious/mystical discourse ("veil of mystery . . . dark inner sanctum") by scientific discourse, et cetera.
I quote it here, however, primarily to point to the ways in which it borrows the
rhetoric of the nature documentary so familiar from television's science and
wildlife series: described as a "shy" but "active little creature," the fetus is figured
as another form of mysterious animal life to be captured and rendered for the
audience's curious looks.

8. For further elaboration of these issues, see, for example, Feuer, "Concept";
Morley, *Family*; and Spigel, "Installing" and *Make Room*.

9. The image of television I refer to here comes particularly from Ellis, *Visible
Fictions*, discussed in the previous chapter. I am indebted to Angela Wall for these
thoughts about the parallel regulatory aspects of televisual and reproductive
technologies.

10. Although my discussion of the exclusion of women within television's
familial space focuses on recent trends within TV history, for an analysis that
reveals the ways in which the mother was similarly marginalized in the domestic
comedies of the 1950s, see Leibman.

11. A number of these shows involve father (or mother) substitutes moving into
familial space as "domestic help," and thus class as well as gender issues are
certainly at stake in these representations.

12. The way in which this resonates with (often homophobic) attacks on "pro-
miscuity," common in the age of AIDS, should also be noted.

13. Given the parameters of television history with which I am concerned in this
book, I discuss these trends primarily in terms of 1980s television. However, more
recent cases can certainly be found: *NYPD Blue*, for instance, provides another
good example.

14. These points are discussed in more detail in the previous chapter; I take them
from Ross, "Masculinity," especially 153; and Fiske, *Television*.

15. In her analysis of debates regarding abortion and reproductive technologies
in Great Britain, Jalma Hanmer also notes the way in which "men identify with
embryos and foetuses, and not mothers," rarely even mentioning women in the
public discourse of reproductive politics "as they are subsumed within men's
identification as embryos, foetuses, children and men within the family" (95).

16. However, whether the failure of *I Married Dora* was due to its representation
of gender and ethnicity, its flirtation with a racially/ethnically mixed romantic
pair, or merely the poor quality of the show is beyond the scope of this argument.

17. According to the 1994 *World Almanac and Book of Facts* (which takes these
figures from the Bureau of Census, U.S. Department of Commerce), in 1980, 14
percent of white children lived with their mothers only (women who were single,
separated/divorced, or widowed), while only 2 percent lived in single-parent
male-headed households; these figures rose to 16 percent and 3 percent respectively in 1990. Forty-four percent of African American children lived in households that were headed by women in 1980, compared to 2 percent that had fathers
alone; these figures rose to 51 percent and 4 percent in 1990. For Hispanic families,

20 percent of the children lived with their mothers alone and 2 percent with their fathers only in 1980, rising to 27 percent and 3 percent in 1990. In addition to demonstrating the gender asymmetry of single-parent households, these statistics clearly reveal a racial and ethnic asymmetry (and this disparity is probably even greater than the numbers suggest since the census excluded persons under eighteen years old who maintained households or family groups). Television's representations of single-parent households may thus be critiqued not only for glossing over issues of gender, but even more so for evading questions of race.

18. Of course, this proclamation of (the superiority of) paternal instinct is just the flip side of Hollywood's mistrust of mothers and "mother-substitutes," seen in films as varied as *Kramer vs. Kramer* (1979) and *Mommie Dearest* (1981) to the more recent *The Hand That Rocks the Cradle* (1991), *Boyz N the Hood* (1991), *Terminator 2: Judgment Day* (1991), and *Mrs. Doubtfire* (1994).

19. Many other feminist theorists have also discussed a masculine appropriation of reproduction. See, for instance, Corea; Martin; Oakley; Mary O'Brien; and Rich.

20. Modleski also makes the important point that the patriarchal sphere has historically been limited by the assumption of mothers' custodial rights only within our own century, and it is in this context that we must read these shows (69).

21. Many feminist critics have noted the rise of fetal protection statutes and incidents of court cases in which women are charged with maternal neglect in relation to fetuses they are carrying, possibly even having their custody challenged prior to birth. See, for example, Eisenstein 125; Hartouni, "Containing" 42; and McNeil 151.

22. This manipulation of "the natural" points to the double bind for women in current reproductive politics that I noted earlier in the text: both the assumption of a "natural" link between women and motherhood, femininity and maternity—and the disruption of this very same link—may be (and have been) equally used against feminism and women's interests. Stabile (179) makes a similar point, as does Angela Wall in "Reconstructing Motherhood," a paper that has been very useful in furthering my thinking on these issues.

23. *Hooperman's* second season opener (November 30, 1988) dealt, in part, with the miscarriage suffered by Harry Hooperman's "girlfriend," Susan Smith, a woman Hooperman met (assuming that she was a man) while hiring a maintenance person for his building. Throughout the first season, Smith had rejected his offers for a serious relationship—a situation altered by the second season's miscarriage story (which carried over into the second episode). However, after deciding to try again for a child, she took a break to recover from her loss and then disappeared from the show.

Thirtysomething's premiere (December 6, 1988) focused on central character Hope's ambivalence about having a second child at her husband's urging after she returns to work and is offered a chance at a desired writing career. Hope finds the mementos of a soldier's wife who once lived in their house, and she becomes drawn into her story (visualized for viewers) of a heartbreaking miscarriage but ensuing decision to try again. Having learned from this woman's tale that there is never a perfect time to try to have a baby, Hope is persuaded to attempt to conceive another child herself. Interestingly, the story of the soldier's wife almost functions as a premonition for the future of the series: later in the season, Hope has a miscarriage as well.

As stated in the text above, both of these stories involve women's choices in regard to family, relationship, and career decisions, and thus, they narrate the conflicts related to contemporary sexual politics in fairly conventional terms, suggesting that reproductive options are matters for middle-class, white women. In my analysis of *Moonlighting's* miscarriage episode (which aired on December 6, 1988; Jay Daniel, executive producer; Glenn Gordon Caron, series creator), I hope to demonstrate not so much how the text *narrates* such conflicts, but how the power struggles at the root of sexual and reproductive politics are actually *embodied* within the program's *mise-en-scène* and the terms of representation itself.

24. The distinction between *histoire* or "story" (in which all marks of enunciation are suppressed in the assumption of third-person narration) and *discours*/"discourse" (in which the positions of speaker and listener are acknowledged and revealed) comes from the linguist Emile Benveniste, *Problems in General Linguistics*. In applying this distinction to film studies, Christian Metz has argued that the classical film disguises its discourse as story by effacing the signs of its own production and by disavowing the presence of the viewer. See Metz "History/Discourse"; and Nowell-Smith, "Note."

While Metz's analysis applies to most forms of classical cinema, it does not account for the ways in which the Hollywood musical and many forms of television acknowledge the viewer or insist on revealing the marks of enunciation so as to create the illusion of a live or shared work in the very process of construction. In regard to the musical, see Feuer, *Hollywood*; and Collins, "Toward." In relationship to television's illusion of liveness and discourse, see Feuer, "Concept"; and Morse, "Television."

25. For an analysis of the ways in which *Moonlighting* creates its own mystique precisely by demystifying the myth it is creating (in other words, how it manages to announce itself as a unique and "quality" show by exposing the production processes of television), see J. P. Williams. Also discussing the text's self-reflexivity and generic hybridity is Vande Berg. On the notion of "quality television" and its relationship to self-reflexivity, see Feuer, "MTM."

26. And the fact that there is vital life in the womb—that the fetus is an "active little creature"—is indeed emphasized. See note 7 above.

27. On the historical impulses behind the musical's "escapist" fantasies, see Dyer, "Entertainment"; and Roth.

28. In a perceptive analysis of the musical comedy which outlines the specificity of the genre and the ways in which musical spectacles may rupture and/or mirror the narratives in which they are placed, Patricia Mellencamp writes:

> [M]usicals depict a literal version of "family romance," a thematic often embedded within another "story" in other genres. Musicals virtually re-enact the ritual of re-creation/pro-creation of the privileged heterosexual couple, the nucleus of patriarchal society. As in classical narrative, the work of musicals is the containment of potentially disruptive sexuality, a threat to the sanctity of marriage and the family. ("Spectacle" 29; see also 34–35)

As I attempt to show throughout this chapter, the literalization of family romance and the containment of a disruptive (female) sexuality is nowhere more apparent than in "A Womb with a View." However, because its "ritual of pro-creation" is enacted through a desire for the paternal Law which is directly expressed (rather than mediated through the conventions of romance), the subversive power of spectacle is negated. Underscoring the patriarchal contract upon which the musical's fantasies are based, the spectacle of Baby Hayes's desire for a dad can only reduplicate and mirror the repression inherent in the narrative itself.

29. I take the description of the fetus as a "homunculus" from Petchesky ("Fetal" 268). The word refers to "a fully formed, miniature human body believed, according to some medical theories of the 16th and 17th centuries, to be contained in the spermatozoon" (*The Random House Dictionary of the English Language*, Second Edition, Unabridged [New York: Random House, 1987], 916). While today's medical science obviously no longer accepts this theory of reproduction, it does still tend to display an unusual amount of identification on the part of male scientists with presumed male embryos and fetuses (usually referred to as "he"). For discussions of this, see the readings of medical discourses provided by Franklin; Martin, "Body" and *The Woman in the Body*; and Petchesky, "Fetal."

These theorists, along with many others (Hartouni, "Containing"; Rapp; Stabile), also stress the ways in which the introduction of scientific discourse and imaging (now combined with religious discourse) has altered reproductive debates.

30. On the function of the musical's dance numbers as a form of "surrogate sex," see, for example, Giles; Collins, "Toward"; and editor Rick Altman's introductory comments for both articles. In her discussion of *Three Men and a Baby*, Modleski also refers to the way in which the term *surrogate mother* derealizes motherhood, minimizing the woman's role in order to present the father as the "real thing" and thus justify his role as surrogate mother in the old sense of the term (69, 80).

In critiquing the use of the term *surrogate mother*, however, I am not trying to construct a general argument against the use of surrogacy (or any reproductive technology) as an alternative to "natural" forms of procreation. To do so, I believe, would oversimplify an issue which, as noted in the text above, is fraught with complications. While opponents of reproductive technologies often attack the ways in which these technologies deny or disrupt natural human processes, to accept this argument uncritically is not only to maintain an essentialist view which equates femininity with biological maternity, it is also to find ourselves within a web of contradictions. Specifically, in order to both avoid the claim that women can legitimately assume a maternal position only if they are biologically ordained as mothers and to evade the confusion involved in attempting to legislate against reproductive technologies without having to also embrace laws that regulate women's reproductive freedoms (our access to birth control and abortion), feminists must reject any argument which rests on "natural" grounds. On the other hand, the attempt to avoid this essentialism by supporting current work in reproductive technologies may also paradoxically result in feminists' aligning themselves with those who demand respect for men's "instinctual needs" to father. The opposition between essentialism and anti-essentialism thus fails to clarify all the problems at hand. A similar case can be made for the ways in which arguments posed in terms of rights (parental rights, children's rights, the right to control one's own body, the right to enter into contracts, et cetera) also fail to untangle the web of contradictions ensuing from the challenges now posed to both the family and ideologies of familialism. For one analysis of these issues that focuses on the issue of surrogacy, see Doane and Hodges. For a discussion that focuses on abortion and the problems involved in the discourse of "rights," see Poovey.

31. In noting the secondary discourses that circulated around the show and figured Cybill Shepherd as a "shrew," I am referring primarily to the tabloids' representations of the battles on the *Moonlighting* set, not to the articles that appeared in women's magazines which featured Shepherd with her twin children or emphasized her ability to combine motherhood with a career. For an analysis that investigates these other discourses (and the question of female narcissism) in order to reveal the complexity of Shepherd's position in women's magazines and in *Moonlighting*'s re-presentation of *The Taming of the Shrew*, see Radner. J. P. Williams also discusses viewers' responses to Cybill/Maddie (and to the blurring of the boundary between character and actress) (93–94).

32. Remarking on the "extraordinary reaction" this cover received, the editors of *Vanity Fair* reported that "in the U.S. alone there were ninety-five different television pieces—an audience of more than 110 million—as well as sixty-four radio shows on thirty-one stations and more than 1,500 newspaper articles and a dozen cartoons. . . . Meanwhile, in the U.K., Germany, Italy, Spain, Japan, and South America, Demi made headlines" ("Readers" 28). See also Stabile's discussion of reproductive imagery, in which she notes, "Some stores and newsstands refused to carry the August [*Vanity Fair*] issue, while others modestly concealed it in the brown wrapper evocative of porn magazines. Nevertheless, the cover displayed no more skin than magazines like *Allure, Cosmopolitan,* and *Vogue* do on a regular basis. What repelled and shocked viewers obviously was the vast

expanse of white, pregnant belly" (190). Featured again in *Vanity Fair* a year later, Moore herself commented on the controversy and its contradictions, responding to the fact that some people "didn't want [the magazine] in a family store because it wasn't appropriate" by stating, "I don't know how much *more* family-oriented I could possibly have gotten" (Conant 118). According to Bruce Willis (discussing the situation on the *Late Show with David Letterman* in August 1994), Moore's January 1994 appearance continued this controversy, raising the ire of many who considered her gymnastic gag (which was actually the work of a body double) to be not only an indecent display but neglectful parental behavior that was harmful to the fetus. Moore's "parturient prominence" thus reveals both the concern with fetal rights and the crisis of maternal representation.

33. Another ironic twist in this is that Cybill Shepherd herself was often figured in women's magazines as a model wife and mother in regard to her own pregnancy and then rearing of twins.

34. On the relationship between femininity/maternity and the monstrous within the genre of horror, see Linda Williams; and Creed, "Horror."

35. For a discussion of how the musical typically manages the tensions inherent to its form by containing the "momentarily subversive fantasy breaks" of spectacle within a suppressive process of narrativization, see Mellencamp, "Spectacle" 34–35.

36. Providing another very interesting analysis, Mia Carter-Reis also discusses the maternal *mise-en-scène* of *Aliens*.

37. The "untraditional" and/or single-parent sitcoms to which Zoglin compares *The Cosby Show* include 1972–1978's *Maude* (noted again for its abortion story), *One Day at a Time* (1975–1984), and *Kate and Allie* (1984–1989).

38. Of course, there are television shows that are also named after their female stars. The power of this reference to Cosby within "A Womb with a View" depends not only the general currency afforded to his name but, more importantly, to both the place of this reference within the narrative structure of the text and to the way in which Cosby's name substitutes for any information concerning Baby Hayes's actual new parents. Once again, granting the child a paternal heritage takes precedence over recognizing the mother.

39. Discussing the musical's "presumed address to a female, or at least feminine, audience," Medhurst quotes, for example, film critic John Grierson who, in 1929, wrote of the musical: "They may have their place, but it is in the exclusively women's theatres which men may know how to avoid" (109, 107). Not only is the audience and the genre itself considered feminine, but, as Steve Neale points out, male musical actors/dancers are typically "feminized" when seen in this form ("Masculinity" 14–15). The need to erect some kind of masculine defense—here, through the assumption of the patriarchal name—is thus even more pressing for the male character in *Moonlighting*'s show.

40. This description of the fetus (from which my section title derives) comes from Barbara Katz Rothman, who writes, "The fetus in utero has become a metaphor for 'man' in space, floating free, attached only by the umbilical cord to the spaceship. But where is the mother in that metaphor? She has become empty space" (114). Zoe Sofia similarly relates the cult of fetal personhood to science fiction imagery, noting in particular the film *2001: A Space Odyssey*—a text which reveals the masculinist logic of extermination underlying the sci-fi fantasy of a technological reproduction which might fully dispense with women. See also Petchesky, who discusses the figuration of "the fetus-as-spaceman" in medical imagery, science fiction, and popular fantasy ("Fetal" 270); and Franklin, who notes the representation of fetus as astronaut or athlete (202).

41. For a discussion of Willis's "wise-guy" star image (one which depends more on voice than body and is more childish/adolescent than paternal) in *Moonlighting, Look Who's Talking*, and especially the *Die Hard* films, see Tasker, especially 238–43.

42. One might also consider the way in which recent reproductive politics have literally turned horrific with the brutal slaying of doctors and clinic workers/defenders by anti-abortion activists.

43. For a discussion of the ways in which the sperm and egg are represented in scientific and mass cultural discourses according to cultural notions of femininity and masculinity, see, for example, Martin, "Body."

44. It is interesting that in both of these texts, the presence of a grandfather takes on a crucial role. In other words, granting the child a paternal legacy is equally (or more) important than supplying him with a man to fill the role of father. As I explain in regard to *Moonlighting*, Cosby's name actually substitutes for any mention of Baby Hayes's new parents. In *Look Who's Talking*, Mikey's search for a father is the primary focus of the text, but significantly, it is the (paternal) grandfather who actually brings the couple together, assumes the legality of their union, and initiates the scene in which James (the hero) will finally be recognized as the legitimate protector of the small child. While Molly's parents are seen near the beginning of the film, not only are they ineffectual (her mother dominates the father, who, in contrast to Mikey, never speaks within the entire film—the "reason" for Molly's own independence and difficulty with men), but they drop out of sight once the hero's family is introduced.

45. Kathleen K. Rowe discusses the resistant potential of Roseanne's bodily display; Mellencamp emphasizes the power of her wit in *High Anxiety* 338–50.

6. "Into the System"

1. For an analysis of the way in which "cybernetic simulation prompts a redefinition of such fundamental terms as life and reality" (37), see Nichols, "The Work of Culture in the Age of Cybernetic Systems." As indicated by his title, Nichols follows the model mapped out by Walter Benjamin in his essay "The Work of Art in the Age of Mechanical Reproduction." In so doing, Nichols suggests that the question posed by postmodern simulation is not whether cyborgian forms can truly be considered "real life," but how the presumption of what life or reality actually *is* has been radically overturned by these cultural transformations. While I disagree with some of the distinctions that he makes between cultural formations, his analysis of cybernetic systems is nonetheless quite illuminating.

2. Interestingly, as Nichols explains, in the legal battles that have ensued from cybernetic simulation (which throws conventional notions of proprietorship into question as it confuses the distinction between subject and object, commodity and consumer, creator and creation), the courts have been "more prone to grant [patent] protection for the fabrication of new life forms, via recombinant DNA experiments, than for the development of computer software," which simply relies on mathematical procedures available to all (39). While these life-forms are, at this point, quite simple, the larger significance of this trend (which literalizes the notion of "commodified life") must be carefully considered. The concern over patents and copyrights, of course, arises as a capitalist market system seeks to preserve itself—to maintain its conceptions of ownership and individual rights/profit—in the face of a historical change that threatens to make these concepts obsolete. In so doing, however, this ideology ties itself up in an interesting knot that is apparent in the controversies over reproductive technologies (in which dominant notions of ownership may conflict with those of the privatized family). If artificially fabricated life falls under proprietary rules, then the commonly voiced objection that babies are not commodities (and thus cannot be treated through these technologies as things to be bought and sold) no longer seems to respond to today's cybernetic conditions. The political implications of reproductive technologies thus become extremely confusing, pitting critics either on the side of proprietary claims or on the side of traditional notions of motherhood and the family. It is only by analyzing the effects of simulation together with relations

of gender that feminists can hope to avoid (or at least think through) these kinds of knots. For a discussion of some of these legal battles, see Nichols 37–45.

3. For an interesting discussion of gender and reproductive politics in cyborg representations that does not limit itself to television, as I do here, but moves across film and TV, see Fuchs, "'Death.'" Rayner discusses some of the same texts as Fuchs while also incorporating readings of novels in a discussion of the cyborg and the boundaries of identity.

4. On the notion of the "video subject," see, for example, Morse, "Television," where she discusses both how television seems to speak to us from a position of subjectivity and how we are then positioned as particular kinds of video subjects ourselves. As the ultimate TV creation, Max embodies all of these positions: he is a part of TV that seems to interact with the viewer (using strategies of direct address and, in the diegesis of the show, actually conversing with people through the tube) as well as an avid TV viewer-consumer himself.

5. Given my own "spliced" postmodernist/psychoanalytic reading of this show, it is also interesting to note that Max's cyber-self-consciousness arises with his acquisition of language, however remixed and stuttered this might be.

6. Max Headroom first appeared on England's Channel 4 as the sarcastic host of a music video/celebrity interview show. In 1984, a Channel 4 TV movie entitled *Rebus: The Max Headroom Story* was produced to explain Max's origin. The U.S. cable station Cinemax aired *Rebus* in 1985 and picked up the ensuing British series in the fall of 1986. In 1987, it began producing the New York version of Max's talk show, titled *Original Max Headroom* to distinguish it from the sci-fi that ABC was doing. This ABC series was itself based on the British *Rebus*, which it "American-ized" and remade. ABC ran *Max Headroom* from March through May 1987, and then picked it up again in the fall of 1987. It was soon cancelled in October 1987, but some previously unseen episodes aired in 1988 to round out ABC's prime-time schedule during the Hollywood writers strike.

7. Of course, not all viewers will accept this "invitation"; I am not, in other words, attempting to (re)create a postmodern version of the "hypodermic needle theory" of audience effects.

8. Most notable for my analysis here is, of course, Haraway, "Manifesto." See also her *Primate Visions* and *Simians, Cyborgs, and Women.* Feminist theorists who discuss postmodernism specifically in relationship to television would include Kaplan, *Rocking around the Clock*; and Mellencamp, *High Anxiety.* For an overview of the relationship between postmodernism and television studies, see Collins, "Postmodernism and Television." For an overview of the relationship between postmodernism and feminism, see Nicholson; and the essays in the section on feminism edited by Docherty.

9. For example, because of the way in which he enacts the theme of male regression, Modleski, in "Incredible," describes Pee-wee Herman as "that essen-tially '80s figure of masculinity" (93). Max Headroom has also been described as paradigmatic of the 1980s postmodern subject for the way in which he embodies the decade's techno-fantasies and/or social formations (such as the new profes-sional middle class). See, for example, Berko; King; and Ross, "Techno-Ethics."

10. The description of Pee-wee Herman as the "part-time boy" comes from Ian Balfour, who analyzes an episode of *Pee-wee's Playhouse* in which Pee-wee prom-ises to tell the story of the "part-time boy": "The part-time boy," Balfour writes, "is, of course, Pee-wee: and this phrase too has to be understood in more than one sense. Part-time *boy,* because Pee-wee is part-time boy and part-time girl, if only in his most hysterical and histrionic moments. But also *part-time* boy because the other part of the time Pee-wee is something like a man" (156). While I largely discuss the nostalgia of *Pee-wee's Playhouse* in terms of psychoanalytic notions of regression, Alexander Doty presents an interesting analysis of the show in terms of historical (gay) nostalgia—specifically, the way in which the program re-views

1950s and 1960s (pre-Stonewall) culture through the lens of a 1980s (post-Stonewall) sensibility (82–83).

11. See, for example, Jameson's analysis of postmodern culture in "Postmodernism."

12. There have, however, been some important attempts to analyze television through psychoanalytic theory, most of which focus on individual programs or genres. One fascinating example would be Robert Stam's "Television News," which develops a different model of the psychic dynamics of televisual looking from the one that I emphasize here. Rather than suggesting that television diffuses the intensity of the cinematic gaze, Stam argues that "the televisual apparatus . . . affords pleasures even more multiform and varied than those afforded by the cinema," granting perhaps an even greater "sense of visual power to its virtually 'all-perceiving' spectator" (24). Evaluating television more in terms of the fragmentation that I discuss in the text above is Sandy Flitterman-Lewis in her very informative discussion of the conceptual bases of psychoanalysis (and psychoanalytic film theory) and its applicability to TV ("Psychoanalysis").

13. Both characters, for instance, have been seen as firmly "depart[ing] from the realm of 'classical' narrative with its attendant centered subjects" (Barry King, commenting on Max Headroom, 182), even "send[ing] up the traditional oedipal [*sic*] narrative of classic Hollywood Cinema" (Modleski, commenting on Pee-wee, "Incredible" 91). For a reading of Max Headroom as a critique of TV from within its own realms, see Rapping, "Max Headroom."

14. Describing how a child he knew was so captivated by the show that she termed the TV set itself *Pee-wee*, Balfour explains that while we may not be able to fully identify Pee-wee with television as this young viewer did, *Playhouse*'s rigorous system of popular culture citations explicitly aligns it with the work of TV (164).

15. Constance Penley describes this original plan, explaining that it was scrapped due to network and parental fears that it would encourage improper consumerism (children would sit too close to the set or destroy it by marking up the screen without the protective plastic sheet), in "Cabinet" 145.

16. Justifying their selection of Max as one of the most intriguing people of the year, the authors write: "Max could max out in the future, but that won't alter his page in the history books or his card in the trivia games"—a statement which is interesting not so much for the way in which it attempts to establish Max's historical import, but for its equation of historical importance with trivia game recognition.

17. My analysis of the cyborg derives largely from Haraway, who analyzes scientific, technological, ideological, and social trends which link or interface humans, animals, and machines along an integrated economic and cultural circuit ("Manifesto"). Nichols also discusses the origin and conceptual parameters of the term *cyborg*, explaining that its vision of a new identity (that of a cybernetic organism) does not so much reduce humans to automata as elevate simulacra (including humans) to the organic, again confusing the distinction between animal, human, and postmodern machine (35).

18. She also discusses holographic models in science on 75–76 and the general paradigm shift to holistic modes of thought on 76–78. Martin Schwab likewise suggests the rise of holistic models in the essay "In the Mirror," which appears in the same volume, a special issue of *Discourse* entitled "On Technology (Cybernetics, Ecology, and the Postmodern Imagination)." In discussing the rise of holographic paradigms in scientific as well as cultural movements, it is perhaps interesting to note that most of us are familiar with holograms, not through science, but through consumption—specifically, through the presence of holograms on credit cards as a means of control against fraud. More than an amusing coincidence, the connection that exists between these emblems of "the new

holism" and consumerism—not to mention the function of the hologram as a guarantee of "authenticity" for proper spending—points to the contradictions of postmodern simulation.

19. Despite its counter-cultural origins in "oriental" philosophy, "native" spirituality, and gynocentric mysticism, the popularity of the New Age movement was notably on the rise throughout the 1980s, particularly among the young, professional, white middle class—a fact that points to a disturbing appropriation and the problematic position of New Ageism within contemporary politics. First popularized (and made into a marketing success) by actress-turned-author Shirley MacLaine, New Age thought seems to have recuperated principles of spiritual unity and natural harmony for a capitalist laissez-faire view. For, as MacLaine explains in the TV movie *Out On a Limb* (a two-part televised account of her own "spiritual awakening," which aired on ABC in January 1987), if we all choose the lives that we are re-born into, then (to paraphrase MacLaine) the poor peasants that she sees in South America must be happy with their lot (and so, by extension, should all other poor people). Not only could New Ageism be taken up in such troubling ways in considering the "other," but its views on the "self" were also made to correspond to bourgeois precepts. Indeed, the self-actualization promoted by New Age thought proved to be quite compatible with, and good for, American business, and many corporations in the 1980s attempted to capitalize on its success. For instance, according to a 1988 article in *The New York Times Magazine*, more than 50 percent of Fortune 500 companies purchased training tapes from a company which marketed its curriculum as "New Age Thinking" and employed its discourse of utopian self-transformation for the goal of financial and high-tech advance (Bordewich).

20. See McLuhan and my discussion of McLuhan in chapter 4; Balfour also uses the pun "Globy Village" in describing *Pee-wee's Playhouse*'s utopian vision of multiracial, ethnic, and cultural harmony (161). Baudrillard presents his dystopic vision of today's hyperreality (and the masses within it) as "a black hole which engulfs the social" in *In the Shadow* 4.

21. The phrase "new orality" and the pun on the double meaning of "formula" come from Ong 136; see also Gabriele Schwab's discussion of Ong and the recuperation of holistic perspectives (76–77). Fiske and Hartley specifically align television with an "oral logic" in their section "Oral and Literate Traditions in Television Discourse" in *Reading Television* 116–126; and Haraway too discusses the breakdown of the distinction oral vs. literate ("Manifesto" 93). For a fascinating discussion of the cyborg and an "oral logic," see Morse, "What Do."

22. Given this discursive connection of technological "second nature" and the feminine, it is suggestive that the first user-friendly computer had a woman's name—Lisa. More important, though, than the feminization of any one particular cybernetic or technological "being" (which may not stand out from the customary way in which machines in this culture tend to be gendered as female) is the way in which the *entire* process of cybernetic simulation/reproduction is rendered within gendered terms. Unlike the earlier robot who may have been figured as humanized and therefore gendered so as to ward off fears of a mechanized life, the very operations of cybernetic reproduction involve fantasies of sexuality and generation. The displacement of sexual difference onto cybernetic systems thus takes place at a different level than it did in the past—the maternal/feminine merges into the site of simulation itself, yielding paradoxical, new forms of gender figuration. I discuss the management of the ensuing anxieties concerning reproductive technologies in more detail in chapter 5.

23. The example of Edison Carter and Max Headroom may be seen as a literal case of a "difference that returns as the same." In the series' opening episode, the computer-generated Max is created from the mind of Edison Carter. As I elaborate later in the chapter, in the series' second "start up" (when the show briefly returned in the spring of 1988), the same computer genius who "delivered" Max

saves Edison from losing his mind by reinjecting the contents of Max's memory back into Edison's brain, thus recreating Edison from Max.

24. Freud analyzes the compulsion to repeat and its relationship to the "death drive" in *Beyond the Pleasure Principle.*

25. This discussion of man as a "prosthetic god" resonates with Stam's description of how the "the televisual apparatus . . . prosthetically extends human perception" (24)—a statement which, of course, also resonates with McLuhan's theory of the media as "extensions" of man.

26. The ambivalence expressed in the mirror stage and in its projections (involving, for instance, both narcissism and a sense of hostility / inadequacy, the illusion of omnipotence brought together with the terror of insecurity, the instability of an identity that is nonetheless figured as a fortress, the coexistence of fantasies of the fragmented body with an image of the self as immovable statue, et cetera) is repeated in figurations of the cyborg which are similarly ambiguous: partial fragmentation leads to a new kind of fusion and totality, narcissistic fantasies of creation and reproduction are intertwined with those of destruction and death, the openness of unformed identities coexists with the goal of absolute control, and so on. Such ambiguity hints at the way in which the cyborg may function either to extend our life capacities or, on the other hand, to signal the end of all life itself.

27. In chapter 5, I referred to Barbara Katz Rothman's analysis of the fetus as "a metaphor for 'man' in space, floating free, attached only by the umbilical cord to the spaceship," the mother who has simply become "empty space" (114).

28. Reviewing "those things . . . [and] events . . . which are able to arouse . . . a feeling of the uncanny," Freud mentions "'doubts whether an apparently animate being is really alive; or conversely, whether a lifeless object might not be in fact animate'; . . . wax-work figures, artificial dolls and automatons . . . [and] epileptic seizures and the manifestations of insanity, because these excite in the spectator the feeling that automatic, mechanical processes are at work, concealed beneath the ordinary appearance of animation" (132). As an automated body which is controlled from elsewhere, the cyborg incorporates all of these traits, confounding the self precisely because it seems to be at once more present yet more absent than the subject. As an object, a commodity, it has a certain material presence that lacks the gap of desire that constitutes the subject (the split between consciousness and the unconscious). Yet as an entity lacking agency and a mind of its own, it is also less accessible; it has the absence that characterizes ephemeral forms.

29. Penley also provides an interesting discussion of the use of the uncanny in *Pee-wee's Playhouse*—the way in which Pee-wee's house is a "haunted house," filled with the terror of sexual investigation. Furthermore, in her argument, she discusses the ways in which *Pee-wee's Playhouse* is both familiar and unfamiliar, like and unlike the surrounding (commodified) world of Saturday morning TV (see "Cabinet," especially 138–41 and 142–43).

30. The fact that *Pee-wee's Playhouse* stood out among Saturday morning children's shows (largely cartoon programs) for its use of live characters—even though these characters often seemed like puppets or cartoons—also worked to increase the sense of uncanniness that the show provoked, further confusing the distinction between life and death, reality and fantasy.

31. Using Freud's theory of wit and the unconscious, Bryan Bruce explains that the humor of *Pee-wee's Playhouse* does more than allow for uninhibited play: "Freud also points to a more 'sinister' side of the comic impulse . . . , a manifestation of humour 'in the service of hostile aggression.' There is definitely an edge to Pee-wee . . . [serving] a similarly antagonistic purpose, promoting a rebellion against authority which Freud describes as another function of humour" (6).

32. Doty sees the female characters in *Pee-wee's Playhouse* as doubles of Pee-wee himself (88); this articulates a relationship between femininity and gay male identity, but arguably, it also denies anything other than a mirroring function to female subjectivity.

33. Gabriele Schwab comments on children's—especially male children's—play with cyborgs, analyzing the fantasies of domination involved in these games which teach boys to exert power over technology just as they learn to exert it over nature (68–69). While I agree that control over cyborgs is largely presented as a male prerogative, I would argue that this is not because cybersimulation itself is seen as masculine. On the contrary, the cyborg has been linked to cultural fantasies of the lacking / excessive feminine body, and thus (according to our culture's social and psychological demands) it must be tamed and brought under men's command.

34. One interesting account of the TV cyborg that is relevant to my comments on the "holism" of the video subject (both on and in front of the screen) is provided by Morse, "Sport." Using the theories of Heinrich von Kleist, Morse discusses the televised athlete in terms of the "cultural fantasy of the body as perfect machine . . . flowing into the instinctual patterns of nature in a 'harmonious oneness of being.' . . ." Suggesting how television viewers are drawn into this fantasy, she goes on to add, "Not just athletes but also spectators of sport ritual participate vicariously in this 'flow' . . ." (56). In chapter 4, I further elaborate how this image of grace, harmony, and flow is linked to figurations of femininity.

35. Both Baudrillard and Gabriele Schwab differentiate the cyborg from the automaton and / or the robot. Their arguments are too long to summarize here, but, in effect, they each conclude that rather than compensating for their human creators or contrasting with the societies in which they existed (as did previous mechanical beings), cyborgs become fully a part of a "decentered" postmodernity, merging into the surrounding cybersimulated environment (Schwab 72–73; Baudrillard, *Simulations* 83–102). Because of this new position of the cyborg within our culture—particularly its position within the realm of television, where decentered subjectivity seems to be the norm—the video cyborg would not subvert our expectations in the same way that the mechanical creatures that Freud describes do; this video being may therefore exist somewhat beyond the uncanny's affective regime (failing to provoke the dread inspired by their cinematic counterparts). In this sense, the television cyborgs who exist within the sphere of hyperreality are a bit like the beings who populate the imaginary worlds of fiction: according to Freud, unless a writer models his fictional world on the supposedly rational order of "common reality," the effects of his craft will not be felt as uncanny, for they do not break the rules of expected possibility ("'Uncanny'" 158–61). However, I would disagree with theorists who (somewhat hysterically) argue that we are all beyond all sense of rational expectation. Clearly, neither postmodernism nor television has overthrown this logic even if they have shifted our culture in transitional ways. While television cyborgs may then operate within a new cultural formation (and hence with new psychic consequences that require further exploration), the dynamics of gender that Freud associates with the uncanny are still crucial to examine.

36. Not only does Pee-wee's name suggest castration anxiety because of its association with denigrations of size, but it also invokes the idea of bed-wetting, which, according to psychoanalysis, often prompts the parental threats leading to this anxiety. In *Pee-wee's Playhouse*, then, the male name (which usually functions as the assertion of patriarchal identity) merely refigures the anxieties that the paternal Law is meant to replace.

37. See also where Penley details some of the episodes dealing with sexual investigation and gender roles (also calling attention to Pee-wee's famous refrain, "I know you are, but what am I?") ("Cabinet" 133–38).

38. There have, however, been some interesting reception and audience analyses of this show. For discussions of two very different viewing populations (children in the one case and gay men in the other), see Jenkins, "Going Bonkers!"; and Doty.

39. This episode, the series pilot (and a remake of the text originally broadcast on

England's Channel 4), aired on ABC on March 31, 1987, and was produced by Peter Wagg. It starred Matt Frewer as both Edison Carter and Max Headroom, Amanda Pays as Theora Jones (Edison's computer "controller"), Chris Young as Bryce Lynch (the computer whiz-kid), and Charles Roket as Mr. Grossberg (the melodramatic villain aligned with the Zic-Zac corporation).

40. In an article on commercials that make stars—particularly ironic in the case of *Max Headroom* given the explicitly anti-commercial message of the British TV film on which the series was based—Max Headroom is compared to such characters as Ronald McDonald, Morris the Cat, and the California Raisins (see Montesano). Coca-Cola enlisted Max in its fight against Pepsi in 1986, the same year that Cinemax began its video/talk show, and Video Storyboard voted the Max Headroom ads the best-remembered commercials of that year (Ross, "Techno-Ethics," n. 14, 155).

41. *Max Headroom* was revived (in order to fill in a "programming vacuum" created by the writers strike [Ross, "Techno-Ethics" 153]) on April 28, 1988.

42. Writing on the relationship between cybernetic simulation and consumerism, Nichols explains: "Just as the mechanical reproduction of copies revealed the power of industrial capitalism to reorganize and reassemble the world around us, rendering it as commodity art, the automated intelligence of chips reveals the power of post-industrial capitalism to simulate and replace the world around us, rendering not only that exterior realm but also interior ones of consciousness, intelligence, thought and intersubjectivity as commodity experience" (33). This seems to me to be exactly the case in *Pee-wee's Playhouse* and *Max Headroom*: rather than endorsing consumerism by explicitly promoting it (and, in fact, while even doing the opposite), these shows bring the interior conditions of consumer consciousness to the surface of their texts.

43. Penley makes a related point about the program's ostensible rejection of the "blatantly manipulative commercialism that pervades children's television programming." Discussing an episode in which Pee-wee finally takes up his offer and invites the Salesman in (during a party in which everyone receives a present except for Pee-wee), Penley quips that "everyone has a price" and then explains: "Repeatedly in the Playhouse, a moral stance is established—here, an objection to the kind of corporate decision-making that turns every kids show into a half-hour commercial—and then blithely undermined" ("Cabinet" 141). In contrast, Balfour interprets this same episode as a carnivalesque event that overturns traditional social rules and offers a politically utopian vision because the Salesman really *does* have an incredible offer: free foil for Pee-wee's foil ball. "This entry of the salesman with his offer of free foil clearly marks it as the most patently utopian moment of the show because as everyone knows, there is no such thing as free foil" (165). In addition to being unsure of what it would even mean to single out one moment on *Pee-wee's Playhouse* as exceptionally carnivalesque, I would also argue that in order to evaluate *Pee-wee's Playhouse* in regard to consumerism, the critic must look at more than the program's "plot." In other words, while it is true that Pee-wee often takes a stand against commercialism within the diegesis, the very rhythm and structure of the text (not to mention its context on Saturday morning TV) seems to replicate the kinds of conditions associated with consumerism (the merging of identities discussed in the text above). The fact that, in this encounter with the Salesman, Pee-wee undermines his own moral position thus reveals something more than a lapse on his part: it once again points to the decentered nature of Pee-wee's cyborgian universe in which oppositions (even polar opinions) easily coexist—a universe which is custom-made for the promotion of consumption in its most general mode of operation, even if no particular product is advertised.

44. On the centering effect of the image of the star in otherwise decentered music videos, see Kaplan, *Rocking* 47.

45. Discussing the publicly sanctioned fantasies of popular fiction and the

reoccurring figure of an invincible hero, Freud writes, "Through the revealing characteristic of invulnerability we can immediately recognize His Majesty the Ego, the hero alike of every daydream and of every story" ("On Creative Writing" 150). *Max Headroom* and *Pee-wee's Playhouse* might have been seen as ground-breaking texts, but clearly their heroes (Edison Carter and Pee-wee Herman) continue this tradition.

46. I take the pun about "Pee-wee's misadventure" from Paul Gray. For another interesting commentary on this scandal, see "Pee-wee's Bad Trip."

47. Such a valorization can be found, for example, in Bruce's reading of *Pee-wee's Playhouse*: while he admits that audiences accept Pee-wee's "sexual difference" because it is "situated . . . before the constraints of a repressed, adult sexual identity," he nonetheless views this as a radical ambiguity in the text (6, 5). I would hasten to add, however, that this ambiguity does not prevent *Pee-wee's Playhouse* from being quite misogynist. In his discussion of the show, Doty attempts to balance his recognition of this problem with his regard for *Pee-wee's Playhouse* as an important gay text, arguing that a "'one-size-fits-all' approach to male misogyny . . . is not very sensitive to how the particular position of gay men within patriarchy has been constructed in relation to concepts of 'woman' and the 'feminine'" (86). Here, he explicitly takes issue with Modleski's scathing critique of the appropria-tion of/attack on femininity in *Pee-wee's Playhouse*, and the implicit debate be-tween Modleski and Doty raises fascinating and vexing issues about the relation-ship between sexism and heterosexism, feminism and gay male theory. Of course, one of the critical initiators of this conversation between feminist and anti–homophobic approaches is Eve Kosofsky Sedgwick; for an analysis of the con-tinuum that links male homosociality to male homosexual desire (a continuum that might help us understand both the misogyny and the queer sensibility of this and other texts), see Sedgwick's *Between Men*.

48. Arguing that *Pee-wee's Playhouse* deconstructs masculinity (and thus sub-verts the kind of hypermasculinity that I discuss in chapter 4), Penley writes:

> [T]he interest of this show lies in the way it re-presents masculinity right at the edge of the territory of the child, that morally quarantined and protected area. It is almost as if the show "recognizes" that as long as infantile sexuality remains conceptually off limits, it will not be possible to rethink sexual roles and sexed identities, masculine or otherwise. This is because the adult fantasy of childhood simplicity and happiness is a founding fantasy, one that offers the possibility of innocence to those who need to retain the idea of innocence itself. As long as this fantasy remains unex-amined, so too will the fantasy of masculinity. ("Cabinet" 151)

While I find Penley's argument quite interesting, I would argue that although *Pee-wee's Playhouse* hints at such a radical requestioning of both infantile and mascu-line sexuality, it actually evades these issues by buying into this very fantasy of childhood simplicity whenever the tensions provoked by its sexual questioning seem about to erupt.

49. While I find Sontag's comments on camp productive for my discussion of camp's ambiguous relationship to the politics of postmodernity, I don't want to suggest that she gives the definitive statement on camp; many others have written about this cultural formation, offering a variety of interpretations of its uses and implications. See, for example, the essays collected in the anthologies edited by Bergman and Meyer.

50. Seeing poignancy and charm in what supposedly is without value—con-sumer culture's leftovers—camp paradoxically both exposes and subverts the idea of expendability so central to consumer capitalism even as it celebrates consumption and mass culture by treasuring its debris.

51. Penley offers a more positive assessment of the way in which camp may

correlate with postmodern subjectivity. Considering the historical shifts in a camp sensibility revealed by *Pee-wee's Playhouse*, she writes:

> In [his/her] plea for tolerance and acceptance, . . . the camp figure typically exhibits a bitter wit, a form of "gay angst," the sadness of those who have internalized straight society's opinion of them. But the Pee-wee persona appears to offer a new version of camp subjectivity in that one finds here no inner pathos, no inner struggle, no problem of feeling abnormal or wanting to hide it. . . . Perhaps this oscillation without anxiety represents a new postmodernist stage of camp subjectivity, one distinguished by a capacity for zipping through sexual roles that is as fast and unremarkable as zapping through the channels. ("Cabinet" 149)

While an oscillation of sexual identity without anxiety or tension may be an admirable aspect of the show, this may also reveal how a camp position no longer stands out as a particular stance toward society but has instead become subsumed within cyborgian culture as a whole. Modleski makes this same point when she argues that "camp coincides with postmodern aesthetics in general" ("Incredible Shrinking" 101).

52. On the notion of hypersimulation, see, for example, Baudrillard, *In the Shadow* 33. For a discussion of postmodern pastiche, see Jameson, "Postmodernism" 64–65.

53. Debating Modleski's reading, Doty reminds us that this attitude of course also depends on the position of the camp reader (83–84). Nonetheless, this does not depose Pee-wee from his own position as clubhouse leader, the "virtual playboy" in charge of his world.

54. As O'Brien writes, "Pee-wee has adopted youth as an avocation. And in doing so he has become a great symbol of America, where everyone attempts to be younger than they are . . ." (90). In addition to offering a compelling sense of regression, the appeal of *Pee-wee's Playhouse* for the adult viewer may also have lied in the fact that it nostalgically "returned" to (or more accurately, it actually fabricated) a time untainted by political struggle—a childhood whose history is rewritten in order to evade any sense of cultural conflict, a childhood focused only on playing with one's toys. Contrary to some critics' claims, *Pee-wee's Playhouse* was not the first children's show to employ double meanings and therefore have cross-over appeal to both adults and children: in the early 1960s, for example, *The Bullwinkle Show* had a similar success. One difference between *Pee-wee's Playhouse* and that text, however, is that the *Bullwinkle* plots involved a spoof of cold war politics (Rocky and Bullwinkle's struggles against the Russian spies, Boris and Natasha) and thus drew adults through an acknowledgment of political power struggles. Pee-wee, on the other hand, seems to have attracted some audiences because his (and the show's) regression allowed viewers to evade any such issues.

55. Making a similar allusion, Balfour notes that "for all we know, Pee-wee may have generated spontaneously into the adolescent age he is stuck in" (162). This sense of spontaneous generation does not just describe the particularities of Max's and Pee-wee's own conditions, but seems to be part of the very imaginary of cybernetic simulation. Detailing the difference between this simulation and previous forms of "reproduction," Nichols writes:

> The photographic image, as Roland Barthes proposed, suggests "having been there. . . ." The computer simulation suggests only a "being here" and "having come from nowhere" of what it presents, drawing on those genetic-like algorithms that allow it to bring its simulation into existence, *sui generis*. . . . The individual becomes nothing but an ahistorical position within a chain of discourse marked exhaustively by those shifters that place him or her within speech acts ("I," "here," "now," "you," "there," "then"). (30)

While Nichols is referring to cybernetic subjectivity, the same point about this sense of "nowness" and "immediacy" can be made about television and the video subject. As video cyborgs, Max and Pee-wee constantly refer to themselves in this "now," activating the "I" that finds its place only in discourse even more than is typical on television; they break into the flow of their texts to speak of themselves with an almost hysterical insistence.

56. The myth of Athena is itself filled with similarly paradoxical gender figurations which Freud discusses in two of his essays, "Genital Organization of the Libido" and "Medusa's Head," both in *Sexuality and the Psychology of Love*. Given the conditions of Athena's ascension as Athens's patron, she might be considered the original 'token woman,' a goddess whose position of prestige merely masks a patriarchal rule. As Freud notes, however, she wore the image of the Medusa's Head—"the mythological symbol of loathing" that represents the uncanny female sex on her armor (174). In so doing, she became the ultimate "virgin goddess": "a woman who is unapproachable and repels all sexual desires—since she displays the terrifying genitals of the Mother . . . , a being who frightens and repels because she is castrated" (212–13). Yet Freud goes on to explain that while her decapitation suggests castration, the snakes that make up Medusa's hair "nevertheless serve actually as a mitigation of the horror, for they replace the penis, the absence of which is the cause of the horror" (212). Furthermore, the belief that the sight of this decapitated head "makes the spectator stiff with terror, turns him to stone" also acts as an assuagement, "for becoming stiff means an erection. Thus in the original situation it offers consolation to the spectator: he is still in possession of a penis, and the stiffening reassures him of the fact" (212). Apparently proclaiming the power of the mother, Athena then actually reneges on this threat. In fact, she is, in many ways, just like Pee-wee and Max: she is, like them, strangely desexed and unapproachable, confusing sexual figurations and largely undermining (rather than unleashing) their possibilities. And just as they combine symbols of femininity/castration with assurances that work to contain the fear that this brings, Athena takes her place as a powerful feminine figure only by channeling disgust at the female sex and confirming the male subject's own phallic potency.

57. As Balfour writes, "Pee-wee often dons a helmet that features a single eye, giving him three in all, which identifies tangentially with Oedipus, at least in one reading of the Oedipus myth. 'Oedipus had one eye too many,' Hölderlin could write" (162). Penley also refers to the Sphinx and Pee-wee's sexual investigation ("Cabinet" 136).

58. Balfour also notes the way in which the Sphinx (given its fragmented form) seems to be the perfect Pee-wee character. In discussing the Sphinx and the Oedipal myth, he states: "The classical sphinx proposed a riddle, a question whose answer, as only Oedipus knew, was 'man.' And the consequence of a wrong answer to the riddle was death. In *Pee-wee's Playhouse*, 'man' is the question not the answer, but a question whose consequences are only somewhat less grave" (166). In contrast to this reading, I would suggest that Pee-wee (shielded under the Sphinx's wing and thus protected from any dire consequences) simply evades the question altogether.

59. On the notion of television's "ahistory," see White, "Television."

60. A discussion of communications, cybernetic, and information sciences can be found in Nichols; Haraway, "Manifesto" 81–85; and in several of the articles in *Discourse*'s special issue, "On Technology." See especially the essay by Porush, in which he explains how cybernetics tamed the more radical implications of irreducible uncertainty that scientists had previously emphasized:

> The way cybernetics one-upped Heisenbergian physics ranks as one of the great, sneaky philosophical tricks of the century. . . . [It] took the formula for thermodynamic randomness (*entropy*) and used it to define the randomness from which information arises, and then also called it *entropy*. This ingenious trick had powerful consequences. It appropriated the idea that humans introduced uncertainty into the system and defined it as nothing more

or less than a precondition for having a quantifiable amount of information. Cybernetics thereby managed to subsume the messiness of the human observer's role under a system of positive math. (55)

In this way, the potentially subversive "free play" of the cyborg is contained within a controllable system of measurable data.

61. In other words, both the rejections and endorsements of postmodern disruption fail to think of simulation's play in anything other than traditional terms of evaluation. As Martin Schwab writes:

A tradition of cultural criticism extending from Romanticism to the Frankfurt School has acclaimed or regretted the dissolution of classical grand form and interprets the phenomenon as a transition from connectedness to disconnectedness, from teleology to randomness. . . . Post-Nietzschean positions, exemplified for instance by Lyotard, which interpret the same phenomenon in terms of a liberation from the constraints of order seem to me to differ from the conservative cultural criticism mainly by reversing the evaluation. They see liberation where its opponents perceive alienation. But in all these instances the exact nature of the *transformation* and the chances to participate in its course are lost in the global perspective of a struggle between the forces of order and of chaos. (92–93)

Trapped within these limited terms, critics are unable to develop a full (or fully engaged) theory of postmodernity—one that would go beyond description to indicate spaces of intervention as well.

62. *The American Heritage Dictionary* 328. Also see Porush, who notes that cybernetic science was named after the Greek word for *governor, kybernos* (55). On the military origin of cybernetic systems, see Nichols (35). See also De Landa.

63. Seminal pieces on the utopian longings found in mass culture are: Jameson, "Reification" and Dyer, "Entertainment."

64. Doty explains (justifies?) many of the problems in *Pee-wee's Playhouse* by reading it as a late 1980s (that is, post-Stonewall) version of a 1950s (pre-Stonewall) gay sensibility, with all of the problems that this entails (see, for example, 82, 89). His argument is intriguing and convincing, but as stated in the text above (and as Doty himself acknowledges), this does not negate the aspects of the show that reinforce a traditional male domination.

65. This information comes from Stephan Oakes, executive producer of the first season of *Pee-wee's Playhouse*, cited by Penley ("Cabinet" 144–45).

66. One example cited by Ross, for example, involved a video pirate who took over the signals of two Chicago TV stations in order to make a brief appearance as Max Headroom—here complete with a body whose bottom was bared to the camera ("Techno-Ethics" 138).

7. Networking

1. While it is my central focus throughout this study, I am not trying to argue that gender is the only significant interpretive category; other categories (regional, racial, ethnic, class, age, and other diversities) are, of course, equally important to explore. Indeed, as postmodernism calls into question totalizing "master narratives" that operate at a global level, it directs our attention to a number of (intersecting) issues and concerns at the local level, all of which raise important questions for analysis. TV's own shift from "broadcasting" to "narrowcasting" might be seen as paralleling—and demanding—a critical project which looks to these various sites. The challenge, as I suggest here, is attempting to "network" all of these concerns—a problem that I certainly wouldn't claim to solve in this book.

2. *Broadcast News* was written and directed by James L. Brooks for 20th Century Fox in 1987; *Network* was directed by Sidney Lumet from a screenplay by Paddy Cheyefsky for United Artists in 1976. Although this film was made a decade before

most of the television shows that I examine in this study, its exploration of the relationships between television and gender, multinational capitalism and the manipulation of spiritual values, money and sex, politics and consumerism almost presages the fraught relations that I interrogate here. In fact, in their analysis of political conspiracy films and "the failure of liberalism," Douglas Kellner and Michael Ryan note that *Network* was appealing to "those populist themes of the culture (the small-guy hero, resentment against the system, distrust of power and big institutions) whose libertarian, individualist, traditionalist, and antiauthoritarian strains would be exploited by the Right later in the decade" (101) and into the 1980s (particularly because *Network* also targets for criticism any radical alternative in its mockery of socialist, feminist, and black power movements). In this way, *Network*'s affirmation of "the individual" (construed, of course, as a male individual) against "the system" paves the way for the kinds of projections that I discuss throughout this book.

3. This "psychic battering" takes contrasting forms in the two films. As I note in the chapter, Jane, the heroine of *Broadcast News*, falls for Tom, the rising reporter (later to become anchorman), when she sees his story on date rape, which includes a cut-away to Tom's emotional face (eyes brimming with tears) as he conducts an interview. All of the women in the newsroom are moved by the story, including the initially resistant Jane, much to the sarcastic dismay of the male reporter (Aaron Altman, played by Albert Brooks) who is Tom's romantic and professional rival. After a newsroom shake-up (in which most workers are fired, Aaron resigns, Tom gets promoted, and Jane takes over for her laid-off boss, becoming the network's first female bureau chief), Aaron tries to dissuade Jane of her feelings for Tom, pointing out that Tom's tearful reaction to the earlier date rape story must have been faked: there was only one camera shooting the interview, so the cut-away shot was surely filmed later (an obvious fact that Jane, as news producer *extraordinaire*, certainly should have been able to pick up on her own). Having been sucked into an identification with the raped woman as well as with Tom, Jane is wounded to learn that she has in fact been seduced and betrayed—thus solidifying her identification with the rape victim while firmly breaking hers with Tom— and she abruptly ends the relationship with Tom, refusing to go off on a vacation they had planned. In opposition to Jane's "battering" through this "feminine" position (her alignment with a raped woman), *Network*'s heroine, Diana, is shown to have no female identifications whatsoever. She is represented as psychically impaired through her loss of all sensitivity and feeling, all "womanliness"—a loss that is chalked up to her immersion in the cutthroat world of broadcasting.

Both of these women, though, are represented as successful in their careers, moving to heights unprecedented (according to the narratives) for women in TV. But while they may be empowered in their diegeses, I would argue that they are disempowered by the films. *Network*'s Diana is a charismatic but ultimately very unlikable character, and the film ends with the suggestion that she will never have another human connection again in her life—which the film's hero furthermore predicts will be cut short by her own psychic failings. *Broadcast News*'s Jane is smart and appealing, and in the film's coda (seven years later), she seems about to attain both her personal and her professional goals: we learn that she has a boyfriend (one even willing to do some commuting for the relationship) and that she is about to accept the job of network news managing editor, making her Tom's (the new anchorman's) boss. Thus, by the end of the film, she is presented as the woman who can have it all (man plus high-powered career)—the cliché, in other words, of the postfeminist "superwoman." Viewers, however, are never afforded a glimpse of how she pulls this off (or even if she does). We never see the guy or the job, and so we are left with the image of Jane established earlier in the text: that of a woman who calls herself "a basket case" for her inability to integrate her private and her public selves, television and "real life." In this way, it is the film itself that has it all: it can claim a "positive" image of a conquering heroine without having actually to represent this achievement—or determine what would have to be transformed in order for such a thing to be in fact achieved.

4. Tom might be seen as a male version of "the dumb blond" who achieves success despite—or because of—what is marked in the film as his stupidity. Tom does have an array of skills, but they are stereotypically "feminine" ones: he has good clothes sense and knows a number of tricks concerning appearance, posing, and self-image—precisely the skills that his competitor, Aaron, lacks.

5. One could argue that this, indeed, is what occurs. Not only is Jane figured as participating in a "masculine" discourse in her promotion of "hard" news reporting over the encroachment of emotion and entertainment values (a "soft" news approach), but in the scene I discuss above, most of Jane's information (which she then passes on to Tom through his earpiece) actually comes from Aaron, who gives it to Jane through the phone (that is, through her own earpiece). She is, in other words, precisely a relay between the two men, a component in a circuit that runs between these two male poles.

6. While I do not discuss computer possibilities and/or communities here, it would be interesting to trace the gender connotations of this new mode of "mediation" in order to analyze if and how the dynamics that I discuss in this study might be applied—or need to be altered—to fit that example.

7. My language here only begins to point toward the sexual coding of televised/televisual warfare (the place of gender, that is, within an industrial/military/media complex); others, however, have offered very interesting sustained analyses of these issues, particularly in relationship to TV's coverage of the Gulf War. See, for example, Castonguay, "The Masquerade"; Marks; and Wiegman, "Missiles."

8. Jameson himself discusses the aesthetic potential of video (yet not necessarily television) to challenge modernist forms in "Reading without Interpretation." A point similar to the one that I make in the text above about the relationship between TV, economics, and postmodernism can be found in Hayward and Kerr 5, 7.

9. For discussions of how TV no longer refers to an outside reality, but instead seems to refer only to itself, see White, "Crossing Wavelengths"; and Eco, "Guide."

10. The notion of the feminine as both the repressed matrix/ground from which the male must separate and the excessive object which must be investigated as Other is a common one in feminist psychoanalytic thought. For just one influential discussion of this, see Irigaray, *Speculum*.

11. Because of this, it is important not only to analyze the relations that bind gender, television, and postmodernism, but to see these relations as productive ones, allowing for the construction of new knowledges and activities (as TV articulates a sexually commodified address, gender produces various positions of viewing and consuming, postmodernism creates new alignments of power and pleasure, and the languages of all of these provide cultural critics with conceptual tools). While not specifically dealing with the media, for similar assessments of the centrality of sexual difference to cultural theories of postmodernism, see, among others, Jardine, *Gynesis*; and Morris, "Introduction," especially 11–16.

12. Works which employ a dystopian model of postmodernism are too numerous to list here. For some representative and influential examples, see Jameson, "Postmodernism"; Baudrillard in, for example, *Simulations* and *In the Shadow*; and Kroker and Cook in *The Postmodern Scene*.

13. Sandy Flitterman discusses the relationship between the open-ended narrative structure of the soap opera and the effectivity of the commercials which offer oases of closure on daytime TV in "Real Soap Operas." While this juxtaposition may be most marked on daytime television, the multiplicity, interruption, and nonclosure of the soap opera is, in many ways, simply an extreme case of the general structure of television narrative, and thus this relationship can be said to hold true of all of TV: in television series, the same faults are re-exposed in new

enactments each week, and in serials, the solutions to such faults are endlessly deferred; the commercials, however, assure us of the possibility of narrative solutions, simply through purchasing the products they promote.

14. Fiske, supplementing Barthes's distinction between the "readerly" and the "writerly" text so as to allow for a third category in which he places TV, writes: "The producerly text shows many of the characteristics . . . [of] the radical text . . . : it draws attention to its own textuality, it does not produce a singular reading subject but one that is involved in the process of representation rather than a victim of it, it plays with the difference between the representation and the real . . . , and it replaces the pleasures of identification and familiarity with more cognitive pleasures of participation and production" (*Television* 95; Fiske refers here to Barthes, *S/Z*; and to Kaplan's discussion of radical texts in *Women and Film*). Other positive appraisals of postmodernism or television include, for example, Robert Allen, "On Reading"; and Collins, "Postmodernism."

15. The phrase "waning of affect," used to describe postmodern culture, comes from Jameson, "Postmodernism" 61.

16. Deleuze and Guattari develop the notion of the nomadic subject in *A Thousand Plateaus*.

17. The debates arising around the meaning of the term *post* in *postmodernism* also attest to the controversy surrounding the claim of an absolute historical break. For a similar critique of postmodern theories' "disjunctive dilemmas" and the ways in which they are mapped onto historical scenarios, see Montag.

18. On the death of "grand narratives" in our culture, see Lyotard.

19. Polan 53; and Nichols.

20. Modleski, "Rhythms" 71. Her notion of "the art of being off center" is derived from Walter Benjamin, "On Some Motifs in Baudelaire" 176. Modleski and Benjamin are speaking of housewives and the unemployed respectively, but these comments also have a particular resonance for our media-literate youth: a "preoccupied" and "decentered" subjectivity—not to mention un- or multiple employment—are clichéd components of the stereotype of the "Generation X slacker."

21. Discussing the ways in which the operations of simulation threaten the difference between true and false, real and imaginary, Baudrillard writes:

> Psychology and medicine stop at this point, before a thereafter undiscoverable truth of the illness. For if any symptom can be "produced," and can no longer be accepted as a fact of nature, then every illness may be considered as simulatable and simulated, and medicine loses its meaning since it only knows how to treat "true" illnesses by their objective causes. Psychosomatics evolves in a dubious way on the edge of the illness principle. As for psychoanalysis, it transfers the symptom from the organic to the unconscious order: once again, the latter is held to be true, more true than the former—but why should simulation stop at the portals of the unconscious? Why couldn't the "work" of the unconscious be "produced" in the same way as any other symptom in classical medicine? Dreams already are. . . . What can psychoanalysis do with the reduplication of the discourse of the unconscious in a discourse of simulation that can never be unmasked, since it isn't false either? (*Simulations* 5–7)

Yet the very example of dreams that Baudrillard uses undermines his argument, for it indicates that the unconscious was never theorized by Freud or Lacan as a realm of simple truth and reality outside of the work of signifying systems. Structured like a language, the unconscious necessarily involves a mediation and/or production of "the truth," always involves what Baudrillard considers simulation. Simply because signification has no direct relationship to reality does not mean that it has no cultural or psychic effectivity, and a model (such as the one that Baudrillard offers) that posits a historical break from an era of reference to an era of codes misinterprets the work of both signification and the unconscious.

22. Commenting on the ways in which postmodern critics disallow the possibility of resistance by insisting on the totality of postmodern domination, Montag also notes this misinterpretation of psychoanalytic theory (found, for instance, in Jameson, "Postmodernism" 87):

> Both Jameson and Lyotard seem to agree that such . . . instances [possible spaces of resistance] once existed but have now vanished into the purely present. Jameson cites two examples of what he calls "pre-capitalist enclaves" which by virtue of their "extraterritoriality," that is, their exteriority to a given conjuncture, permit "critical effectivity." Faced with the puzzling assertion that one of these "enclaves" is the unconscious, we can only ask in what sense it is possible to speak of the unconscious as an "enclave" (let alone "pre-capitalist"). Such an assertion belongs more properly to Jungian psychology than to psychoanalysis as understood by Freud and Lacan. In fact, the claim to transcendentality brings to mind the Hegelian Beautiful Soul of which Lacan spoke so many times. The Beautiful Soul denounces the disorder of a world from which it has withdrawn precisely to avoid having to recognize the extent of its own participation in that disorder. (95)

23. Also noting the ways in which postmodern theorists may disavow difference(s) by rejecting a theory of the unconscious, James Collins critiques Baudrillard as follows:

> The failure to recognise the persistence of belief in differences within the masses is most obvious in Baudrillard's misappropriation of Octave Mannoni's "je sais bien, mais quand-même" ("I know, but all the same"). He asserts, "One both believes it and doesn't believe it at the same time, without questioning it seriously, an attitude that may be summed up in the phrase, 'Yes, I know, but all the same.'" For Baudrillard the phrase signifies an intellectual shrug of the shoulders, yet for Mannoni the phrase describes the basis of fetishistic belief which, if anything, means the insistence on differentiation, the denial of neutrality. The basis for fetishistic pleasure is always a specific object, and as such totally refutes Baudrillard's belief that differences are no longer important. The suspension of disbelief or the leap of belief that makes the "quand-même" possible in a given individual depends upon a specific object or text of desire. ("Postmodernism" 13)

While I agree with Collins's critique of Baudrillard, it is interesting that Collins himself perpetuates a certain denial of difference—that of gender—in his explanation. It is not simply that fetishism is based upon processes of differentiation or a specific text of desire—these processes and this text are precisely that of sexual differentiation, a crucial point which Collins fails to note. In other words, by denying difference in the gesture of rejecting psychoanalysis, postmodern critics also deny (or fail to analyze) the structures of sexual difference operative in our culture. The fact that the "quand-même" is also central to Christian Metz's famous analysis of cinema as an imaginary signifier also suggests the continued importance of film theory—a key site for the analysis of sexual difference(s)—for television and postmodern studies.

24. Pfeil, "'Making'." See also Pfeil, "Potholders"; and Barry King.

25. Many feminist theorists have addressed this issue. For one sustained analysis, see Jardine.

26. For a sarcastic example of this, see Pfeil's readings of two novels (one involving a man who murders his wife and the other concerning a boy's initiation into manhood as a result of a seduction by a "young black swamp-woman" [68]) in "Potholders." Commenting on these books' deployment of destabilizing textual strategies, he writes, "[W]e have a quintessentially postmodern text which meets these feminist-poststructuralist demands . . . ; what more could [Hélène] Cixous wish for . . . ?" (65). While Pfeil poses this rhetorical question in order to argue against the value of using a "feminist-poststructuralist" approach in analy-

ses of postmodernism, I would argue that even—indeed, especially—within this approach, we could find a lot more to ask for from such texts. While feminist theory may strive to disrupt the unification of the realist text (and the centered male subject thereby constructed), clearly not all disruptions from order would be equally valorized; it is recognizing the differences within difference that is essential to feminist criticism.

27. Morris makes a similar observation about the feminist use of the genre of "woman's complaint," "a speech-genre all too familiar in everyday life, as well as in pantomime, cartoons, and sitcoms." Defined by "unsuccessful repetition," this mode combines self-expression with negation, failing, as Morris writes, "to produce the desired effects of difference that might allow the complaint to end" (*Pirate's* 15). TV, defined by successful repetition, may then provide an ideal arena for critics to analyze the terms of these complaints. In either case, we can only continue to work to construct such differences within postmodern and TV criticism, hoping that this may shift not only the position of the feminist cultural theorist, but the very networks that define mass-mediated life.

WORKS CITED

Adorno, Theodor W. "Culture Industry Reconsidered." *New German Critique* 6 (Fall 1975): 12–19.

———. "Television and the Patterns of Mass Culture." In Rosenberg and White 474–88.

Allen, Jeanne. "The Film Viewer as Consumer." *Quarterly Review of Film Studies* 5.4 (1980): 481–99.

Allen, Robert, ed. *Channels of Discourse: Television and Contemporary Criticism.* Chapel Hill: U of North Carolina P, 1987.

———, ed. *Channels of Discourse, Reassembled: Television and Contemporary Criticism.* 2nd ed. Chapel Hill: U of North Carolina P, 1992.

———. "On Reading Soaps: A Semiotic Primer." In Kaplan, *Regarding* 97–108.

———. *Speaking of Soap Operas.* Chapel Hill: U of North Carolina P, 1985.

Altman, Karen E. "Television as a Gendered Technology: Advertising the American Television Set." *Journal of Popular Film and Television* 17.2 (1989): 46–56.

Altman, Rick. *Genre: The Musical.* London: BFI/Routledge, 1981.

American Heritage Dictionary of the English Language. Boston: Houghton, 1976.

Anders, Gunther. "The Phantom World of TV." In Rosenberg and White 358–67.

Ang, Ien. *Desperately Seeking the Audience.* New York: Routledge, 1991.

———. *Watching Dallas: Soap Opera and the Melodramatic Imagination.* New York: Methuen, 1985.

Ang, Ien, and Joke Hermes. "Gender and/in Media Consumption." In Curran and Gurevitch 307–28.

Arditti, Rita, Renate Duelli Klein, and Shelley Minden, eds. *Test Tube Women: What Future for Motherhood?* Boston: Routledge, 1984.

Aspinall, Sue, and Robert Murphy, eds. *Gainsborough Melodrama.* London: BFI, 1983.

Avery, Robert K., and David Eason, eds. *Critical Perspectives on Media and Society.* New York: Guilford, 1991.

Baehr, Helen, and Gillian Dyer, eds. *Boxed In: Women and Television.* New York: Pandora, 1987.

Bakhtin, Mikhail. *Rabelais and His World.* Trans. Helene Iswolsky. Cambridge: MIT P, 1968.

Balfour, Ian. "The Playhouse of the Signifier: Reading Pee-wee Herman." *Camera Obscura* 17 (May 1988): 155–67.

Barnouw, Erik. *Tube of Plenty: The Evolution of American Television.* 2nd rev. ed. New York: Oxford UP, 1990.

Barthes, Roland. *Camera Lucida: Reflections on Photography.* Trans. Richard Howard. New York: Farrar, 1981.

———. *S/Z.* Trans. Richard Miller. London: Cape, 1975.

———. "Upon Leaving the Movie Theatre." In Cha 1–4.

Bathrick, Serafina. "*The Mary Tyler Moore Show*: Women at Home and at Work." In Feuer et al. 99–131.

Baudrillard, Jean. *Baudrillard Live: Selected Interviews.* Ed. Mike Gane. Trans. Mike Gane et al. New York: Routledge, 1993.

———. "The Ecstasy of Communication." Trans. John Johnston. In Foster 126–34.

———. *In the Shadow of the Silent Majorities . . . Or the End of the Social and Other Essays.* Trans. Paul Foss, John Johnston, and Paul Patton. New York: Semiotext(e), 1983.

———. *Simulations.* Trans. Paul Foss, Paul Patton, and Philip Beitchman. New York: Semiotext(e), 1983.

Benjamin, Walter. *Illuminations.* Ed. Hannah Arendt. Trans. Harry Zohn. New York: Schocken, 1969.

Bennett, Tony, Susan Boyd-Bowman, Colin Mercer, and Janet Woollacott, eds. *Popular Television and Film: A Reader.* London: BFI, 1981.

Bennett, Tony, and Janet Woollacott. *Bond and Beyond: Fiction, Ideology, and Social Process.* London: Macmillan, 1987.

Benveniste, Emile. *Problems in General Linguistics.* Trans. Mary Elizabeth Meek. Coral Gables: U of Miami P, 1971.

Bergman, David. *Camp Grounds: Style and Homosexuality.* Amherst: U of Massachusetts P, 1993.

Berko, Lili. "Simulation and High Concept Imagery: The Case of Max Headroom." *Wide Angle* 10.4 (1988): 50–61.

Betterton, Rosemary, ed. *Looking On: Images of Femininity in the Visual Arts and Media.* London: Pandora, 1987.

Beusse, Robert B., and Russell Shaw. "Maude's Abortion: Spontaneous or Induced?" *America* 3 (Nov. 1973): 324–26.

Bhabha, Homi. "Of Mimicry and Man: The Ambivalence of Colonial Discourse." *October* 28 (Spring 1984): 125–33.

———. "The Other Question . . ." *Screen* 24.6 (1983): 18–36.

Bloch, Ernst, et al. *Aesthetics and Politics.* Ed. and trans. Ronald Taylor. London: NLB, 1977.

Boddy, William. *Fifties Television: The Industry and Its Critics.* Urbana: U of Illinois P, 1990.

———. "Loving a Nineteen-Inch Motorola: American Writing on Television." In Kaplan, *Regarding* 1–11.

Bogle, Donald. *Toms, Coons, Mulattoes, Mammies and Bucks: An Interpretive History of Blacks in American Films.* New York: Bantam, 1973.

Bonner, Frances, et al., eds. *Imagining Women: Cultural Representations and Gender.* Cambridge: Polity, 1992.

Boorstin, Daniel. *The Image: A Guide to Pseudo-Events in America.* New York: Atheneum, 1971.

Bordewich, Fergus M. "Colorado's Thriving Cults." *New York Times Magazine* 1 (May 1988): 36–44.

Bowlby, Rachel. *Just Looking: Consumer Culture in Dreiser, Gissing, and Zola.* New York: Methuen, 1985.

Brantlinger, Patrick. *Bread and Circuses: Theories of Mass Culture as Social Decay.* Ithaca: Cornell UP, 1983.

Brooks, Peter. *The Melodramatic Imagination: Balzac, Henry James, Melodrama and the Mode of Excess.* New Haven: Yale UP, 1976.

Brooks, Tim, and Earle Marsh. *The Complete Directory to Prime Time Network TV Shows, 1946–Present.* 5th ed. New York: Ballantine, 1992.

Brown, Mary Ellen. *Soap Opera and Women's Talk: The Pleasure of Resistance.* Thousand Oaks, CA: Sage, 1994.

———, ed. *Television and Women's Culture: The Politics of the Popular.* London: Sage, 1990.

Bruce, Bryan. "Pee Wee Herman: The Homosexual Subtext." *CineAction* 9 (July 1987): 3–6.

Brunovska, Kristine, and Henry Jenkins. *Classical Hollywood Comedy.* New York: Routledge, 1994.

Brunsdon, Charlotte. "*Crossroads*: Notes on Soap Opera." In Kaplan, *Regarding* 76–83.

———. "Television: Aesthetics and Audiences." In Mellencamp, *Logics* 59–72.

Brunsdon, Charlotte, and David Morley. *Everyday Television: "Nationwide."* London: BFI, 1978.

Butler, Jeremy G. "*Miami Vice*: The Legacy of Film Noir." *Journal of Popular Film and Television* 13.3 (1985): 127–38.

———. "Notes on the Soap Opera Apparatus: Televisual Style and 'As the World Turns.'" *Cinema Journal* 25.3 (1986): 53–70.

———. *Television: Critical Methods and Application.* Belmont, CA: Wadsworth, 1994.

Butler, Judith. *Bodies That Matter: On the Discursive Limits of "Sex."* New York: Routledge, 1993.

———. *Gender Trouble: Feminism and the Subversion of Identity.* New York: Routledge, 1990.

Butler, Judith, and Joan W. Scott, eds. *Feminists Theorize the Political.* New York: Routledge, 1992.

Camera Obscura: Special Issue on "The Spectatrix." Ed. Janet Bergstrom and Mary Ann Doane. 20–21 (1989).

Carroll, Noël. "The Image of Women in Film: A Defense of a Paradigm." *Journal of Aesthetics and Art Criticism* 48.4 (1990): 349–60.

Carson, Diane, Linda Dittmar, and Janice R. Welsch, eds. *Multiple Voices in Feminist Film Criticism.* Minneapolis: U of Minnesota P, 1994.

Carter-Reis, Mia. "De-Feminizing the Future: Cleaning up the Outer Limits in *Aliens.*" Unpublished paper, University of Wisconsin–Milwaukee, 1987.

Case, Sue-Ellen. "Toward a Butch-Femme Aesthetic." *Discourse* 11.1 (1988–89): 55–73.

Castleman, Harry, and Walter Podrazik. *Watching TV: Four Decades of American Television.* New York: McGraw-Hill, 1982.

Castonguay, James. "Domesticating the Gulf War." Paper presented at the Society for Cinema Studies Conference, Pittsburgh PA, May 1992.

———. "The Masquerade of Massacre: Rethinking the 'Crisis of Masculinity' after the 'Crisis in the Gulf.'" Paper presented at the Society for Cinema Studies Conference, Syracuse NY, March 1994.

Certeau, Michel de. *The Practice of Everyday Life.* Trans. Steven Rendall. Berkeley: U of California P, 1984.

Cha, Theresa Hak Kyung, ed. *Apparatus.* New York: Tanam, 1981.

Chodorow, Nancy. *The Reproduction of Mothering: Psychoanalysis and the Sociology of Gender.* Berkeley: U of California P, 1978.

Chow, Rey. "Postmodern Automatons." In Butler and Scott 101–17.

Cohan, Steven, and Ina Rae Hark, eds. *Screening the Male: Exploring Masculinities in Hollywood Cinema.* New York: Routledge, 1993.

Cohen, Ed. "Who Are 'We'? Gay 'Identity' as Political (E)motion (A Theoretical Rumination)." In Fuss 71–92.

Collins, James. "Postmodernism and Cultural Practice: Redefining the Parameters." *Screen* 28.2 (1987): 11–26.

———. "Television and Postmodernism." In Allen, *Channels* (2nd. ed.) 327–53.

———. "Toward Defining a Matrix of the Musical Comedy: The Place of the Spectator within the Textual Mechanisms." In Rick Altman 134–45.

———. *Uncommon Cultures: Popular Culture and Postmodernism.* New York: Routledge, 1989.

———. "Watching Ourselves Watch Television, Or Who's Your Agent?" *Cultural Studies* 3 (1989): 261–81.

Conant, Jennet. "Demi's Body Language." *Vanity Fair* (Aug. 1992): 112–18, 188–92.

Connor, Peter. *Postmodernist Culture: An Introduction to the Theories of the Contemporary.* New York: Blackwell, 1989.

Cook, Pam, ed. *The Cinema Book.* London: BFI, 1985.

Cook, Pam, and Philip Dodd, eds. *Women and Film: A Sight and Sound Reader.* Philadelphia: Temple UP, 1993.

Corea, Gena. *The Mother Machine: Reproductive Technologies from Artificial Insemination to Artificial Wombs.* New York: Harper, 1985.

Corea, Gena, et al., eds. *Man-Made Women: How New Reproductive Technologies Affect Women.* Bloomington: Indiana UP, 1987.

Coward, Rosalind. "Come Back Miss Ellie: On Character and Narrative in Soap Operas." *Critical Quarterly* 28.1–2 (1986): 171–78.

―――. *Female Desires: How They Are Sold, Bought, and Packaged.* New York: Grove, 1985.

Cowie, Elizabeth. "Women, Representation and the Image." *Screen Education* 23 (Summer 1977): 15–23.

Creed, Barbara. "From Here to Modernity: Feminism and Postmodernism." *Screen* 28.2 (1987): 47–67.

―――. "Horror and the Monstrous-Feminine: An Imaginary Abjection." *Screen* 27.1 (1986): 44–71.

Cubitt, Sean. "Top of the Pops: The Politics of the Living Room." In Masterman 46–48.

Curran, James, and Michael Gurevitch. *Mass Media and Society.* New York: Arnold, 1991.

Curti, Lidia. "Genre and Gender." *Cultural Studies* 2.2 (1988): 152–67.

D'Acci, Julie. "The Case of *Cagney and Lacey.*" In Baehr and Dyer 203–25.

―――. "Defining Women: The Case of *Cagney and Lacey.*" In Spigel and Mann 169–200.

Davis, Angela Y. *Women, Race, and Class.* New York: Vintage, 1981.

De Landa, Manuel. *War in the Age of Intelligent Machines.* New York: Zone, 1991.

de Lauretis, Teresa. *Alice Doesn't: Feminism, Semiotics, Cinema.* Bloomington: Indiana UP, 1984.

―――. *Technologies of Gender: Essays on Theory, Film, and Fiction.* Bloomington: Indiana UP, 1987.

de Lauretis, Teresa, and Stephen Heath, eds. *The Cinematic Apparatus.* New York: St. Martin's, 1980.

Deleuze, Gilles, and Félix Guattari. *A Thousand Plateaus: Capitalism and Schizophrenia.* Trans. Brian Massumi. Minneapolis: U of Minnesota P, 1987.

Deming, Robert. "The Return of the Unrepressed: Male Desire, Gender, and Genre." *Quarterly Review of Film and Video* 14.1–2 (1992): 125–47.

Derrida, Jacques. "Living On/Borderlines." Trans. James Hulbert. *Deconstruction and Criticism.* Ed. Harold Bloom, et al. New York: Seabury, 1979. 75–176.

―――. *Spurs/Eperons: Nietzsche's Styles.* Trans. Barbara Harlow. Chicago: U of Chicago P, 1978.

Derrida, Jacques, and Christie V. MacDonald. "Choreographies." *Diacritics* 12 (1982): 66–76.

Derry, Charles. "Television Soap Opera: Incest, Bigamy, and Fatal Disease." *Journal of the University Film and Video Association* 35.1 (1983): 4–16.

Diawara, Manthia, ed. *Black American Cinema.* New York: Routledge, 1993.

Dinnerstein, Dorothy. *The Mermaid and the Minotaur: Sexual Arrangements and Human Malaise.* New York: Harper, 1976.

Doane, Janice, and Devon Hodges. *Nostalgia and Sexual Difference: The Resistance to Contemporary Feminism.* New York: Methuen, 1987.

―――. "Risky Business: Familial Ideology and the Case of Baby M." *differences* 1.1 (1989): 67–81.

Doane, Mary Ann. *The Desire to Desire: The Woman's Film of the 1940s.* Bloomington: Indiana UP, 1987.

―――. "Film and the Masquerade—Theorising the Female Spectator." *Screen* 23.3–4 (1982): 74–88.

―――. "Information, Crisis, Catastrophe." In Mellencamp, *Logics* 222–39.

―――. "Masquerade Reconsidered: Further Thoughts on the Female Spectator." *Discourse* 11.1 (1988–89): 42–54.

―――. "Technophilia: Technology, Representation and the Feminine." *Body/Politics: Women and the Discourses of Science.* Ed. Mary Jacobus, Evelyn Fox Keller, and Sally Shuttleworth. New York: Routledge, 1990. 163–76.

Doane, Mary Ann, Linda Williams, and Patricia Mellencamp. *Re-vision: Essays in Feminist Film Criticism.* Frederick, MD: University Publications of America, 1984.

Docherty, Thomas, ed. *Postmodernism: A Reader.* New York: Columbia UP, 1993.

Doty, Alexander. "The Sissy Boy, the Fat Ladies, and the Dykes: Queerness and / as Gender in Pee-wee's World." *Making Things Perfectly Queer: Interpreting Mass Culture.* Minneapolis: U of Minnesota P, 1993. 81–95.

Douglas, Ann. *The Feminization of American Culture.* New York: Avon, 1977.

Drummond, Phillip, and Richard Paterson, eds. *Television in Transition: Papers from the First International Television Studies Conference.* London: BFI, 1986.

During, Simon, ed. *The Cultural Studies Reader.* New York: Routledge, 1993.

"Duty and Honor." *Miami Vice.* Prod. Michael Mann. Perf. Dr. Haing S. Ngor, Michael Wright, Edward James Olmos, Don Johnson, and Philip Michael Thomas. NBC. 6 February 1987.

Dyer, Richard. "Don't Look Now." *Screen* 23.3–4 (1982): 61–73.

———. "Entertainment and Utopia." In Rick Altman 175–89.

———. *Heavenly Bodies: Film Stars and Society.* New York: St. Martin's, 1986.

Echols, Alice. "The Taming of the Id: Feminist Sexual Politics, 1968–1983." *Pleasure and Danger: Exploring Female Sexuality.* Ed. Carole Vance. Boston: Routledge, 1984. 50–72.

Eco, Umberto. "A Guide to the Neo Television of the 1980s." *Framework* 25 (1984): 18–25.

———. *Travels in Hyperreality.* New York: Harcourt, 1986.

Eisenstein, Zilla. *The Female Body and the Law.* Berkeley: U of California P, 1988.

Ellis, John. *Visible Fictions: Cinema, Television, Video.* Boston: Routledge, 1982.

Elsaesser, Thomas. "Tales of Sound and Fury: Observations on the Family Melodrama." *Monogram* 4 (1972): 2–15.

Erens, Patricia, ed. *Issues in Feminist Film Criticism.* Bloomington: Indiana UP, 1990.

Fanon, Frantz. *Black Skin, White Masks.* Trans. Charles Lam Markmann. New York: Grove, 1967.

Felman, Shoshana. "Women and Madness: The Critical Phallacy." *Diacritics* 5.4 (1975): 2–10.

Feuer, Jane. "The Concept of Live Television: Ontology as Ideology." In Kaplan, *Regarding* 12–22.

———. *The Hollywood Musical.* London: BFI, 1982.

———. "Melodrama, Serial Form and Television Today." *Screen* 25.1 (1984): 4–16.

———. "The MTM Style." In Feuer, Kerr, and Vahimagi 32–60.

———. "Narrative Form in American Network Television." In MacCabe 101–14.

———. "Reading *Dynasty*: Television and Reception Theory." *South Atlantic Quarterly* 88.2 (1989): 443–60.

Feuer, Jane, Paul Kerr, and Tise Vahimagi, eds. *MTM: Quality Television.* London: BFI, 1984.

Fiedler, Leslie. "Come Back to the Raft Ag'in, Huck Honey." *The Collected Essays of Leslie Fiedler.* Vol. I. New York: Stein, 1971. 142–51.

Findlay, A. L. R. *Reproduction and the Fetus.* London: Arnold, 1984.

Firestone, Shulamith. *The Dialectic of Sex: The Case for Feminist Revolution.* New York: Morrow, 1970.

Fiske, John. "British Cultural Studies and Television." In Robert Allen, *Channels* (2nd ed.) 284–326.

———. *Media Matters: Everyday Culture and Political Change.* Minneapolis: U of Minnesota P, 1994.

———. "*Miami Vice,* Miami Pleasure." *Cultural Studies* 1.1 (1987): 113–19.

———. "Moments of Television: Neither the Text Nor the Audience." In Seiter, Borchers, Kreutzner, and Warth 56–78.

———. *Television Culture.* New York: Methuen, 1987.

Fiske, John, and John Hartley. *Reading Television.* New York: Methuen, 1978.

Flitterman, Sandy. "The *Real* Soap Operas: TV Commercials." In Kaplan, *Regarding* 84–96.

———. "Thighs and Whiskers: The Fascination of *Magnum, p.i.*" *Screen* 26.2 (1985): 42–58.

Flitterman-Lewis, Sandy. "All's Well That Doesn't End: Soap Operas and the Marriage Motif." *Camera Obscura* 16 (Jan. 1988): 119–27.

———. "Psychoanalysis, Film, and Television." In Robert Allen, *Channels* (2nd ed.) 203–46.

Foster, Hal, ed. *The Anti-Aesthetic: Essays on Postmodern Culture.* Port Townsend, WA: Bayp, 1983.

Foucault, Michel. *Foucault Live (Interviews, 1966–84).* Ed. Sylvère Lotringer. Trans. John Johnston. New York: Semiotext(e), 1989.

———. *Language, Counter-Memory, Practice: Selected Essays and Interviews.* Ed. and intro. Donald F. Bouchard. Trans. Donald F. Bouchard and Sherry Simon. Ithaca: Cornell UP, 1977.

———. *Power/Knowledge: Selected Interviews and Other Writings 1972–1977.* Ed. Colin Gordon. Trans. Gordon et al. New York: Pantheon, 1980.

Franklin, Sarah. "Fetal Fascinations: New Dimensions to the Medical-Scientific Construction of Fetal Personhood." In Franklin, Lury, and Stacey 190–205.

Franklin, Sarah, Celia Lury, and Jackie Stacey, eds. *Off-Centre: Feminism and Cultural Studies.* London: Harper, 1991.

Fraser, Nancy. *Unruly Practices: Power, Discourse, and Gender in Contemporary Social Theory.* Minneapolis: U of Minnesota P, 1989.

Freud, Sigmund. *The Basic Writings of Sigmund Freud.* Ed. A. A. Brill. New York: Random, 1966.

———. *Beyond the Pleasure Principle.* Trans. James Strachey. New York: Norton, 1961.

———. *Civilization and Its Discontents.* Trans. James Strachey. New York: Norton, 1961.

———. "Creative Writers and Day-Dreaming." *The Standard Edition of the Complete Psychological Works of Sigmund Freud.* Vol IX. Trans. and ed. James Strachey. London: Hogarth, 1974. 143–53.

———. "Femininity." *New Introductory Lectures in Psychoanalysis.* Trans. James Strachey. New York: Norton, 1964. 99–119.

———. *Sexuality and the Psychology of Love.* Ed. Philip Rieff. New York: Collier, 1963.

———. *The Standard Edition of the Complete Psychological Works of Sigmund Freud.* 24 vols. Trans. and ed. James Strachey. London: Hogarth, 1974.

———. *Three Essays on the Theory of Sexuality.* Trans. James Strachey. New York: Basic, 1962.

———. "The 'Uncanny.'" *On Creativity and the Unconscious.* New York: Harper, 1958. 122–61.

Friedan, Betty. *The Feminine Mystique.* New York: Dell, 1963.

Friedberg, Anne. *Window Shopping: Cinema and the Postmodern.* Berkeley: U of California P, 1993.

Fuchs, Cynthia J. "The Buddy Politic." In Cohan and Hark 194–210.

———. "'Death Is Irrelevant': Cyborgs, Reproduction, and the Future of Male Hysteria." *Genders* 18 (Winter 1993): 113–33.

Fuss, Diana, ed. *Inside/Out: Lesbian Theories, Gay Theories.* New York: Routledge, 1991.

Gaines, Jane. "White Privilege and Looking Relations: Race and Gender in Feminist Film Theory." *Cultural Critique* 4 (Fall 1986): 59–79.

Gans, Herbert. *Popular and High Culture: An Analysis and Evaluation of Taste.* New York: Basic, 1974.

Gates, Henry Louis, Jr., ed. *Reading Black, Reading Feminist: A Critical Anthology.* New York: Meridian, 1990.

Geraghty, Christine. *Women and Soap Opera: A Study of Prime Time Soaps.* Cambridge: Polity, 1991.

Giles, Dennis. "Show-making." In Rick Altman 85–101.

Gilligan, Carol. *In a Different Voice: Psychological Theory and Women's Development.* Cambridge: Harvard UP, 1982.

Ginsburg, Faye, and Anna Lowenhaupt Tsing, eds. *Uncertain Terms: Negotiating Gender in American Culture.* Boston: Beacon, 1990.

Gitlin, Todd. *Inside Prime-Time.* New York: Pantheon, 1983.

———, ed. *Watching Television.* New York: Pantheon Books, 1986.

———. "'We Build Excitement.'" In Gitlin, *Watching* 136–61.

———. *The Whole World is Watching: Mass Media in the Making and the Unmaking of the New Left.* Berkeley: U of California P, 1980.

Gledhill, Christine. "Developments in Feminist Criticism." In Doane, Williams, and Mellencamp 18–48.

———, ed. *Home Is Where the Heart Is: Studies in Melodrama and the Women's Film.* London: BFI, 1987.

———. "Speculations on the Relationship between Soap Opera and Melodrama." *Quarterly Review of Film and Video* 14.1–2 (July 1992): 103–24.

Glynn, Eugene David, M.D. "Television and the American Character—A Psychiatrist Looks at Television." *Television's Impact on American Culture.* Ed. William Y. Elliott. East Lansing: Michigan State UP, 1956. 175–82.

Goodwin, Andrew, and Garry Whannel, eds. *Understanding Television.* London: Routledge, 1990.

Gray, Ann. "Behind Closed Doors: Video Recorders in the Home." In Baehr and Dyer. 38–54.

Gray, Herman. "Recodings: Possibilities and Limitations in Commercial Television Representations of African American Culture." *Quarterly Review of Film and Video* 13.1–3 (1991): 117–30.

Gray, Paul. "Pee-wee's Misadventure." *Time* 12 August 1991: 58.

Grossberg, Lawrence. "The In-Difference of Television." *Screen* 28.2 (1987): 28–45.

Grossberg, Lawrence, Cary Nelson, and Paula Treichler, eds. *Cultural Studies.* New York: Routledge, 1992.

Hall, Stuart. "Culture, the Media, and the 'Ideological Effect.'" In Curran, Gurevitch, and Woollacott 315–48.

———. "Encoding/Decoding." In Hall, Hobson, Lowe, and Willis 128–38.

———. "The Rediscovery of 'Ideology': Return of the Repressed in Media Studies." *Culture, Society, and the Media.* Ed. Michael Gurevitch et al. New York: Methuen, 1982. 56–90.

Hall, Stuart, Dorothy Hobson, Andrew Lowe, and Paul Willis, eds. *Culture, Media and Language.* London: Hutchinson, 1980.

Hanmer, Jalna. "Transforming Consciousness: Women and the New Reproductive Technologies." In Corea et al. 88–109.

Haraway, Donna. "A Manifesto for Cyborgs: Science, Technology, and Socialist Feminism in the 1980s." *Socialist Review* 15.2 (1985): 65–107.

———. *Primate Visions: Gender, Race, and Nature in the World of Modern Science.* New York: Routledge, 1989.

———. *Simians, Cyborgs, and Women: The Reinvention of Nature.* New York: Routledge, 1991.

Harmetz, Aljean. "Maude Didn't Leave 'em Laughing." *New York Times* 10 Dec. 1972, sec. 2: 3.

Harrison, Michael R. et al. "Management of the Fetus with a Correctable Congenital Defect." *Journal of the American Medical Association* 246 (1981): 774–77.

Hartouni, Valerie. "Containing Women: Reproductive Discourse in the 1980s." In Penley and Ross. 27–56.

———. "Fetal Exposures: Abortion Politics and the Optics of Allusion." *Camera Obscura* 29 (May 1992): 128–49.

Haskell, Molly. *From Reverence to Rape: The Treatment of Women in the Movies.* Baltimore: Penguin, 1974.

Hastie, Amelie. "A Fabricated Space: Assimilating the Individual on *Star Trek: The*

Next Generation." Enterprise Zones: Liminal Positions on Star Trek. Ed. Taylor Harrison, Sarah Projanski, Kent Ono, and Elyce Rae Helford. Boulder, CO: Westview, forthcoming 1996.

Hayward, Phillip, and Paul Kerr. "Introduction to *Postmodern Screen." Screen* 28.2 (1987): 2–8.

Heath, Stephen. "Representing Television." In Mellencamp, *Logics* 267–302.

Hebdige, Dick. *Hiding in the Light: On Images and Things.* London: Comedia, 1987.

———. *Subculture: The Meaning of Style.* London: Methuen, 1979.

Hegel, Georg W. F. *Phenomenology of Mind.* Trans. J. B. Baillie. New York: Harper, 1967.

Hickey, Neil. "A Look at What the Neilsen Figures Reveal about America's Television Habits." *TV Guide* 7 Dec. 1985: 40.

Hobson, Dorothy. *"Crossroads": The Drama of a Soap Opera.* London: Methuen, 1982.

———. "Soap Operas at Work." In Seiter, Borchers, Kreutzner, and Warth 150–67.

Holmlund, Chris. "Masculinity as Multiple Masquerade." In Cohan and Hark 213–29.

Horkheimer, Max, and Theodor W. Adorno. *The Dialectic of Enlightenment.* Trans. John Cumming. New York: Continuum, 1987.

Houston, Beverle. "Viewing Television: The Metapsychology of Endless Consumption." *Quarterly Review of Film Studies* 9.3 (1984): 183–95.

Hughes, Patrick. "Today's Television, Tomorrow's World." In Goodwin and Whannel 165–82.

Hutcheon, Linda. *The Politics of Postmodernism.* New York: Routledge, 1990.

Huyssen, Andreas. *After the Great Divide: Modernism, Mass Culture, Postmodernism.* Bloomington: Indiana UP, 1986.

Irigaray, Luce. *Speculum of the Other Woman.* Trans. Gillian C. Gill. Ithaca: Cornell UP, 1985.

———. *This Sex Which Is Not One.* Trans. Catherine Porter. Ithaca: Cornell UP, 1985.

Jameson, Fredric. "Postmodernism, or the Cultural Logic of Late Capitalism." *New Left Review* 146 (1984): 53–92.

———. "Reading without Interpretation: Postmodernism and the Video-Text." *The Linguistics of Writing: Arguments between Language and Literature.* Ed. Derek Attridge, Alan Durant, Nigel Fabb, and Colin McCabe. New York: Methuen, 1987. 199–233.

———. "Reification and Utopia in Mass Culture." *Social Text* 1 (Fall 1979): 130–48.

Jardine, Alice. *Gynesis: Configurations of Woman and Modernity.* Ithaca: Cornell UP, 1985.

Jardine, Alice, and Paul Smith. *Men in Feminism.* New York: Methuen, 1987.

Jeffords, Susan. "Can Masculinity Be Terminated?" In Cohan and Hark 245–62.

———. *Hard Bodies: Hollywood Masculinity in the Reagan Era.* New Brunswick: Rutgers UP, 1994.

———. *The Remasculinization of America: Gender and the Vietnam War.* Bloomington: Indiana UP, 1989.

Jeffords, Susan, and Lauren Rabinovitz, eds. *Seeing through the Media: The Persian Gulf War.* New Brunswick: Rutgers UP, 1994.

Jenkins, Henry. "*Star Trek* Rerun, Reread, Rewritten: Fan Writing as Textual Poaching." *Critical Studies in Mass Communication* 5.2 (1988): 85–107.

———. *Textual Poachers: Television Fans and Participatory Culture.* New York: Routledge, 1992.

Jenkins III, Henry. "'Going Bonkers!' Children, Play and Pee-wee." *Camera Obscura* 17 (May 1988): 169–93.

Johnston, Claire. "Feminist Politics and Film History." *Screen* 16.3 (1975): 115–24.

Journal of Communication. Special Issue on "Ferment in the Field." 33 (Summer 1983).

Journal of Communication Inquiry. Special Issue on Music Television. 10.1 (1986).

Kaplan, E. Ann. "Feminism/Oedipus/Postmodernism: The Case of MTV." In Kaplan, *Postmodernism* 30–44.

————. "Feminist Criticism and Television." In Robert Allen, *Channels* (2nd ed.) 247–83.

————, ed. *Postmodernism and Its Discontents: Theories, Practices.* New York: Verso, 1988.

————, ed. *Regarding Television: Critical Approaches: An Anthology.* Frederick, MD: University Publications of America, 1983.

————. *Rocking around the Clock: Music Television, Postmodernism, and Consumer Culture.* New York: Methuen, 1987.

————. *Women and Film: Both Sides of the Camera.* New York: Methuen, 1984.

Katz, Elihu, and Tamar Liebes. "Decoding Dallas: Notes from a Cross-Cultural Study." In Newcomb (4th ed.) 419–32.

————. "On the Critical Abilities of Television Viewers." In Seiter, Borchers, Kreutzner, and Warth 204–22.

Kellner, Douglas. *Jean Baudrillard: From Marxism to Postmodernism and Beyond.* Stanford, CA: Stanford UP, 1989.

————. *The Persian Gulf TV War.* San Francisco: Westview, 1992.

Kellner, Douglas, and Michael Ryan. *Camera Politica: The Politics and Ideology of Contemporary Hollywood Film.* Bloomington: Indiana UP, 1988.

Kervin, Denise. "Reality according to Television News: Pictures from El Salvador." *Wide Angle* 7.4 (1985): 61–71.

King, Barry. "The Burden of Max Headroom." *Screen* 30.1–2 (1989): 122–38.

King, Scott Benjamin. "Sonny's Virtues: The Gender Negotiations of *Miami Vice.*" *Screen* 31.3 (1990): 281–95.

Kirkham, Pat, and Janet Thumin, eds. *You Tarzan: Masculinity, Movies, and Men.* New York: St. Martin's, 1993.

Kottak, Conrad Phillip. *Prime-Time Society: An Anthropological Analysis of Television and Culture.* Belmont, CA: Wadsworth, 1990.

Kristeva, Julia. *The Kristeva Reader.* Ed. Toril Moi. Trans. Léon S. Roudiez and Seán Hand. New York: Columbia UP, 1986.

————. *Powers of Horror: An Essay on Abjection.* Trans. Léon S. Roudiez. New York: Columbia UP, 1982.

Kroker, Arthur, and David Cook. *The Postmodern Scene: Excremental Culture and Hyper-Aesthetics.* New York: St. Martin's, 1986.

Kuhn, Annette. "Women's Genres." *Screen* 25.1 (1984): 18–28.

Lacan, Jacques. *Ecrits: A Selection.* Trans. Alan Sheridan. New York: Norton, 1977.

————. *Feminine Sexuality: Jacques Lacan and the école freudienne.* Trans. and intro. Juliet Mitchell and Jacqueline Rose. New York: Norton, 1983.

Lamb, Patricia Frazer, and Diana L. Veith. "Romantic Myth, Transcendence, and *Star Trek* Zines." *Erotic Universe: Sexuality and Fantastic Literature.* Ed. Donald Palumbo. New York: Greenwood, 1986. 235–55.

Landy, Marcia, ed. *Imitations of Life: A Reader on Film and Television Melodrama.* Detroit: Wayne State UP, 1991.

Lazarsfeld, Paul. "Remarks on Administrative and Critical Communications Research." *Studies in Philosophy and Social Science* 9 (1941): 2–16.

Lears, T. J. Jackson. "From Salvation to Self-Realization: Advertising and the Therapeutic Roots of Consumer Culture, 1880–1930." *The Culture of Consumption: Critical Essays in American History, 1880–1980.* Ed. Richard Wightman Fox and T. J. Jackson Lears. New York: Pantheon, 1983. 3–38.

————. *No Place of Grace: Antimodernism and the Transformation of American Culture, 1881–1920.* New York: Pantheon, 1981.

Lehman, Peter. *Running Scared: Masculinity and the Representation of the Male Body.* Philadelphia: Temple UP, 1993.

Leibman, Nina. "Leave Mother Out: The Fifties Family in American Film and Television." *Wide Angle* 10.4 (1988): 24–41.

Leo, John R. "The Familialism of 'Man' in American Television Melodrama." *South Atlantic Quarterly* 88.1 (1989): 31–51.

Lewis, Justin. "Are You Receiving Me?" In Goodwin and Whannel 153–64.

Logan, Michael. "Return Engagement." *TV Guide* 16 Oct. 1993: 12–15.

Long, Elizabeth. "Feminism and Cultural Studies." In Avery and Eason 114–25.

Lopate, Carol. "Daytime Television: You'll Never Want to Leave Home." *Radical America* 11.1 (1977): 32–49.

Lowenthal, Leo. "Historical Perspectives of Popular Culture." In Rosenberg and White. 46–58.

———. *Literature, Popular Culture, and Society.* Englewood Cliffs, NJ: Prentice Hall, 1961.

Luker, Kristin. *Abortion and the Politics of Motherhood.* Berkeley: U of California P, 1984.

Lull, James. "Family Communication Patterns and the Social Uses of Television." *Communication Research* 7.3 (1980): 319–34.

———. "A Rules Approach to the Study of Television and Society." *Human Communication Research* 6 (1982): 197–209.

Lyotard, Jean-François. *The Postmodern Condition: A Report on Knowledge.* Trans. Geoff Bennington and Brian Massumi. Minneapolis: U of Minnesota P, 1984.

MacCabe, Colin, ed. *High Theory/Low Culture: Analysing Popular Television and Film.* New York: St. Martin's, 1986.

MacDonald, Dwight. "A Theory of Mass Culture." In Rosenberg and White 59–73.

Marc, David. *Demographic Vistas: Television in American Culture.* Philadelphia: U of Pennsylvania P, 1984.

———. "TV Auteurism." *American Film* (Nov. 1981): 52–81.

Marcuse, Herbert. *One Dimensional Man: Studies in the Ideology of Advanced Industrial Society.* Boston: Beacon, 1962.

Marks, Laura. "Tie a Yellow Ribbon around Me: Masochism, Militarism and the Gulf War on TV." *Camera Obscura* 27 (Sep. 1991): 54–75.

Martin, Emily. "Body Narratives, Body Boundaries." In Grossberg, Nelson, and Treichler 409–23.

———. *The Woman in the Body.* Boston: Beacon Press, 1987.

Marx, Karl. *Capital.* Vol. I. Trans. Ben Fowkes. Harmondsworth: Penguin, 1976.

Masterman, Len, ed. *Television Mythologies: Stars, Shows, and Signs.* London: Comedia, 1984.

Mattelart, Armand, et al. *International Image Markets.* London: Comedia, 1987.

Mayne, Judith. *Cinema and Spectatorship.* New York: Routledge, 1993.

———. "*L.A. Law* and Prime-Time Feminism." *Discourse* 10.2 (1988): 30–47.

———. *The Woman at the Keyhole: Feminism and Women's Cinema.* Bloomington: Indiana UP, 1990.

McKeegan, Michele. *Abortion Politics: Mutiny in the Ranks of the Right.* New York: Free, 1992.

McLuhan, Marshall. *Understanding Media: The Extensions of Man.* New York: McGraw-Hill, 1964.

McNay, Lois. *Foucault and Feminism: Power, Gender, and the Self.* Boston: Northeastern UP, 1993.

McNeil, Alex. *Total Television: A Comprehensive Guide to Programming from 1948 to the Present.* 3rd ed. New York: Penguin, 1991.

McNeil, Maureen. "Putting the Alton Bill in Context." In Franklin, Lury, and Stacey 149–59.

McRobbie, Angela. *Feminism and Youth Culture: From Jackie to Just Seventeen.* Boston: Unwin, 1991.

———. "Settling Accounts with Subcultures: A Feminist Critique." *Screen Education* 34 (1980): 37–49.

Medhurst, Andy. "The Musical." In Cook 106–109.

Media Report to Women 21.1 (1993).

Mellencamp, Patricia. *High Anxiety: Catastrophe, Scandal, Age, and Comedy.* Bloomington: Indiana UP, 1992.

———, ed. *Logics of Television: Essays in Cultural Criticism.* Bloomington: Indiana UP, 1990.

———. "Situation and Simulation." *Screen* 26.2 (1985): 30–40.

———. "Situation Comedy, Feminism, and Freud: Discourses of Gracie and Lucy." In Modleski, *Studies* 80–95.

———. "Spectacle and Spectator: Looking through the American Musical Comedy." *Ciné-tracts* 1.2 (1977): 28–35.

———. "TV Time and Catastrophe, or *Beyond the Pleasure Principle of Television.*" In Mellencamp, *Logics* 240–66.

Melosh, Barbara, ed. *Gender and American History Since 1890.* New York: Routledge, 1993.

Merritt, Bishetta D. "Bill Cosby: TV Auteur?" *Journal of Popular Culture* 24.4 (1991): 89–102.

Metz, Christian. "History / Discourse: Note on Two Voyeurisms." Trans. Susan Bennett. *Edinburgh '76 Magazine* 1 (1976): 21–25.

———. *The Imaginary Signifier: Psychoanalysis and Cinema.* Trans. Celia Britton, Annwyl Williams, Ben Brewster, and Alfred Guzzetti. Bloomington: Indiana UP, 1982.

Meyer, Moe, ed. *The Politics and Poetics of Camp.* New York: Routledge, 1994.

Meyersohn, Rolf B. "Social Research in Television." In Rosenberg and White 345–57.

Miller, Nancy, ed. *The Poetics of Gender.* New York: Columbia UP, 1986.

———. "The Text's Heroine: A Feminist Critic and Her Fictions." *Diacritics* 12.2 (1982): 48–53.

Mitchell, W. J. T. "From CNN to JFK: Paranoia, Melodrama, and American Mass Media in 1991." *Afterimage* 19 (May 1992): 13–17.

Modleski, Tania. "Femininity as Mas[s]querade: A Feminist Approach to Mass Culture." In MacCabe 37–52.

———. *Feminism without Women: Culture and Criticism in a "Postfeminist" Age.* New York: Routledge, 1991.

———. "The Incredible Shrinking He(r)man: Male Regression, the Male Body, and Film." In Modleski, *Feminism* 90–111.

———. *Loving with a Vengeance: Mass-Produced Fantasies for Women.* Hamden, CT: Archon, 1982.

———. "The Rhythms of Reception: Daytime Television and Women's Work." In Kaplan, *Regarding* 67–75.

———, ed. *Studies in Entertainment: Critical Approaches to Mass Culture.* Bloomington: Indiana UP, 1986.

———. "The Terror of Pleasure: The Contemporary Horror Film and Postmodern Theory." In Modleski, *Studies* 155–66.

———. "Three Men and Baby M." *Camera Obscura* 17 (May 1988): 69–81.

Moi, Toril. *Sexual/Textual Politics: Feminist Literary Theory.* New York: Methuen, 1985.

Monaghan, Patricia. *The Book of Goddesses and Heroines.* New York: Dutton, 1981.

Montag, Warren. "What Is at Stake in the Debate on Postmodernism?" In Kaplan, *Postmodernism* 83–103.

Montesano, Anthony P. "Commercial Characters Make It Big in '80s: Temporarily Leave Adland for TV Shows and Movies." *Backstage* 5 Jan. 1990: 1–3.

Montrelay, Michèle. "Inquiry into Femininity." *m/f* 1 (1978): 83–102.

Moore, Suzanne. *Looking for Trouble: On Shopping, Gender, and the Cinema.* London: Serpent's Tail, 1991.

Morley, David. "Changing Paradigms in Audience Studies." In Seiter, Borchers, Kreutzner, and Warth 16–43.

———. *Family Television: Cultural Power and Domestic Leisure.* London: Comedia, 1986.

——. The *"Nationwide" Audience: Structure and Decoding.* London: BFI, 1980.

——. *Television, Audiences, and Cultural Studies.* London: Routledge, 1992.

Morris, Meaghan. "Banality in Cultural Studies." *Discourse* 10.2 (1988): 3–29. Rpt. in Mellencamp, *Logics* 14–43.

——. *The Pirate's Fiancée: Feminism, Reading, Postmodernism.* New York: Verso, 1988.

Morrison, Toni, ed. *Race-ing Justice, En-gendering Power: Essays on Anita Hill, Clarence Thomas, and the Construction of Social Reality.* New York: Pantheon, 1992.

Morrow, Lance. "But Seriously Folks . . ." *Time* 1 June 1992: 29–31.

Morse, Margaret. "Sport on Television: Replay and Display." In Kaplan, *Regarding* 44–66.

——. "Talk, Talk, Talk—The Space of Discourse in Television." *Screen* 26.2 (1985): 2–15.

——. "The Television News Personality and Credibility: Reflections on the News in Transition." In Modleski, *Studies* 55–79.

——. "What Do Cyborgs Eat? Oral Logic in an Information Society." *Discourse* 16.3 (1994): 86–123.

Mulvey, Laura. "Afterthoughts on 'Visual Pleasure and Narrative Cinema' Inspired by *Duel in the Sun.*" *Framework* 15–17 (Summer 1981): 12–15.

——. "Melodrama In and Out of the Home." In MacCabe 80–100.

——. "Visual Pleasure and Narrative Cinema." *Screen* 16.3 (1975): 6–18.

Mumford, Laura Stempel. "Plotting Paternity: Looking for Dad on the Daytime Soaps." *Genders* 12 (Winter 1991): 45–61.

Neale, Steve. "Masculinity as Spectacle." *Screen* 24.6 (1983): 2–16.

——. "Melodrama and Tears." *Screen* 27.6 (1986): 6–22.

Nemecek, Larry. *The Star Trek: The Next Generation Companion.* New York: Pocket, 1992.

Newcomb, Horace, ed. *Television: The Critical View.* 4th ed. New York: Oxford UP, 1987.

——, ed. *Television: The Critical View.* 5th ed. New York: Oxford UP, 1994.

——. "Texas: A Giant State of Mind." In Newcomb, *Television* (4th ed.) 221–28.

——. *TV: The Most Popular Art.* Garden City, NY: Anchor/Doubleday, 1974.

Nichols, Bill. "The Work of Culture in the Age of Cybernetic Systems." *Screen* 29.1 (1988): 22–46.

Nicholson, Linda J., ed. *Feminism and Postmodernism.* New York: Routledge, 1990.

Nietzsche, Friedrich. *The Gay Science.* Trans. Walter Kaufmann. New York: Vintage, 1974.

Nochimson, Martha. *No End to Her: Soap Opera and the Female Subject.* Berkeley: U of California P, 1992.

Norris, Christopher. *What's Wrong with Postmodernism?* Baltimore: Johns Hopkins UP, 1990.

Nowell-Smith, Geoffrey. "Minnelli and Melodrama." *Screen* 18.2 (1977): 113–19.

——. "A Note on History/Discourse." *Edinburgh Magazine* 1 (1976): 26–32.

Oakley, Ann. *The Captured Womb: A History of the Medical Care of Pregnant Women.* Oxford: Blackwell, 1984.

O'Brien, Glenn. "Pee-wee Hermeneutics." *ArtForum* 25.10 (1987): 90–93.

O'Brien, Mary. *The Politics of Reproduction.* Boston: Routledge, 1981.

O'Connor, John E., ed. *American History/American Television: Interpreting the Video Past.* New York: Ungar, 1983.

Ong, Walter. *Orality and Literacy. The Technologizing of the Word.* New York: Methuen, 1982.

"On Technology (Cybernetics, Ecology, and the Postmodern Imagination)." Special Issue. *Discourse* 9 (Spring-Summer 1987).

Owens, Craig. "Posing." *Difference: On Representation and Sexuality,* Catalog for The New Museum of Contemporary Art's Exhibition, "Difference." Curator Kate Linker. New York: The New Museum of Contemporary Art, 1985. 7–17.

Parker, Rozsika, and Griselda Pollock, eds. *Framing Feminism: Art and the Women's Movement 1970–1985*. London: Pandora, 1987.

"Pee-wee's Bad Trip." *The Nation* 26 Aug. 1991: 213.

Penley, Constance. "Brownian Motion: Women, Tactics, and Technology." In Penley and Ross 135–61.

———. "The Cabinet of Dr. Pee-wee: Consumerism and Sexual Terror." *Camera Obscura* 17 (May 1988): 133–53.

———. "Feminism, Psychoanalysis, and the Study of Popular Culture." In Grossberg, Nelson, and Treichler 479–500.

Penley, Constance, and Andrew Ross, eds. *Technoculture*. Minneapolis: U of Minnesota P, 1991.

Penley, Constance, and Sharon Willis. "Introduction." In Penley and Willis vii–xix.

———, eds. *Male Trouble*. Minneapolis: U of Minnesota P, 1993.

Petchesky, Rosalind. *Abortion and Women's Choice: The State, Sexuality and Reproductive Freedom*. New York: Longman, 1984.

———. "Fetal Images: The Power of Visual Culture in the Politics of Reproduction." *Feminist Studies* 13.2 (1987): 263–92.

Petro, Patrice. "Mass Culture and the Feminine: The 'Place' of Television in Film Studies." *Cinema Journal* 25.3 (1986): 5–21.

Pfeil, Fred. "'Making Flippy-Floppy': Postmodernism and the Baby Boom PMC." *The Year Left*. Ed. Mike Davis, Michael Sprinker, and Fred Pfeil. London: Verso, 1985. 263–95.

———. "Potholders and Subincisions: On *The Businessman, Fiskadoro*, and Postmodern Paradise." In Kaplan, *Postmodernism* 59–78.

Polan, Dana. "Postmodernism and Cultural Analysis Today." In Kaplan, *Postmodernism* 45–58.

Pollock, Griselda. "Report on the Weekend School." *Screen* 18.2 (1977): 105–13.

———. "What's Wrong with Images of Women?" *Screen Education* 24 (Autumn 1977): 25–33.

Poovey, Mary. "The Abortion Question and the Death of Man." In Butler and Scott 239–56.

Porter, Dennis. "Soap Time: Thoughts on a Commodity Art Form." *College English* 38.8 (1977): 782–88.

Porush, David. "Reading in the Servo-Mechanical Loop." *Discourse* 9 (Spring-Summer 1987): 53–62.

Poster, Mark. *The Mode of Information: Poststructuralism and Social Context*. Chicago: U of Chicago P, 1990.

Press, Andrea L. *Women Watching Television: Gender, Class, and Generation in the American Television Experience*. Philadelphia: U of Pennsylvania P, 1991.

Probyn, Elspeth. "New Traditionalism and Post-Feminism: TV Does the Home." *Screen* 31.2 (1990): 147–59.

Rabinovitz, Lauren. "Sitcoms and Single Moms: Representations of Feminism on American TV." *Cinema Journal* 29.1 (1989): 3–19.

Radner, Hilary. "Quality Television and Feminine Narcissism: The Shrew and the Covergirl." *Genders* 8 (Summer 1990): 110–28.

Radway, Janice. *Reading the Romance: Women, Patriarchy, and Popular Culture*. Chapel Hill: U of North Carolina P, 1984.

Ramazanoglu, Caroline. *Up Against Foucault: Explorations of Some Tensions between Foucault and Feminism*. New York: Routledge, 1993.

Random House Dictionary of the English Language. 2nd ed. Unabridged. New York: Random, 1987.

Rapaport, Herman. "Gazing in Wonderland: The Disarticulated Image." *Enclitic* 6.2 (1982): 57–77.

Rapp, Rayna. "Constructing Amniocentesis: Maternal and Medical Discourses." In Ginsburg and Tsing 28–42.

Rapping, Elayne. *The Looking Glass World of Nonfiction TV*. Boston: South End, 1987.

————. "Max Headroom: V-V-Very Bigtime TV." *Socialist Review* 17.6 (1987): 30–43.

————. *The Movie of the Week: Private Stories/Public Events*. Minneapolis: U of Minnesota P, 1992.

Rayner, Alice. "Cyborgs and Replicants: On the Boundaries." *Discourse* 16.3 (1994): 124–43.

"Readers Bite Back." *Vanity Fair* (Oct. 1991): 28–40.

Real, Michael. "Media Theory: Contributions to an Understanding of American Mass Communications." *American Quarterly* 32.3 (1980): 238–58.

Rich, Adrienne. *Of Woman Born: Motherhood as Experience and Institution*. New York: Norton, 1976.

Riviere, Joan. "Womanliness as a Masquerade." *Psychoanalysis and Female Sexuality*. Ed. Hendrik Ruitenbeek. New Haven: College and UP, 1966. 209–20.

Rodowick, D. N. "The Difficulty of Difference." *Wide Angle* 5.1 (1982): 4–16.

Rogin, Michael. *Ronald Reagan: The Movie, and Other Episodes in Political Demonology*. Berkeley: U of California P, 1987.

Rojek, Chris, and Bryan S. Turner, eds. *Forget Baudrillard?* New York: Routledge, 1993.

Root, Jane. *Open the Box*. London: Comedia, 1986.

Rose, Jacqueline. *Sexuality in the Field of Vision*. London: Verso, 1986.

Rosen, Marjorie. *Popcorn Venus: Women, Movies, and the American Dream*. New York: Coward, 1973.

Rosen, Philip, ed. *Narrative, Apparatus, Ideology: A Film Theory Reader*. New York: Columbia UP, 1986.

Rosenberg, Bernard, and David Manning White, eds. *Mass Culture: The Popular Arts in America*. New York: Free, 1957.

Ross, Andrew. "Masculinity and *Miami Vice*: Selling In." *Oxford Literary Review* 8.1–2 (1986): 143–54.

————. "*Miami Vice*: Selling In." *Communication* 9.3/4 (1987): 305–34.

————. "Techno-Ethics and Tele-Ethics: Three Lives in the Day of Max Headroom." In Mellencamp, *Logics* 138–55.

Roth, Mark. "Some Warners Musicals and the Spirit of the New Deal." In Rick Altman. 41–56.

Rothman, Barbara Katz. *The Tentative Pregnancy: Prenatal Diagnosis and the Future of Motherhood*. New York: Viking, 1986.

Rowe, Kathleen. "Roseanne: Unruly Woman as Domestic Goddess." *Screen* 31.4 (1990): 408–19.

Rowe, Robert. "Sarah Higley: Writer of Holodeck Pursuits." *Star Trek: The Next Generation Magazine* 16 (1991): 20–24.

Russo, Mary. "Female Grotesques: Carnival and Theory." *Feminist Studies/Critical Studies*. Ed. Teresa de Lauretis. Bloomington: Indiana UP, 1986. 213–29.

Saussure, Ferdinand de. *Course in General Linguistics*. Trans. Wade Baskin. New York: McGraw-Hill, 1959.

Sawicki, Jana. *Disciplining Foucault: Feminism, Power, and the Body*. New York: Routledge, 1991.

Schiller, Herbert. *Culture Inc*. New York: Oxford UP, 1989.

————. *Who Knows? Information in the Age of the Fortune 500*. Norwood, NJ: Ablex, 1981.

Schor, Naomi. "Dreaming Dissymmetry: Barthes, Foucault, and Sexual Difference." In Jardine and Smith 98–110.

Schulze, Laurie Jane. "*Getting Physical*: Text/Context/Reading and the Made-for-Television Movie." *Cinema Journal* 25.2 (1986): 35–50.

————. "The Made-for-TV Movie: Industrial Practice, Cultural Form, Popular Reception." In Newcomb, *Television* (5th ed.) 155–75.

Schwab, Gabriele. "Cyborgs. Postmodern Phantasms of Body and Mind." *Discourse* 9 (Spring-Summer 1987): 64–84.

Schwab, Martin. "In the Mirror of Technology." *Discourse* 9 (Spring-Summer 1987): 85–105.

Schwock, James. "Cold War, Hegemony, Postmodernism: American Television and the World-System, 1945–1992." *Quarterly Review of Film and Video* 14.3 (1993): 9–24.

Scott, Joan. "'Experience.'" In Butler and Scott 22–40.

Sedgwick, Eve Kosofsky. *Between Men: English Literature and Male Homosocial Desire.* New York: Columbia UP, 1985.

———. *The Epistemology of the Closet.* Berkeley: U of California P, 1990.

Seiter, Ellen. "Men, Sex and Money in Recent Family Melodramas." *Journal of the University Film and Video Association* 35.1 (1983): 17–27.

———. "The Role of the Woman Reader: Eco's Narrative Theory and Soap Operas." *Tabloid* 6 (1981): 36–43.

Seiter, Ellen, Hans Borchers, Gabriele Kreutzner, and Eva-Maria Warth. "'Don't Treat Us Like We're So Stupid and Naïve': Towards an Ethnography of Soap Opera Viewers." In Seiter, Borchers, Kreutzner, and Warth 223–47.

Seiter, Ellen, Hans Borchers, Gabriele Kreutzner, and Eva-Maria Warth, eds. *Remote Control: Television, Audiences, and Cultural Power.* New York: Routledge, 1989.

Seldes, Gilbert. "The People and the Arts." In Rosenberg and White 74–97.

Shaviro, Steven. *The Cinematic Body.* Minneapolis: U of Minnesota P, 1993.

Showalter, Elaine, ed. *The New Feminist Criticism: Essays on Women, Literature, and Theory.* New York: Pantheon, 1985.

Silverman, Kaja. *The Acoustic Mirror: The Female Voice in Psychoanalysis and Cinema.* Bloomington: Indiana UP, 1988.

———. *Male Subjectivity at the Margins.* New York: Routledge, 1992.

Smith, David Lionel. "The Thomas Spectacle: Power, Impotence, and Melodrama." *The Black Scholar* 22.1–2 (Winter 1991): 93–95.

Sofia, Zoe. "Exterminating Fetuses: Abortion, Disarmament, and the Sexo-Semiotics of Extraterrestrialism." *Diacritics* 14.2 (1984): 47–59.

Sontag, Susan. "Notes on Camp." *A Susan Sontag Reader.* New York: Vintage, 1983. 105–19.

Sorkin, Michael. "Faking It." *Watching Television.* Ed. Todd Gitlin. New York: Pantheon, 1986. 162–82.

Spigel, Lynn. "From Domestic Space to Outer Space: The 1960s Fantastic Family Sit-Com." *Close Encounters: Film, Feminism, and Science Fiction.* Ed. Penley et al. Minneapolis: U of Minnesota P, 1991. 205–35.

———. "Installing the Television Set: Popular Discourses on Television and Domestic Space, 1948–1955." *Camera Obscura* 16 (Mar. 1988): 11–46.

———. *Make Room for TV: Television and the Family Ideal in Postwar America.* Chicago: U of Chicago P, 1992.

Spigel, Lynn, and Denise Mann, eds. *Private Screenings: Television and the Female Consumer.* Minneapolis: U of Minnesota P, 1992.

Spivak, Gayatri Chakravorty. "Displacement and the Discourse of Woman." *Displacement: Derrida and After.* Ed. Mark Krupnick. Bloomington: Indiana UP, 1983. 169–95.

Stabile, Carole A. "Shooting the Mother: Fetal Photography and the Politics of Disappearance." *Camera Obscura* 28 (Jan. 1992): 176–205.

Stam, Robert. "Mobilizing Fictions: The Gulf War, the Media, and the Recruitment of the Spectator." *Public Culture* 4.2 (1992): 101–26.

———. "Television News and Its Spectator." In Kaplan, *Regarding* 23–43.

Stanworth, Michelle, ed. *Reproductive Technologies: Gender, Motherhood, and Medicine.* Minneapolis: U of Minnesota P, 1987.

Sterling, Christopher, and John Kittross. *Stay Tuned: A Concise History of American Television.* Belmont, CA: Wadsworth, 1978.

Studlar, Gaylyn. *In the Realm of Pleasure: Von Sternberg, Dietrich, and the Masochistic Aesthetic.* Urbana: U of Illinois P, 1988.

Sutton, Martin. "Patterns of Meaning in the Musical." In Rick Altman 190–96.

Tasker, Yvonne. "Dumb Movies for Dumb People: Masculinity, the Body, and the Voice in Contemporary Action Cinema." In Cohan and Hark 230–44.

Taylor, Ella. *Prime Time Families: Television Culture in Postwar America.* Berkeley: U of California P, 1989.

Thompson, Robert. "Stephen J. Cannell: An Auteur Analysis of the Adventure/ Action Genre." *Television Criticism: Approaches and Applications.* Ed. Leah R. Vande Berg and Lawrence A. Wenner. New York: Longman, 1991. 112–26.

Thorburn, David. "Television Melodrama." In Newcomb, *Television* (4th ed.) 628–44.

Tichi, Cecilia. *Electronic Hearth: Creating an American Television Culture.* New York: Oxford UP, 1991.

Timberg, Bernard. "The Rhetoric of the Camera in Television Soap Opera." *Journal of American Culture* 6.3 (1983): 76–81.

Torres, Sasha. "Melodrama, Masculinity, and the Family: *thirtysomething* as Therapy." *Camera Obscura* 19 (Jan. 1989): 86–107.

Tuchman, Gaye. "Women's Depiction by the Mass Media." *Signs* 4.3 (1979): 528–42.

Tuchman, Gaye, et al. *Hearth and Home: Images of Women in the Mass Media.* New York: Oxford UP, 1978.

"The 25 Most Intriguing People of '86." *People Weekly* 22 Dec. 1986: 100–101.

Vande Berg, Leah R. Ekdom. "Dramady: *Moonlighting* as an Emergent Generic Hybrid." *Communication Studies* 40.1 (1989): 13–28.

Vanity Fair 54.8 (Aug. 1991); photographs by Annie Leibovitz.

Van Zoonen, Liesbet. "Feminist Perspectives on the Media." In Curran and Gurevitch 33–54.

Wall, Angela. "Reconstructing Motherhood: Technologies of Reproduction and the Challenge of Norplant." Paper presented to the Society for Science and Literature, New Orleans, Nov. 1994.

Wallis, Brian, ed. *Art after Modernism: Rethinking Representation.* New York and Boston: The New Museum of Contemporary Art/Godine, 1984.

Waters, Harry F., with Janet Huck and Vern E. Smith. "Mad about M-M-Max." *Newsweek* 20 Apr. 1987: 58–64.

Wedel, Mrs. Theodore O., Robert B. Beusse, and Russell Shaw. "The 'Maude' Case: Pressure or Persuasion." *America* 15 Dec. 1973: 464–66.

Weibel, Kathryn. *Mirror, Mirror: Images of Women Reflected in Popular Culture.* Garden City, NY: Anchor, 1977.

Whetmore, Edward Jay. *Mediamerica: Form, Content, and Consequence of Mass Communication.* 4th ed. Belmont, CA: Wadsworth, 1991.

White, Mimi. "Crossing Wavelengths: The Diegetic and Referential Imaginary of American Commercial Television." *Cinema Journal* 25.2 (1986): 51–64.

———. "Ideological Analysis and Television." In Robert Allen, *Channels* (2nd ed.) 161–202.

———. *Tele-Advising: Therapeutic Discourse in American Television.* Chapel Hill: U of North Carolina P, 1992.

———. "Television: A Narrative—A History." *Cultural Studies* 3.3 (1989): 282–300.

———. "What's the Difference? *Frank's Place* in Television." *Wide Angle* 13.3–4 (1991): 82–93.

Whitfield, Stephen E., and Gene Roddenberry. *The Making of Star Trek.* New York: Ballantine, 1968.

Wiegman, Robyn. "Feminism, 'The Boyz,' and Other Matters Regarding the Male." In Cohan and Hark 173–93.

———. "Missiles and Melodrama (Masculinity and the Televisual War)." In Jeffords and Rabinovitz 171–87.

Wilcox, Rhonda. "Shifting Roles and Synthetic Women in *Star Trek: The Next Generation.*" *Studies in Popular Culture* 13.2 (1991): 53–65.

Williams, J. P. "The Mystique of *Moonlighting*: 'When You Care Enough to Watch the Very Best.'" *Journal of Popular Film and Television* 16.3 (1988): 90–99.

Williams, Linda. "When the Woman Looks." In Doane, Mellencamp, and Williams 83–99.

Williams, Raymond. *Television: Technology and Cultural Form.* New York: Schocken, 1974.

Wollen, Peter. "Ways of Thinking about Music Video (and Post-Modernism)." *Critical Quarterly* 28.1–2 (1986): 167–70.

Wren-Lewis, Justin. "The Encoding-Decoding Model: Criticisms and Redevelopments for Research on Decoding." *Media, Culture, and Society* 5 (Apr. 1983): 179–97.

Zoglin, Richard. "Where Fathers and Mothers Know Best." *Time* 1 June 1992: 33.

INDEX

Boldface indicates pages with illustrations.

LYNNE JOYRICH is an Associate Professor in the Department of English and Comparative Literature at the University of Wisconsin–Milwaukee, where she teaches film and television studies.